BUILD YOUR OWN
MINIMUM–COST
SOLAR HEATING SYSTEM

BUILD YOUR OWN MINIMUM-COST SOLAR HEATING SYSTEM

BY ROBERT P. HAVILAND

TAB BOOKS Inc.
BLUE RIDGE SUMMIT, PA. 17214

FIRST EDITION

FIRST PRINTING

Copyright © 1982 by TAB BOOKS Inc.

Printed in the United States of America

Library of Congress Cataloging in Publication Data

Haviland, Robert P.
    Build your own minimum-cost solar heating system.

    Includes index.
    1. Solar heating.   I. Title.
TH7413.H38   697'.78   81-18241
ISBN 0-8306-0091-4   AACR2
ISBN 0-8306-1411-7 (pbk.)

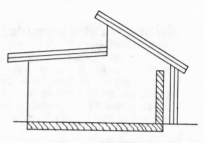

Contents

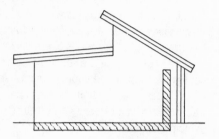

Introduction

This book is particularly addressed to the do-it-yourself homeowner who feels the need to maintain comfort by using the sun. But, it is also addressed to all homeowners to show them that residential solar energy is viable, at costs no greater, and sometimes less, than the methods it replaces. Architects, designers, builders, and workmen will also find the book useful.

WHY SOLAR ENERGY?

Before starting on the details of solar energy use in low cost ways, it seems well to look at the reasons why every homeowner, indeed everybody, must think about this form of energy and should start using it. The basic reason is very simple:

THE WORLD IS RUNNING OUT OF FOSSIL FUEL!

Note that this statement is set off and is in caps for emphasis. Perhaps you don't believe this or don't want to believe it. So let's say it again: if you are of average age, and we keep using fossil fuels at the rate we are now, oil supplies will effectively be gone in your lifetime. Natural gas will effectively be gone before your children are grown. Even coal supplies will be critical in your lifetime, and your children or grandchildren will be faced with effective exhaustion of coal.

Not convinced? Look at the data on reserves of oil, gas, and coal in the *U.S. Book of Statistics and Information*, widely sold as *The American Almanac*. Look at *The Global 2000 Report to the*

President, which should be available at your library. Just for example, Table 11-5 of this report estimates that the *world* reserve of crude oil will be exhausted in thirty years at the 1978 rate of use. At the current rate of use, oil will be exhausted about twenty-five years from now.

This period may be extended if great new discoveries are found, but there are natural laws which govern both the rate of discoveries and their usefulness. Basically, these laws state that the amount of a resource can be increased by expending more energy in extracting the resource. This applies to all resources—coal and oil, iron and copper, even fish in the sea.

There is a catch in this, though. It would take almost an infinite amount of energy to catch the last fish in the seas. The principle applies to energy resources also; it will take an infinite amount of energy to extract the last gallon of petroleum—far, far more energy than the gallon of oil it will yield. In fact, the point of energy equality is reached long before the oil reserve is exhausted.

If you think about this a little, you will see a cost-availability relation. When it requires one unit of energy to extract one unit of an energy resource, the cost of the resource has become infinitely high. The cost comes down as the energy expended gets less, but the basic fact is simple. Costs, and therefore prices, must go up as resources become more and more exhausted.

To homeowners, these basic principles add up to problems. First, the cost of the energy required to keep the home going will increase, and increase again and again. Eventually, if we stick to the common types of fuels, there won't be any at any price.

Additionally, it must be remembered that the cost of fuel enters into every other facet of life. The cost of materials and food is going to go up and up. In fact, in the United States the cost of food will go up faster than the cost of energy because our agricultural processes use more energy from fuel than is produced in food.

The increase in material costs carries a warning: don't wait too long before abandoning conventional fuels. The cost of changeover is tolerable now; it will be less tolerable in the future. If you wait too long, you might find that you just can't hack it. Then what do you do?

If you want to philosophize, you might find it worthwhile to think about comparing the meanings of the words *different* and *worse*, or equally, *different* and *better*. The next fifty years are certainly going to be different than the present. That doesn't mean that they must be worse, or even that they can't be better we must simply recognize that life is going to be different. We won't be able to take energy for granted and to forget it. Whether this makes a better life for you is a matter within your control.

That is the real purpose of this book, to help you try to find a way to have a good life, even a better one, while still adjusting to the differences that energy scarcities will bring.

One final word. Perhaps you are still unconvinced. All I can say is that's too bad—for you, for your family, and for your children. Please take the time and make the effort. Open your eyes and your ears and rethink the entire matter.

Let's turn now to the specific purpose of this book—the use of solar energy to meet part of the demand now being made of fossil fuel energy sources, particularly in energy for the home. It is ironic that this use of solar energy does not depend on great new discoveries. Just the opposite. Effective use of solar energy now depends on ideas that are tens, hundreds, even thousands of years old. Indeed the use of solar power depends on ideas that primitive people took for granted—and that modern man has ignored, then forgotten. Now we are rethinking these matters, and discovering that primitive men weren't so primitive after all; and they certainly weren't stupid.

The easiest answer to the question "what happened" is simple. Call it a fossil-fuel binge if you wish; it is a good description. The trend started just after the Middle Ages with the first use of coal as fuel. It was compounded by new developments in mass production, these in turn being based on the increased use of energy. Life became easier for some at first, then for more and more. The taste for "The Good Life," "La Dolce Vita" spread and spread.

The twin impact of petroleum exploitation and the mass production of automobiles turned this developing taste into an addiction. Combined with mass communication, it became a binge.

We were led to scrap the old precepts of "use it up", "wear it out," and "make it do" and to replace these with "planned obsolescence", "last year's model", and "you owe it to yourself." Throwaway became a way of life. We were really suckered in!

Simultaneously, changes in living patterns and housing concepts came along. Suburbia came into being, with individual houses designed for "the open life". This meant houses which consumed fossil fuel energy, and which paid no attention to natural sources; indeed, fossil fuel energy was often used in brute-force ways. A prize example is the simultaneous operation of a heating plant and an air-conditioning plant to give "optimum internal environment." It mattered not that the outside temperature was ideal. The energy use continued unthinkingly.

Many changes, both great and small, will have to be made over the next 50 years or so to correct the consequences of this fossil fuel binge. We shall concentrate on a particular family of small changes that can be made by one person for one family in his own habitation.

THE APPROACH TO SOLAR DESIGN

Now that we've discussed the "whys" of solar heating, let's turn to the "hows." The first part of this book covers the basic concepts of using solar energy for heating. Then follows a review of the technical factors and techniques that govern solar heating design. In this discussion, technical material is presented as:

Guidelines

Tabulations and graphs

Relations and tables of design

The intent is to bring the concepts to the point that using them is no more difficult than balancing a checkbook.

This preparatory material is followed by a series of simple designs, covering typical application techniques. All are slanted to the basic goal of keeping costs low. Some of these are my own, others were worked out by individuals and by centers dedicated to solar applications.

Finally, you will find a list of reference material. Some references are particularly recommended for their insightfulness; others are included for their coverage of specific topics.

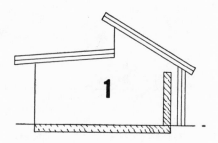

Solar Heat Concepts

Let us review the concepts of various solar heating systems to determine which ones best solve our particular problems. For this, it will help us to look at the modern concept, then to look back at the history of its development.

The idea of solar heating can be seen in its simplest possible form in the *direct gain* system illustrated in Fig. 1-1. Here, in its modern form, we have a south-facing wall that is transparent to incoming solar radiation. Ideally, the wall is opaque or reflective to the long-wave radiation of objects at comfortable room temperature and is not a good conductor of heat. There are no materials that meet this ideal, but glass is quite good, and two separated layers are excellent.

The sunlight passing through this wall is mostly absorbed by the floor, shown as a massive "heat absorber." This is shown insulated, as it should be for cold-climate use. During the day, sunlight warms the floor. The choice of flooring material is important so that the surface does not get too hot. This means that the material should be a fairly good conductor of heat, with all parts of the mass being warmed. However, with a perfect conductor, insulation becomes very important to prevent loss of heat to the outside. The floor should be a good absorber, but should also be practical and attractive. Again, there are no ideal materials, although dark red clay tiles cemented to a concrete subfloor do very well.

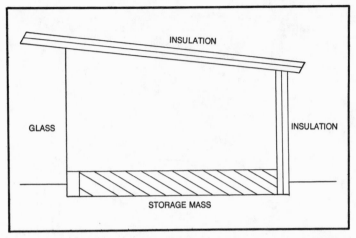

Fig. 1-1. This version of the direct gain of solar energy for heating uses a south-facing glass wall. Heat is stored inside the house, usually in a massive floor as shown. Walls, roof, and basement should be well insulated, and the glass should be one, two, or three layers thick, depending on the local climate. The basic principle is very old.

The other walls of the area need to be insulated, as does the roof. Doors and windows are provided, of course, but these also need insulation.

During the night, or on days when the sun is cloud-covered, the floor gives off the heat it has stored, becoming cooler. The mass of storage and insulation needed is to limit the amount of temperature drop, keeping indoor temperature in the comfort range.

The purpose of the southward orientation can be seen in Fig. 1-2, which shows a southward-facing house, with several sun positions. Morning sun can shine through an east wall, with the greatest amount coming in midsummer when it is not needed. Similarly, for the west wall, the greatest amount would come in the afternoon in midsummer, when it is usually too hot anyway. The south wall gives heat gain over the whole day at midwinter but only part of the day at midsummer.

Looking back at Fig. 1-1, note that the roof is shown with an overhang. This important development is shown in Fig. 1-3. At midwinter, the sun is low in the sky, and sunlight covers the entire floor of the room at noon, and most of it at other times. At midsummer, when the sun is high in the sky, the overhang completely shades the room—no solar input, matching the fact that heat will not be needed.

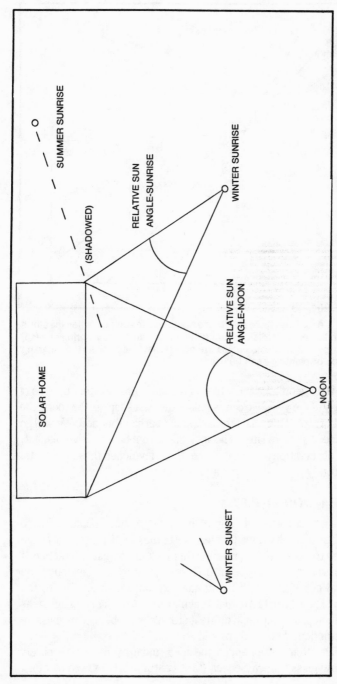

Fig. 1-2. The horizontal sun angles show how the solar house captures energy through its south wall during the entire day in winter, subject to cloudiness and local shading. In summer the south wall is shadowed for a period after sunrise by the east wall.

3

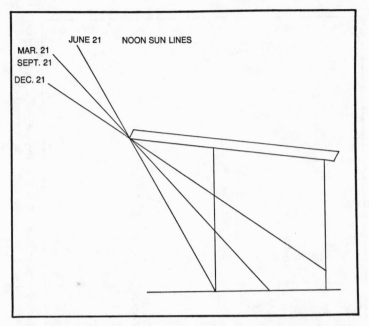

JUNE 21   NOON SUN LINES
MAR. 21
SEPT. 21
DEC. 21

Fig. 1-3. A roof overhang shades the south wall in summer, when the sun is high in the sky. In winter, the entire floor is in sunshine; in spring and fall, only a part is. Movable panels are sometimes used for further shading control, or plantings can be used.

With geometry and tables of the sun's position for any time of any day of the year, we can calculate the best shape of the room, the effect of roof slope, and the amount of overhang needed. We will go into these matters later. The ancients did not have these tools, but, from observation and experience, they developed these concepts, apparently in stages, over a period of time.

SOME ANCIENT HISTORY

The early story is, of course, incomplete, but Socrates, in the fourth century B.C., made reference to the Greek practice of facing houses to the south, contrasting this with the barbarian practice of underground living. Classical Greek architecture developed the central courtyard, with living quarters on the side, open to the south. They did not have glass but may have used fabric hangings as a method of thermal control. Heat storage was obtained by massive construction of stone or rubble and mortar.

The Romans extended the idea, using walls of transparent window glass, which Seneca (first century A.D.) noted as being developed in his lifetime. A major use appears to have been in the public baths, which had a *heliocaminus,* literally a solar furnace, facing south or southwest, and kept very warm by the sun. Sand or stone floors and stone walls provided heat storage.

The importance of solar heating was recognized by Roman courts, which held that a heliocaminus had a right to the sun and could not be shaded by a later building. This principle was later affirmed in the Code Justinian in the sixth century A.D.

It should be noted that the window wall does not have to be vertical. In fact, for maximum heat gain during the coldest months, a tilted window is better. The mathematics of this will be covered later.

HEAT WALLS

In addition to this form of direct solar heat gain, there is another probably older and certainly more widespread form. The construction is shown schematically in Fig. 1-4. The walls and roof were of massive construction of masonry or brick, either fired or unfired. As we will see, heat on the outside of the surfaces propagates relatively slowly through the wall or roof, reaching the inside six to twelve or more hours after the peak temperature outside. Effectively, therefore, the room was cooled during the heat of the day, and heated during the cool hours of the evening or night.

In this figure, insulation is shown at the north wall and under the floor. Most likely, this insulation was provided by additional rooms, often storerooms, at the rear of the living area and by tier construction, forming levels of apartments. This construction form is used in the pueblos of the American Southwest, both current and ancient, and also in the cliff dwellings. These appear to date back as early as A.D. 700, with most constructed around A.D. 1200.

In some respects, the cliff dwellings are closer in form to Fig. 1-1. Both natural overhang of the cliff and a constructed overhang were used. Insulation was provided by tier construction and by nesting the apartments in the hollows of the cliff.

Variations of these two construction modes are found in many parts of the world. There are material variations, of course, as dictated by local availability. There are also great variations in layout, many probably dictated by weather, others by need for defense, or perhaps by custom.

Much of the technology involved has been forgotten. For example, paper has been known for thousands of years; when oiled, it becomes translucent. Was it used for walls and window screens,

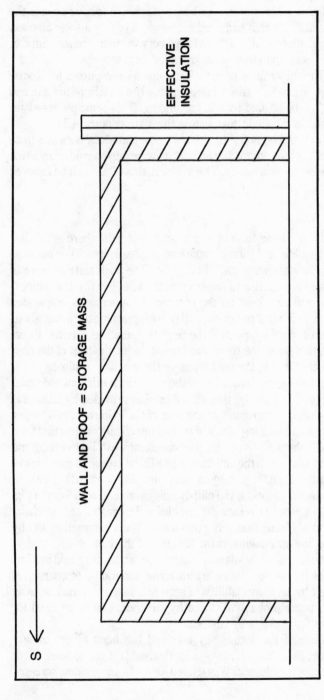

Fig. 1-4. Many ancient houses secured internal comfort through thick walls of masonry, rubble, brick, or mud, oriented to the south. Heat from the sun warms the wall through the day, reaches the inside during the evening or night hours. Storage rooms or cliff provide effective insulation for north face.

as is common in Japan and China? It is probable that oiled paper, sheepskin parchment, sheep gut, and mica were all used for windows in various parts of the world.

This early technology is now being studied in earnest. For those who want to explore it further, the books *A Golden Thread* and *Architecture without Architects* are suggested as a good starting point (see Bibliography). The first covers the use of solar energy in a number of ancient areas, with good coverage of the past one-hundred years. The second does not deal with solar energy use, but the excellent, widespread photographic coverage of ancient construction provides a clear view of applied solar energy concepts.

STORAGE WALLS

To return to the basic concepts of solar energy, Fig. 1-5 shows another variation of the direct gain system—the *storage wall* technique. In this, a large mass is placed close to the inside of the southward facing window. It functions both as the heat storage element and as a delay element to control the release of heat to the room. There may be additional control elements, such as closable wall vents to allow air circulation, and window and wall coverings.

The storage mass may be solid or liquid. Typical solids are cast-in-place concrete and brick or stone masonry. This form is often called a Trombe wall, after the French designer who constructed such a house in 1967. The technique, however, is much older, having been used by the Romans. The original designer is unknown.

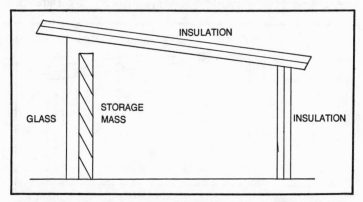

Fig. 1-5. Storage wall system with the storage mass inside house. If the mass is water in tanks, it is called a water wall; if the mass is masonry, a Trombe wall, after the modern experimenter and advocate. The idea is very old and was used in the Baths of Caracalla in Imperial Rome.

The liquid storage wall appears to be a modern invention. Water in containers is a common storage element. The containers can be as simple as 1- or 5-gallon plastic jugs, 55-gallon steel drums, or sections of spiral grooved culvert pipes. The sun facing side of the container is usually painted black or green. There is considerable freedom in design, which allows an arrangement which is architecturally sound and esthetically pleasing.

THE GREENHOUSE OR SOLARIUM

Still another variation in the basic design is the greenhouse or solarium construction shown in Fig. 1-6. This is also a very old technique, having been used by the Romans. At one time it was very popular in England and can still be found in the Spanish architecture of New Mexico where it may take the form of a glass-covered section of the common central patio. This can be used for dining, as well as for growing vegetables.

In the modern form, it is common to include thermal storage in the greenhouse. This may be a masonry back wall; or heavy masonry or concrete growing tables; or drums, barrels, or jugs of water. A few designs include movable inside or outside insulation to keep night-time temperatures high. There may be air circulation passages between the greenhouse and the adjacent space, plus some provision for limiting maximum temperature, usually vents.

THE HAY ROOF POND

Some of the remaining solar design concepts appear to be modern. One of these is the patented *roof pond* system of Fig. 1-7. Here the

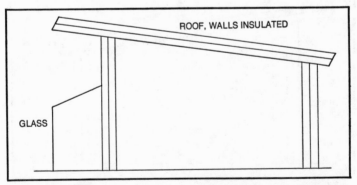

Fig. 1-6. The greenhouse, solarium or atrium makes a good add-on to an existing house. Primarily a daytime system, it can be made into a day/night system by adding storage mass inside it. In cold climates, double or triple glazing is used.

8

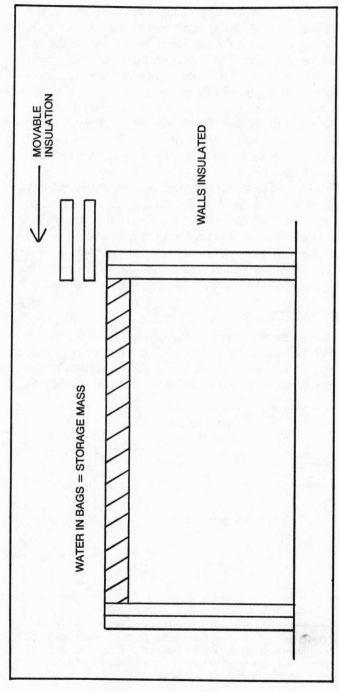

MOVABLE INSULATION

WATER IN BAGS = STORAGE MASS

WALLS INSULATED

Fig. 1-7. The roof pond heating/cooling system uses water for solar heating in winter and radiation cooling in summer. The panels are closed during winter nights to hold absorbed heat in. During the summer they are closed during the day to keep out solar heat, opened at night to let heat escape.

9

roof of a building is strengthened to support water in black bags to a depth of one to three feet. Movable insulating panels cover the water at night, keeping the temperature high. During the day (unless heavily overcast), the insulation panels are rolled back, allowing solar heat gain in the water. Space heating is by conduction through the supporting roof structure.

In addition to having heat gain through walls, heat gain through the roof works well. The general principle is illustrated in Fig. 1-8, showing a skylight set into the roof. This allows the heat storage element to be moved to the rear of the room space. Heat gain through the front wall occurs also, of course.

A variation of this makes the heat gain opening a clerestory window, as shown in Fig. 1-9. This window may be vertical, as shown, or tilted for maximum heat transmission during the coldest months. Overhang can now be used to control heat gain in summer, whereas the skylight must be covered. In very cold climates, internal insulating shutters are desirable and possibly necessary in either application. These can also serve as summer heat control.

WINDOW VARIATIONS

To capture as much energy possible, skylights and clerestories must be large, which may lead to architectural or constructional problems. To increase the heat gain through small windows, a reflective surface on the roof can be used. One such arrangement,

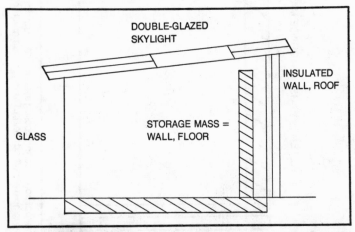

Fig. 1-8. Direct-gain systems are limited in the depth of house from south to north by shadowing. The skylight can admit sunlight to areas not otherwise reached. This permits use of northern walls for heat storage. The wall may be integral with the structure.

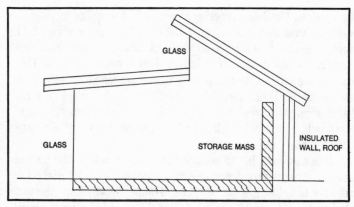

Fig. 1-9. The clerestory system can be used instead of skylights to admit solar heat. They are often preferable, since they are easier to keep sealed against water leaks.

sometimes called a *suncatcher* is shown in Fig. 1-10. A reflector is placed on the southern roof of the house, and also under the overhang of the clerestory. Depending on solar position, one or two reflections to the window area occur, in addition to direct capture. (The roof angles shown are illustrative and should be determined by ray plotting.)

Reflectors have also been used with the direct gain system of Fig. 1-1. A simple form places a patio of white concrete in front of

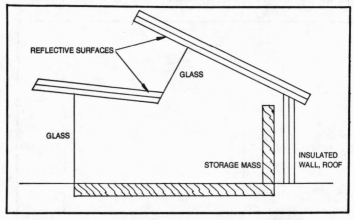

Fig. 1-10. The sun-catcher uses a reflective surface on the roof of one house section and under the eaves of another roof section to increase the effective capture area for solar radiation. Various diffusers may be used to reduce glare. Note that the surfaces may be curved rather than flat to give stronger than normal light intensity.

the window. Outdoor carpeting covers this during hot months. A bed of white stone can also be used. A complex version of Fig. 1-11 places the reflective surface on the inside of a drop-down insulated shutter, raised to reduce heat loss at night or on cloudy days. This form is often found in combination with a greenhouse. Reflection can also be used with the roof panel system, as shown in Fig. 1-12. Again, shapes and angles are illustrative only—the reflective surface would probably be full height, to the second story of a two-story house.

It is also possible to separate the heat gain from the heated area. One method of doing this is shown in Fig. 1-13. Here the collector is below the house space. Trapped heat warms the air, causing it to rise, and is replaced by cool air coming down the back of the absorber area. Height of the absorber is important, so the system is usually found on hillside houses. However, there is a simple variation, sometimes called a *window trap,* shown in Fig. 1-14. Here a glazed-front box is placed against an existing structure. Openings at the top and bottom of the box allow escape of the warmed air and its replacement by cooler air from the floor of the heated room. In both, covers for the circulation openings are needed.

Because these two designs separate heat gain from the basic solar collector, they are often easiest to use in existing structures, thus solving the retrofit problem. However, they may not be the best for a new design, simply because they take more material.

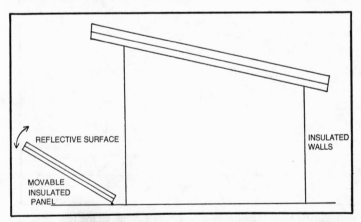

Fig. 1-11. Both reflective surfaces and insulation may be movable to increase solar input or reduce heat losses. They may be combined for a direct gain system. Rarely used in houses, it is an easy add-on, especially useful in very cold climates.

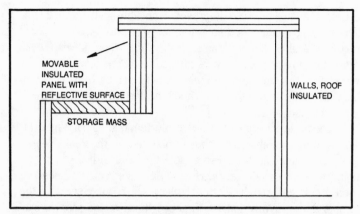

Fig. 1-12. Combinations of solar heating and insulating modes can be worthwhile—most new solar-heated houses use at least two modes of absorption and storage. Shown here, a version of the solar pond, with reflector, and necessary insulation.

ACTIVE SYSTEMS

All of these designs, except the roof pond, are *passive* in that they can operate without moving elements or without an external power

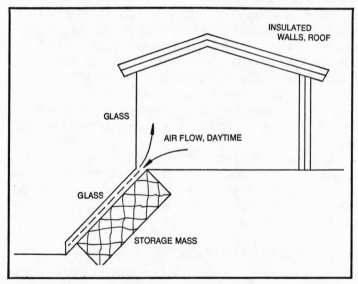

Fig. 1-13. Thermo-siphon solar system. It is not necessary to integrate the solar absorber and heat storage into the house. During the day, sunlight heats up the storage mass. Air flows down the divided passage due to the difference in temperature. At night flow design reverses. If a fan is used to improve air circulation, the system would be termed semiactive.

source (although many are improved if movable shutters are used). There is, however, another large family of solar systems which require movable elements and some type of external power. These *active* systems are not always attractive to the homeowner for general heating but do have their uses. Active systems are often best for applications other than home heating. A number of these are discussed later.

The basic principle of the active system is shown in Fig. 1-14. There is a solar absorber, shown mounted on the roof. Heat is captured, then transferred to a working fluid, either water or a liquid which does not freeze. Heated fluid is stored until needed, then circulated through radiators to warm the room. Generally, the temperatures involved are well above those of the passive systems; 120° to 180° F for an active system in contrast to the 65° to 80° F of the passive system.

There are many variations in these active systems. For example, the heated liquid may be circulated through pipes in the floor or used as a "back-up" in coils placed in a hot air furnace for very cold or cloudy weather. There are a large number of design variations possible in the collector; some heat air directly, others store the heat in pebble beds.

While the active systems are more complex, they do have advantages. It is often easier to install such a system in an existing structure. Also, it is often easier to integrate them as a back-up system into the design of existing structures. Finally, the amount of bad-weather reserve is determined by the amount of storage, which can be quite larger in an active heating system.

Both active and passive solar heating systems have their place. For the home owner, the following rules of thumb appear to apply:

■ If you are building new, consider the passive systems. They are probably best for you—at least for most sites.

■ If you are planning to add solar heating, look carefully at both active and passive systems. Site and building construction will determine the final decision.

BASIC ELEMENTS IN A SOLAR SYSTEM

A review of the various forms of solar heating shows that there are elements which are common to all systems, active or passive. For example, we can identify

An energy collector

An energy transport mechanism

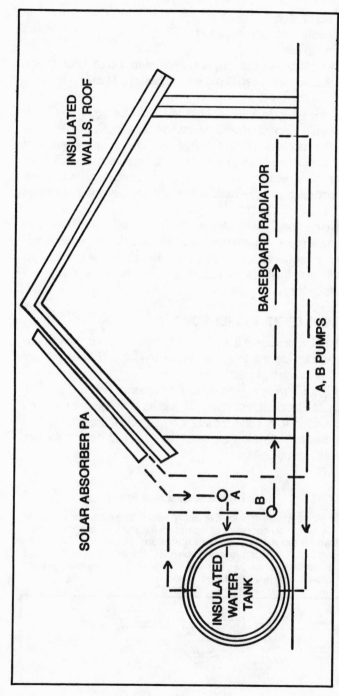

Fig. 1-14. This design separates absorber, storage, and use. Pumps circulate the working fluid, water; separate circuits are provided for absorption and withdrawal. The design is especially useful for existing houses with hot water heat.

15

Energy storage
Energy recovery (transport)
Energy use

In some systems a single physical element may accomplish two or more of these functions. This can be an important factor in low cost use of solar energy.

Table 1-1 arranges these functions in block diagram flow form. Below each block are listed the typical techniques by which the particular function can be satisfied. A "system" is obtained by taking one (or sometimes more) of the techniques from each block and providing the necessary interface. For example, the top line of the chart describes the basic direct gain solar heating system of Fig. 1-1.

Given thought, and filled in, a table of this form can be used to catalog all types of systems and to show if there are additional combinations of elements which form desirable new systems. As far as known, this "morphological approach" has not been applied to solar heating.

A NAGGING DOUBT: DO THEY WORK?

At this point, perhaps it is well to ask if these solar heating systems really work. One way to answer this is to look at the cost savings experience of actual installations.

Figure 1-15 is a photo of the experimental house at the University of Florida, Gainesville. This is an active system, using a roof-mounted solar collector and a large liquid storage tank. This house has been lived in for several years, and its performance monitored completely.

Table 1-1. Morphology of Solar Systems.

This flow diagram designates five easily recognized elements of a solar system, with typical construction/operation for each. Systems of various types can be formed by various combinations of elements. The Active System of Fig. 1-14 uses a separate collector, liquid fluid, water tank, and so on. In some systems, two or more functional elements may be combined into a single physical element.

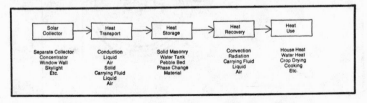

Fig. 1-15. The Experimental Active Solar Heated House at the University of Florida, Gainesville. In this active system, water storage is underground, although originally an above surface tank was used. The house is occupied by the family of a graduate student. Full records of performance are kept.

Table 1-2 shows the actual cost of operation of the solar system for one three-month period during the winter season and the comparative cost had the heating been provided by several conventional means. The solar cost was less than one-fifth as great as the cheapest conventional system using a gas fired furnace. It was one twenty-fifth as expensive as the most convenient conventional system using electric heat strips.

Also shown in the table is the cost per unit of the energy used. Oil has nearly tripled in price since this table was prepared, and gas has about doubled. The cost of electricity has gone up also, but the solar system retains its relative cost ratio: in absolute dollars, the solar system becomes increasingly superior.

Note that these figures are operating costs only. They do not include finance or maintenance costs, but these do not change greatly from one type of heating to another. For new construction, the message is clear—solar energy is by far the cheapest. Over a period of relatively few years, the cost of replacing an existing heating system can be recovered. Thereafter the solar systems savings are obtained.

Another proof of the efficiency of solar heating is to look at the way indoor and outdoor temperatures compare in a solar house. Figure 1-16 shows performance data from the original Trombe Wall, in France, for the 1974 Christmas period. Outside temperatures averaged about 40° F, with lows around 34° F. Temperatures on the inward face of the wall are nearly 80° F on full sunlit days. Even with a very cloudy day, such as the day before Christmas, the wall temperature was still 70° at daybreak the next day. Probably supplemental heat would have felt good early on the morning of Christmas day, although European practice keeps home temperatures lower than in American homes. Supplemental heat would have been required if another cloudy day occurred.

Solar heating works.

OTHER HOME USES OF SOLAR HEATING

Solar heating of homes is by no means the only application of solar energy. A major field is swimming pool heating. In fact, for the first six months of the year 1980, 69 percent of the solar energy capture area installed in Florida was for swimming pool heating.

The principle is exactly that of the active system in Fig. 1-14. A bank of solar collectors is used, often roof mounted. The swimming pool itself is the storage tank, and the pool circulator drives

Table 1-2. Comparison of Heating Costs.

Comparison of costs of heating the home of Fig. 1-15 over a three-month period, based on actual heat used and cost of energy from various sources. Note the adverse cost effect of recent increases on the conventional heating systems.

Operating Cost	Consumption for					Estimated Three Month Total
	Jan	Feb	March	Total		Cost
Solar System, Forced Air Type	72	54	38	164 kWh		$ 8.20
Conventional System						
Heat Pump	999	740	524	2253 kWh		113.15
Natural Gas	107	79	57	248 THERM		47.00
All Electric	1815	1345	950	4110 kWh		205.50
Oil Furnace	80	59	42	181 gal		72.40

Based on: Electricity $ 0.05/kWh
            Gas $ 0.181/THERM
            Oil $ 0.40/gal

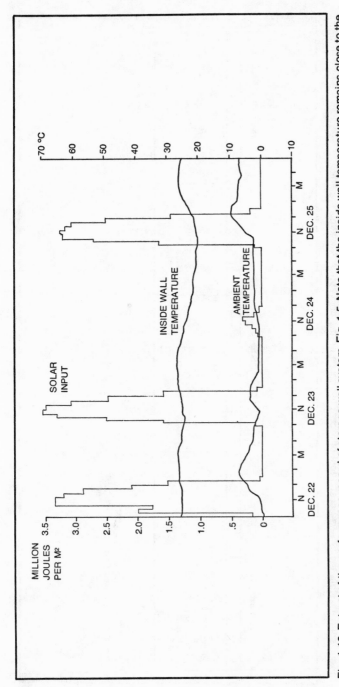

Fig. 1-16. Extract of the performance record of storage wall system, Fig. 1-5. Note that the inside wall temperature remains close to the comfort range 68° to 78°F, despite one cloudy day. Note also that the peak inside wall temperature occurs near M (midnight), although maximum solar input occurs just after N (noon).

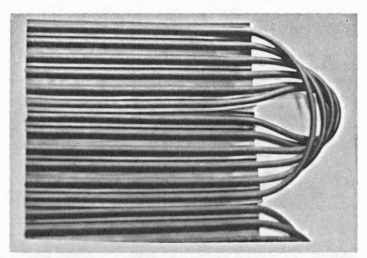

Fig. 1-17. Part of a low-temperature absorber for swimming pool use, formed of plastic tubing molded with a web. The material is made in long strips, cut as needed, and cemented to a metal backing sheet, such as an existing roof. Swimming pool heating was the largest use of solar energy in Florida in 1980.

the water through the collector. The cost is essentially that of the collectors.

Because temperatures do not need to be high, no more than 85°F or so, low-cost absorbers can be used. Figure 1-17 shows one type under testing at the Florida Solar Energy Center. This is made of web-molded plastic, using plastic with an additive to protect against ultraviolet degradation. A second type, also under testing, is shown in Fig. 1-18. This is a wide, extruded sheet of plastic, with water passages molded in. Data on the performance of these and other units can be obtained from the Center.

The second largest amount (18 percent) of solar heating installed in Florida in January-July, 1980, was for hot water heating. (House heating was third at 9 percent.) The principle is also that of the active system of Fig. 1-14, except that the storage element can be the usual hot water tank. If the collector is above the storage tank, as shown in this illustration, a small pump is needed to circulate the heated water, replacing it with cold water. However, if the tank is somewhat above the collector, a thermo-syphon is formed, giving natural circulation. Rules of thumb for these are given later.

Still another use for solar energy around the home is solar water distillation. A typical still is shown in Fig. 1-19. One of these

Fig. 1-18. A second type of swimming-pool absorber made of rigid, rather than flexible, plastic. This material, available in sheets of various lengths, can be attached to headers as needed.

Fig. 1-19. A group of water stills on test at the University of Florida at Gainesville. Water is held in the black trays. The evaporate condenses on the sloping glass cover, trickles into a gutter and on to the measuring jugs, or to point of use.

23

stills will produce from one-half to one pound of fresh water per square foot of pan area, each day of operation. Over the year, this is equal to almost 100 inches of rain. A small still can provide water for cooking and drinking, and water for gardening would not be impossible.

In some countries, solar heat is used for cooking. A simple box with fold-out reflecting flaps can reach temperatures of several hundred degrees Fahrenheit, sufficient for baking and slow roasting. Concentrating collectors have been designed which heat oil to 800° F or so. Relatively small quantities circulated through the walls of an insulated oven will give baking temperatures, and deep-fat frying is not impossible.

Some experimental installations for solar-powered air conditioning and solar-powered refrigeration exist. The usual design uses the principles of the Servel or Electrolux refrigerator, which is usually operated by a small gas flame. (These can be converted to solar operation.) Availability of such air-conditioning units to the general public now awaits an entrepreneur willing to place the device on the market. The current list of air-conditioner manufacturers does not seem to be interested, even though the increasing cost of electrical energy seems destined to drive mechanical air conditioning out of use.

It should be noted that application of the principles developed in solar heating are also of benefit in keeping houses cool. Just for example, the application of four simple design principles to a house in the band between Jacksonville, Florida, and New Orleans, Louisiana, will increase the comfort by about one-fourth. Specifically, these four steps will reduce the heating season from four months to three, and the cooling season from seven months to five. Full application of solar design can reduce the use of the fuel-powered heating system to days. The same gain is possible with solar air conditioning.

INDUSTRIAL USES OF SOLAR ENERGY

Solar energy also has uses outside the home. A very old use is the production of salt from seawater, capturing solar energy in a series of ponds. It will become popular again as fuel costs increase. More widespread is solar power for crop curing. Any good raisin or other dried fruit is prepared this way.

Usually forage crops are dried by being spread in the fields, but superior-quality feed can be obtained by solar heat traps. A simple type being tested at the University of Florida is shown in

Fig. 1-20. A sheet of black plastic is laid on the ground, and a green crop, such as meadow grass, piled on top to cure. Both are covered with clear plastic, held around the edges by dirt piled on it. Blower at right creates low air pressure, making the second plastic form a bubble. Leaks at edges remove water from the curing grass, which becomes top quality hay, free from mildew and mold.

25

Fig. 1-20. Hay is piled on a sheet of black plastic and covered by transparent plastic, held down by dirt piled around the edges. A small electric-powered blower inflates the resulting bag, keeping the upper plastic smooth. Moisture from curing is carried out by the escaping air.

These additional applications are not the subject of this book but are included to show the range of solar-power applications possible. From now on, let us confine our attention to solar power for the home. In the next chapter, we will look at ways to apply the principles of this chapter at low cost. Following chapters will cover design and construction, including some specific projects.

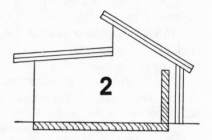

Secrets of Low-Cost Solar Heating

First, to be honest, we should note that there are really no secrets involved. The principles for low-cost design were worked out many, many years ago, but we keep forgetting them, then rediscovering them, and forgetting them again. We have just gone through a 50-year period during which we have forgotten the principles, or at least neglected them on a scale that has been fantastically larger than any previous period in written history. The reason for this has been simple—our reliance on cheap energy from fossil fuels. With enough energy you can do anything—even find a lever long enough to move the world.

We are going to have to go through a period of rediscovery and reapplication of these "secrets." It really isn't that low cost is important in itself—low cost also means low energy consumption, and that's vitally important. But cost is a convenient way of measuring energy use, so let's continue to use the term as a short-term indicator of goals.

NATURE'S RULES OF DESIGN

There is an important fundamental principle underlying all low-cost concepts. This can be expressed in many ways, but the simplest is *How does Nature want it done*? If a given design works against the laws of nature, then it cannot be low cost; it may not involve much expenditure of money, but this is not true economy. If a given thing or process isn't designed with nature, it will work poorly or not at all and be expensive and wasteful.

In buildings, residential and nonresidential alike, architects have expressed this principle in many ways. Frank Lloyd Wright, for example, coined the term "organic architecture" in trying to describe his concepts for use of materials and for fitting them to the land. Others have used the terse "form follows function" as their guide. One sometimes hears the dictum, "build with nature," but the most common expression seems to be "keep it simple."

In making this point about design, Louis Kahn once asked me, "Left to itself, what would a street like to be?" Without reflection, the answer, "a building," seems ridiculous. But if one thinks through the process of street construction in a large city—pave, tear up, and repeat, winding up with a hollow space for a subway with pipes and wires on the sides and a strong roof overhead serving as a pavement—the answer makes sense.

Suppose we phrase the question as "Left to itself, what would a solar house like to be?" Certainly the laws of apparent sun motion, high in the sky in summer and low in winter, indicate that the configuration of Fig. 1-1 is a house in conformity with nature—at least it is an acceptable design.

Solar energy is not enormously intense at our distance from the sun. We are going to have to work to capture it and to get it where it can be used. Because the heating effect is not enormous, we can't afford to waste it. We can't "heat up all outdoors." Solar houses are going to have to be well insulated. That's another thing the solar house would like to be—energy conservative. If you look back at the sketches of Chapter 1, you will see that insulation has been quietly emphasized.

Because of the bad practices which grew out of cheap energy, existing houses are almost all poor energy conservers. A part of conversion to solar heat will necessarily include improvements to reduce heat loss. It will be necessary to take care with any new design, lest the bad practices sneak in. If you hear of an "unsatisfactory" solar heating installation, there's a good chance that the fundamental factor of energy conservation was neglected.

REGIONAL GUIDELINES FOR COMFORT

Recognizing the importance of this factor, the U.S. Department of Housing and Urban Development (HUD) in conjunction with the Department of Energy (DOE) commissioned a project at the AIA Research Corporation. The results of this research are available as the *Regional Guidelines for Building Passive Energy Conserving Homes*. This book, HUD-PDR-355(2) is available from the Gov-

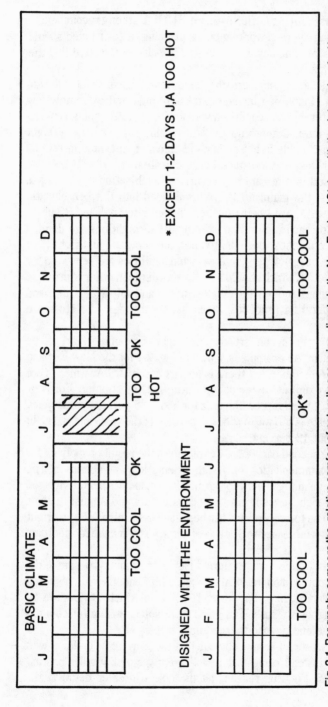

Fig. 2-1. Bar graphs compare the relative comfort of naturally occurring climate in the New England States with the internal no-fuel house environment made possible by "designing with the environment." The "just right" period has been extended from eight weeks to include the period of June through September, less one or two days in July or August where the temperature is too great. This does not include potential gain from use of a solar heating system, just the results of standard housing designs in accord with the environment.

29

ernment Printing Office or from HUD. A strong recommendation—every person working on, or planning, a solar home should have a copy, and anyone interested in solar energy will find the copy helpful.

This book considers the liabilities and assets of different climates. Liabilities include extremely high and extremely low temperatures, wind combined with low temperatures, high humidity, and intense sunshine. Assets include reasonable day/night variations, winds in hot and humid climates, sunshine in cool or cold climates, and moisture in dry climates.

Based on the naturally occurring combination of assets and liabilities, the mainland U.S.A. is divided into thirteen climatic regions, with three being further divided into an A and B subregions. For each region, the existing basic conditions are divided into three calendar periods: too hot, too cool, and just right (like the three bears). Then the assets and liabilities are reviewed for design factors which should be followed, listed in order of priority. Finally, construction techniques, home and lot orientation, and home operating practices which satisfy the design factors are shown.

The gains in comfort, the "just right" time of the year, can be spectacular. An example is shown in Fig. 2-1 for the New England states. Remember that there is no part of the U.S.A. which is not too cool (cold) in winter or too warm (hot) in summer. For New England, too cool predominates for about 75 percent of the year. The climate is too warm about 13 percent of the year, and just right only about 12 percent.

The second part of the figure shows the result of applying the HUD recommendation for design, orientation, and operation. The house is virtually never too warm. This period has been converted into just right (except for a few days in July and August in some years). The too cool period has been decreased also. The just right part is now increased to 37 percent of the year, and the too cool part decreased to 63 percent.

This gain in comfort period has been attained by simple design, layout, and operational choices. This is not the gain resulting from solar heating, but instead, the gain which is possible by designing with nature. The gains from solar heating (or cooling) are above and beyond these simple steps.

However, it seems obvious that the gain from "building with nature" instead of against it will greatly simplify solar heating problems. For this reason, let us look in greater detail at the techniques developed for two general areas of the U.S.A., one where the climate is generally too cold, the other where it is generally too hot. These will be valuable guides for your own conditions.

COMFORT TECHNIQUES

For the New England States, the basic techniques recommended are:

Keep the heat in and the cold out.

Avoid infiltration and heat loss due to wind.

Let in the sunlight.

These are obviously based on the severe winter climate. For year-around comfort, the following should also be included:

Let in the winter sun, but protect from summer sunshine.

Avoid infiltration but allow for natural ventilation.

These modify the three basic recommendations. Note that the three basic recommendations apply equally to conventional housing, housing designed for energy conservation, and for homes that are designed primarily for solar heating. Expressed in the alternate form:

Control heat flow.

Control air flow.

Control sunlight admission.

These are fundamental precepts for good solar design.

For each of the recommendations, the HUD publication shows from two to ten design possibilities that satisfy the precept. Some of these may be startling—thatched roofs, shutters, and even the Eskimo igloo—but the suggestions are sound. Thatch makes an excellent roof and is a wonderful heat insulator, summer or winter. Its worst drawback is that it must be protected from fire. The igloo may well be the most perfect expression of "organic" architecture—built of native material, thoroughly insulated by the characteristics of snow and by internal wall hangings, impervious to air leakage by virtue of jointless construction and an air trap entrance, and heated by body heat plus a small oil lamp, which is also used for cooking and lighting.

Perhaps we haven't completely forgotten all fundamentals; we've just been neglectful or have not understood them.

The lack of understanding can be seen by considering a typical New England or New York colonial dwelling. Typically, there would be a long sloping roof on the northern side with a shed at its low end. The south-facing wall would be high, often with a step, and with a generous roof overhang. In many houses, the south wall would be of brick. Windows would be small, especially on the east and west sides, and would be equipped with shutters. Rooms would have high ceilings. Fireplaces would be massive.

These design features can be translated into the energy recommendations listed above, and a few more that come specifically from solar heating concepts can be added. The sloping roofs block winter winds and create a south-side calm. The sheds provide insulation. The high south wall catches solar heat, especially if it is brick and releases it to the inside during the cool of evening. Window shutters reduce heat loss in winter. Windows, being top and bottom opening, release heat in summer, and allow breeze control. The massive fireplace holds heat through the night. The high ceilings increase room comfort by trapping a "bubble" of hot air above head height, which warms by radiant heat. In these houses one can be comfortable even though air temperature is low.

In contrast to these adaptations to climate, look carefully at the current so-called colonial-style home. They are built without regard to solar or wind orientation: ceilings are low, windows are large, and "shutters," if provided, are immovably fastened to the wall. Fireplaces often look massive, courtesy of a facade of brick veneer, but the heat storage capacity is low. The entire construction shows a lack of comprehension of the original function of the design elements, and the problems they were created to solve.

There is a lesson in this. If you are going to have a good solar design, you must consider the basic problems and the basic functions, and you must work within the limits they set. Look at any design you prepare, or have prepared for you, with suspicion. Ask—"Is this the way it would like to be—the way nature wants it?"

The above precepts are basically valid for all climates in winter, but the relative intensity of the cold, or of the heat in summer, may dictate a different design balance. For example, in the Gulf Coast areas, climatic liabilities are high temperatures, high humidity and strong sunlight in summer, and low temperatures and wind in winter. Climatic assets are winds in summer and good sunlight in winter. Using the assets to overcome the liabilities requires some differences in design from the much colder New England area.

Figure 2-2 shows the relative degree of comfort in this climate, and the comfort gain which can result from application of basic design principles. The gain is not as spectacular as for New

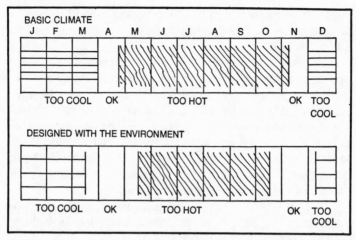

Fig. 2-2. Design with the environment improvement for Texas-Louisiana Gulf Coast shows improvement for hot, humid climate. While there is a long period of too hot conditions, the just right duration has been extended by a factor of nearly three to one. Solar heating is worthwhile for winter months, and solar-driven air conditioning would benefit the summer months.

England but is still appreciable, almost three times in percentage points for the just right part of the year. The recommendations for this climate are:

Isolate from hot summer temperatures.

Allow summer breezes to ventilate and cool.

Protect from summer sun.

Avoid creating additional humidity.

Allow summer ventilation, but prevent winter infiltration.

Let the sunshine in on winter mornings.

Avoid exposure to outside temperature when it's too cool for comfort.

The design principles which conform to these recommendations show in many examples of classical New Orleans architecture. Balconies, trellis work, high ceilings with high windows, extensive planting, and ventilated dormers are basic for summer conditions. With windows closed, high ceilings and stoves give reasonable winter comfort in classical designs. Greater emphasis on solar heating seems desirable, although the trellised balconies and deciduous trees in the planting are good.

In other areas, the climatic problems are different and a different balance of design principles is needed. The overall gain expected for the various areas is summarized in Table 2-1. The gains can be marked from two to three and even four times in percentage points. The largest gains are in reduction of the "too hot" periods.

To obtain further reduction in discomfort periods of the year without using fossil fuel, the principles of solar energy must be applied. At present this is practically limited to solar heating. Solar-powered air conditioning has been demonstrated at several test stations and appears entirely practical. However, no manufacturer has yet started production of suitable components. If you want to try solar cooling, you are entirely on your own. (But, by all means, get in touch with the energy centers, especially at the Universities of Florida, Arizona, and New Mexico.)

In contrast to the solar cooling situation, there is ample experience, data, equipment, and proven design in the solar heating area. (See Sources of Information.)

It must not be thought that solar-oriented design will completely eliminate the "too cool" periods. The extent to which it will reduce duration will depend on the climate, the techniques you adopt, and the amount you are willing to spend on the installation.

As an example of the gain which can be expected, consider Table 2-2. This data is from an early solar design, an experimental solar house at MIT, and is for the 1949-1951 seasons. For each heating month the total amount of heating needed to maintain comfort is shown, with the percentage of this coming from the sun and from fuel sources indicated. Overall, for these seasons, two-thirds of the necessary heating was solar. With conventional heating costs for a house of this size now amounting to around $2000 a year, the savings are important.

This house is in a definitely severe climate. Annual heating costs can be reduced by a much larger fraction in milder climates—down to, say, the eight dollars a month level of the home of Fig. 1-15, as shown in Table 1-2.

As stated above, the degree to which demand for fossil fuel is reduced will depend on the installation. And quite often, the limits to the installation will be set by costs, bringing us to the core of this chapter—low-cost installations.

A FUNDAMENTAL FACTOR IN SOLAR HEATING

Again, there really are no secrets to low-cost solar installations, but this aspect of solar heating has been neglected much too often.

The fundamental factor in developing low-cost solar heating is just as simple as the practice of designing with nature:

USE WHAT HAS TO BE THERE FOR ANOTHER REASON

Again, this is set off and in caps for emphasis.

If we can really do this, get double or even triple use from some component needed in the basic house, we would have an enviable situation—something for nothing. Nature has some laws about this, however, so we probably won't really get the second use "for free," but to the extent that we can, we are ahead.

Let us expand on this concept. A basic house needs:

A floor

Walls

A roof

Access

The access can be for people, for light, or for ventilation. A look at the conceptual solar designs of Chapter 1 will confirm that doors, windows and vents are all being used as an element of solar heating.

By combining a basic element of any house with some component of a solar energy system, we can achieve greater savings and, in many cases, increased performance for both parts. For example, the roof of a typical house is sketched in Fig. 2-3. Just above the roof is a solar absorber. There is only one major and one minor

Table 2-2. Typical Cold Climate Solar System Performance.

The heat load and percent provided by solar heating and conventional fuel for the two year averages, 1949-1951, winter season in Boston. Current practice increases size of the solar system to attain higher solar fraction. Many houses are now being designed for total solar heating. This data is for a single solar heating mode; current practice combines two or more modes into a single house design. (Based on MIT Solar House III, 1949-1951 Seasons.)

Month	Heat Load 10^6 BTU/MONTH	% Solar
Oct.	4.0	100%
Nov.	4.8	86%
Dec.	6.2	69%
Jan.	5.8	56%
Feb.	7.3	50%
Mar.	7.6	85%
Apr.	4.4	95%
Season	40.1	67%

Table 2-1. Comfort Gain Resulting from a "Design with the Environment" Approach.

This table shows the percentage of average year for which the climate is too hot, too cold, and just right, for each major climatic area of the U.S.A. The results of designing with the environment are also tabulated. Note that some areas have greater gains than others, but that gain is possible for all. (Source: AIA, 1980.)

Zone	General Area	Outside			Inside, with Recommended Design		
		Too Hot	OK	Too Cold	Too Hot	OK	Too Cold
1A	New England	13%	12%	75%	0%	37%	63%
1B	Northern Plains	12%	12%	76%	7%	28%	65%
2	Ohio to Nebraska	20%	14%	66%	9%	32%	59%
3	Central-Western Plateaus	11%	12%	77%	1%	38%	61%
4	Rockies	0%	8%	92%	0%	24%	76%
5	Pacific NW	8%	13%	79%	0%	34%	66%
6	California	17%	21%	62%	5%	52%	43%
7A	Mid-Atlantic	42%	12%	46%	33%	34%	33%
7B	Mid-West	35%	13%	52%	24%	34%	42%
8	Piedmont	28%	16%	56%	19%	36%	45%
9	SouthWest	37%	15%	48%	18%	52%	30%
10A	West Texas	26%	19%	55%	10%	53%	37%
10B	Texas-Oklahoma	39%	14%	47%	24%	43%	33%
11	North Florida	52%	12%	36%	39%	36%	25%
12	Gulf	54%	11%	35%	43%	32%	25%
13	South Florida	69%	20%	11%	39%	54%	7%
		80°	68°-80°	68°	80°	68°-80°	68°

difference—the solar absorber uses a transparent watertight layer instead of the opaque one used in the roof, and the absorber includes the energy absorption-transfer panel which is not present in the roof.

Suppose the two were combined into a single entity. Roof performance would not be compromised in any way if the amount of insulation is maintained and proper waterproofing is applied. Solar absorber performance could be increased because of improved insulation. The change in production cost would be the difference in cost between a transparent and an opaque waterproof layer, and the added cost of the absorber—heat interchanger. Total installed

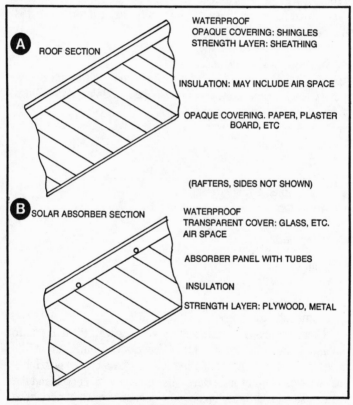

Fig. 2-3. Comparison of roof and absorber construction. Part A shows a cross-section of a typical well-insulated roof, and Part B a section of a typical flat-plate solar absorber. The roof section is designed for climate resistance and opacity, as is the absorber. However, the roof section is designed to withstand wind and snow loads, whereas the absorber has minimum strength. Combining the two gives solar heating with minimal incremental cost.

cost actually might be less if the chosen solar energy roof panel was factory produced and intended for fast installation. Such a unit could shift the reasonable design point of a simple active system from just hot water heating to complete house heating, with several days of reserve.

Such a combined unit appears to justify the statement that a way to low-cost solar energy is to use what has to be there for another reason. This is by no means the only possibility. Several others will be discussed later.

OTHER APPLICATION FACTORS

Of course, we also need to recognize that the principle isn't limited to just "what has to be there." It's actually easier if the concept is extended to include:

What we want to put there.

What we could put there.

We have already mentioned a few of these possibilities in reviewing New England and Texas Gulf house design. Some of the things we might want to put there are:

Sun room
Porch, balcony
Carport
Garage
Tool/implement shed
Workshop
Storage wall
Woodshed

We might even include:

Planting and trellises
Greenhouse
Animal shelter

There are major advantages in working with these items to combine solar heating with other functions. Being out of the "necessity" class, compromise and adaption becomes easier. Inherent qualities often fit in better—the sun room, the porch and the greenhouse all inherently involve the sun, and so are important to current solar design.

Inclusion of an animal shelter may be surprising, but it's an important energy conservation factor in many parts of the world. A human being radiates heat at about the rate of a 150-watt electric heating unit. But a cow or a horse radiates about 500 watts. A herd of cows, as in the Swiss Alps, makes a good furnace, keeping themselves and their owners warm. (There are, of course, problems in sanitation and odor control, but most of these are due to inertia in working out solutions, or to sheer laziness on the part of the owners.) At this time, such a solution would not be possible in cities; whether it will ever be necessary remains to be seen.

There is a subprinciple of some importance which applies to these add-ons, and indeed to the basic concept of building with nature. This can be expressed as "use zoning of areas," but it is also equivalent to temperature zoning. In early houses it was well followed. For example, in cold climates wood, storage sheds, and the unheated pantry were on the coldest, windward side. If the kitchen had a separate chimney, it was on the side toward other rooms. Just the opposite was true in hot climates—often the kitchen was separated from living quarters by a breezeway, and, if possible, the kitchen was down wind from the prevailing summer breezes.

Another basic principle of low-cost solar system design may appear surprising at first. It is "forget efficiency." Here's why.

Suppose we have two different designs of solar systems. One captures half of the sun's energy per unit area to heat a house, i.e., has an efficiency of 50 percent, whereas the second captures only one-fourth of the energy per unit area to do the same heating, at an efficiency of 25 percent. The important factor here is that the fuel cost for these two units is exactly the same—nothing. The two units may be different in other costs—materials, labor, installation, or maintenance, but they are equal in the item of fuel cost.

There are relations between efficiency and some of these other cost factors; the area of the 25 percent efficiency collector must be double that of the 50 percent collector. But if the materials and labor cost less than half that of the high-efficiency collector, the low-efficiency unit would be the most cost attractive. This can easily occur, for example, in a build-it-yourself project, or when preparing a multiple-function design. It's consequences not efficiency that counts, and it is better to look at these directly.

A PRECEPT: USE APPROPRIATE TECHNOLOGY

Another basic precept to follow is: "use appropriate technology." This means the use of common, well-proven materials and methods of construction and often, the use of local materials. This is especially important for the whole house, and for designs based on multiple use. In other words: "keep it simple."

By and large, it is best to avoid using plastics in any application exposed to sunlight. This is certainly true for structural elements, although, as we will see later, plastic covers for the absorber itself may be advantageous, even though they might not last many years. Wood, iron, aluminum, and glass are often going to be the best choices, even though their use involves an increased initial cost.

A strong element in this appropriate technology use is local availability. If brick is made locally, it will be cheaper than brick shipped in. Cement is usually shipped in, but the bulk of low-cost concrete is almost always of local material. Avoid, if possible, those grades of concrete which require shipped-in material. Specify local wood and get it directly from small mills if possible.

This precept may be modified somewhat by the last low-cost precept: "use surplus judiciously." A prime example of this is found in the tanks used for water storage of heat. Cleaned and painted 55 gallon drums are commonly used here. One-gallon milk jugs serve well and are often available for the asking. Five-gallon plastic or metal pails and sonobuoy shipping cases also have been used.

Glass is often available in surplus at attractive prices. It may pay to buy complete sashes from buildings being demolished, even to undertake a "remove and salvage" contract yourself.

For glass, especially, be prepared to modify details of your design to suit available low-cost new or surplus panes. If you can get 4' × 6' plate glass at a good price, don't insist on 16″ × 24″ standard panels. The same principle applies to wood and steel.

One important factor in this is basing your plans on standard dimensions. Plywood in other than 4' × 8' sheets, aluminum in other than 16″ or 36″ wide rolls, or other standard size sheets are always priced at a premium. Then, too, standard sizes are more likely to be found in surplus. Watch the drift in standards with time, though. A 2″ × 4″ once measured two inches by four inches; now it actually measures 1½″ × 3½″.

There is one other principle of low-cost design: if at all possible, do the work yourself. Actually, as we've said before, there are several reasons for this.

It is much less expensive.

If there are any flaws, you know where they are because you put them there.

It's good for the waistline.

Besides, you don't have to pay income tax until you sell the result, and there are ways to avoid it entirely.

If you aren't sufficiently expert in some area, try to work out a work/trade arrangement with a qualified friend.

One final element: to what extent should you do the design yourself, and for what should you get expert assistance? The answer isn't at all simple since it depends on your skill and experience, not only in construction details, but also in esthetics, understanding physical principles, and comprehending the consequences of the change to solar heating.

If you have no experience in an area, you must have qualified assistance. At some point you will be able to do the work yourself but may find it advisable to have your calculations, designs, plans, and/or work reviewed by someone more competent than you. My general recommendation is: plan on quite a bit of consultation in the conceptual and design phases of your projects unless you are truly an expert designer or architect.

Securing aid in the strictly solar aspects may be a problem for you. The number of interested, qualified, and experienced engineers, architects, and builders is increasing, but they are still not common. Look around, and check newspapers and publications for leads. Especially, keep your eyes open, and ask for names when you find an interesting design. Equally, ask for existing designs that you can check when you find likely assistance.

GUARDING AGAINST SELF-SERVING ADS

A final point seems to need discussion. There are a large number of articles, publications, studies, and ads on solar power, energy conservation, and similar matters, with more coming out every day. This book is one. Many of these are very good, and some extremely so; others are misleading, possibly as a result of an old-fashioned viewpoint, or even possibly in attempting to simplify a complex problem. Unfortunately, others are self-serving and presented in the wrong spirit.

An example of the effect of incomplete treatment appeared in *Woman's Day Magazine* late in 1980. The article was entitled "The Cheapest Way to Heat Your House." It included an informative chart, adapted here as Table 2-3. With this, your annual fuel bill is easily determined when you know the heating demand and the cost of fuel. The unfortunate factor is that the chart doesn't really relate to the title. Specifically, it doesn't give a cost figure on what can be the lowest cost way of heating—solar power. While the possibility is mentioned in the article, the chart doesn't even imply it. For a

Table 2-3. Equivalent Fuel Cost.

Alignment chart for the equivalent cost of fuels, based on typical use efficiency and fuel energy content. To use, find your present fuel cost and lay a ruler through it, making the reading at the top and bottom scales the same. Then read the cost of the same amount of energy from any other fossil fuels.

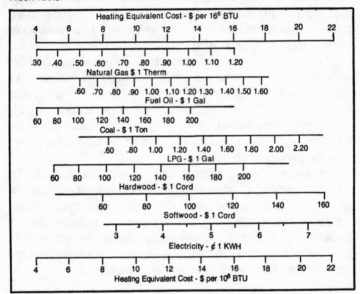

solar-heated house, the chart is a good guide to the cheapest auxiliary fossil fuel. Use it for that purpose.

Self-serving ads especially abound. Figure 2-4 shows schematically a house widely advertised as being "energy efficient," but note especially the way the design "turns its back" on the natural environment, and on solar power. The only possible way to maintain comfort in this house design is to run that air conditioner 24 hours a day, every day of the year. Heating in winter, cooling in summer, and running the fan all of the time deplete fossil fuels. The only merit is that the rate is reduced a little from what it would be otherwise.

You are going to have to think for yourself in these areas. Maybe the kids have a valid point—don't trust anyone over 18!

THE COMFORT ZONE

For conventional heating systems it is customary to design for a fixed house temperature, usually 68° or 70° F in American practice. The system always includes a thermostat for control, starting

42

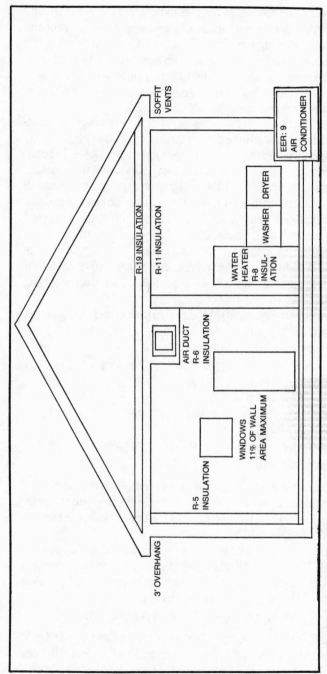

Fig. 2-4. "Energy-efficient" house shows a total rejection of natural ventilation, solar heating, and other "design-with-the-environment" ideas. The air conditioner must run 365 days a year, 24 hours a day—a great waste of energy and a continual drain on the owner's pocketbook.

43

and stopping the furnace as needed to maintain the average temperature. All thermostats include a mechanism to prevent the furnace from cycling too often. Usually this *hysteresis* device is a small magnet which suddenly pulls an arm into the contact position as the temperature falls, and suddenly releases it to the open position as it rises. Most have an adjustment to allow the differential between on and off to be set as desired.

Solar heating systems using separate heat-storage and heat-use components can utilize this method of control, say for starting and stopping a pump in a water storage system or a blower in a rock bed system. Supplementary systems may also have a thermostat.

In passive systems of the integral storage-use type, use of thermostats for control becomes difficult. They do exist, for example, as circulation vent controllers, but more often the system is sized to produce a satisfactorily small range of internal temperature variation by itself, or with occasional manual aid such as pulling a curtain or closing a vent. Note that the temperature variation will occur over a 24-hour period, rather than occurring each hour or so as in a conventional system.

Conventional systems set the design temperature on the basis of comfort, taking into account the effect of moisture in the air. Standard recommended values are:

	RH = 10%	RH = 50%	RH = 100%
Lower Comfort Temperature—10%	68° F	65° F	62° F
Comfort Temperature—100%	77° F	72° F	68° F
Higher Comfort Temperature—10%	83° F	78° F	73° F

RH is the relative humidity, and the percentage is that fraction of people who state that they are comfortable at the given temperature. The "effective" temperatures of the three comfort values are about 62°, 68°, and 73° F.

The values in this table are a simplification of the full comfort situation. Moving air affects comfort markedly, since it changes the heat loss by conduction. It is sometimes expressed by a *wind chill factor*. This can be calculated thusly:

$$\Delta T = 0.634 \ (\log_{10}V - 0.634) \ (°F - 90)$$

Where ΔT is the drop in effective temperature due to a wind of V mph at a temperature of $°F$. A slow breeze, less than four miles per hour or seven feet per second will have no effect on comfort.

In addition to the effect of air temperature, relative humidity, and wind on comfort, the temperature of the surrounding objects is of importance. If walls are colder than the air, there is a feeling of discomfort due to net loss of radiant energy from the body. Warmer walls give a net gain in body radiant energy, allowing lower air temperatures.

There are no current standards for design air temperatures in the presence of warm wall radiation. Indeed, there appears to be very little information on the matter. The ASHRAE Guide, for example, implies only a two-degree difference in comfortable air temperature for summer, as compared to winter, wall temperatures. Edward Mazria states in his book on solar heating, that a range of fifteen degrees is satisfactory in most buildings. For a large restaurant, he used a range of 65 to 75 degrees Fahrenheit for business hours, with a minimum of 60 degrees during the non-business hours.

The range of temperatures is determined by the amount of heat storage provided, whereas the average temperature is determined by the relation between heat gain area and building thermal loss. These factors are covered later.

Pending publication of recommendations, it appears that designs should be based on a range of 65 to 75 degrees Fahrenheit during the hours of normal activity, for normal weather changes. Abnormal weather can be compensated for by such simple steps as manually closing draperies, or opening windows. If extremes in weather must be expected, movable insulators and reflecting shutters would be better.

COMPOSITE SYSTEMS

It is not necessary for the solar heating system to be separated from its back-up system. Equally, it is not necessary for an existing system to be ripped out when solar heating is being added to the house. Both reduced installation cost and excellent backup can be obtained by integrating the two systems, using the best features of the existing system.

Obviously, the existing system will place constraints on the design of the added system. Just for example, it will probably be easier to add an active heat-storage system using water storage to an existing hot water circulator installation. But this may be influenced by home design or by local availability of materials.

Some common combined systems are sketched in Fig. 2-5. The first three are hot water, with A being the common connection

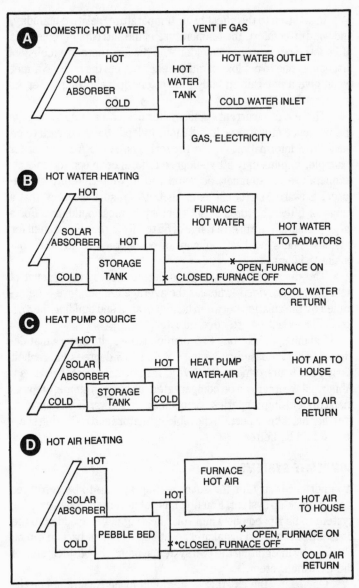

Fig. 2-5. Possible ways of combining solar heating with existing or new conventional heating systems: (A) solar-domestic hot water, (B) solar-hot water, (C) solar-heat pump, (D) solar-heat pump combinations. These designs have the advantage of "built-in" back-up, and can be used to keep costs down in existing houses. The minimum add-on cost is obtained by eliminating heat storage, using solar heat during the day and conventional heat at night. In climates with low daytime temperature, the gain can be very worthwhile.

for the domestic hot water line, rather than house heating. *B* shows a solar heater feeding a heat pump—at the present this is likely to be the system with the least added investment. *C* shows addition of a solar absorber—water storage system to a conventional hot water furnace. If a low temperature collector is used, the furnace will have to run during cold weather periods to satisfy thermostat demand. In moderate weather, the solar system can supply most or all of the heat needed.

Part *D* shows the equivalent for a hot air system, using a hot air solar absorber and a bin (or bed) of large gravel, pebbles or even concrete blocks for heat storage.

Data given later will give guidelines for estimating the size of the components needed.

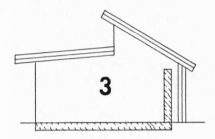

Sizing the System

Let us turn now to the problem of determining how big a solar heating system and its components should be. It is going to be tedious because it will be necessary to go into the various elements in considerable detail, but it's important. If the system is too small, it will not do the heating job and there will be excessive dependence on fossil fuels. If it is too large, areas may become uncomfortably hot and money will have been wasted. Then too, if the various principles of solar heating are not understood and used properly the system may not work correctly, leading to discomfort, dependence on fossil fuel, and waste of time and money. In this and the following chapter, emphasis will be placed on techniques used for arriving at proper design values.

TECHNIQUES FOR SIZING

Because people have different backgrounds, material will be presented in several ways. Basic principles will be covered in both descriptive form with illustrations and in numerical form. The descriptive part is intended to help people who haven't had reason to study the field, understand the basics. The numerical part, in the form of tables, charts, curves, and equations, is intended to provide the data on which to work. Actual working relations also will be presented in conceptual and numerical form. For design, three methods will be covered:

Detail numerical, based on equations
Specific numerical, based on prepared forms
Guidelines, based on experience

The first two of these will give the same results if the particular form fits the individual problem. If not, the detail numerical relations can be used directly, or a new form can be prepared from them. (Reference to other form sources are included.) The work can be done with pencil and paper, the forms being especially adapted to this. A slide rule or calculator can come in handy for the necessary calculations. With one of the small calculators, the work is no more trouble than balancing a check book.

The guidelines are included as a way of checking the results of detail or form calculations. If those results don't agree with the values of the guides, there is probably something wrong. It may be a numerical error, such as transposing two numbers, or taking a number from the wrong column of a table. It may be a basic misunderstanding of the meaning of a table entry, perhaps because its description was poorly worded. In any event, re-check if guidelines and calculations don't agree.

The guidelines are not really intended for design or construction. If you don't want to undertake at least the tabular work, get someone to help—preferably someone with experience like an architect or engineer. It is a good idea to have a professional check the work you do yourself. He can spot errors and problems much quicker than you. Of course, you can turn the whole job over to him.

ELEMENTS OF HEAT THEORY

Let us now review the basics of the heat theory. For solar work, we will be concerned with energy in two forms: one is the internal energy of bodies, manifested in the form of *temperature;* the second is a transient form of energy, specifically heat, which is energy being transferred from one place to another because of a difference in temperature. Heat may be transferred by *conduction,* which requires a single body having a temperature difference within it, or by contact between two bodies at different temperatures. Heat may also be transferred by *radiation* which does not require contact. The houses we will be concerned with gain solar energy by radiation, increasing their internal energy as shown by a rise in temperature. They lose this absorbed energy by heat conduction to the outside world.

We will also be concerned with *convection,* in which the energy is temporarily stored in a moving fluid, often called a *working fluid.* Air and water are the working fluids which will concern us. When we get into details, we will have convective terms in some heat transfer relations.

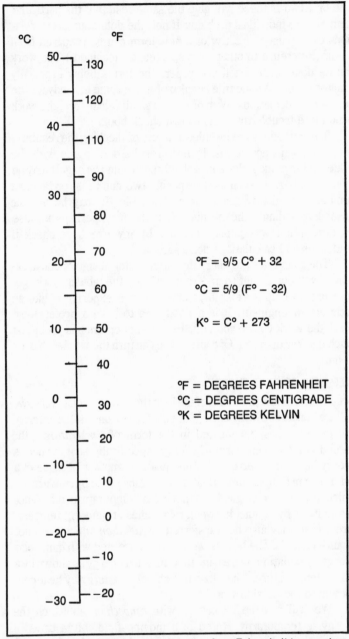

Fig. 3-1. Thermometer scale for converting from Fahrenheit temperature scale to Centrigrade scale. Equations for these conversions and for the Kelvin, or absolute, scale are also shown.

Because of the existence of several measuring systems, and also because of different starting points, we will have to face the problems of measuring quantities by different scales. For temperature, there are four scales, but only two are of importance. These are the *Fahrenheit* (° F) scale, and the *centigrade* (° C) scales. (The small circle with the letter indicates degrees.) Their relation is illustrated in Fig. 3-1 as a linear chart and as a pair of equations. Much of our work will be concentrated in the center of the zone of human comfort, around 65-70° F, or around 20-22° C, easy numbers to remember. (Fig. 3-1 also shows one relation to a third or Kelvin scale, widely used in scientific work.)

There are two basic units of heat energy based on each of the above temperature scales. One is called the *British thermal unit* (BTU) and was originally the amount of energy needed to raise one pound of water 1° F, averaged over the range from freezing to boiling. The second is the *calorie* (cal), originally the energy required to raise one gram of water 1° C. This is sometimes referred to as the *gram-calorie* (gm-cal). Multiples of these units are used, the most common being the kilocalorie (= 1000 cal) and the Mega-BTU, (MBTU or one million BTU).

Because there are many forms of energy, other units may be encountered. A table of conversion factors is shown in Fig. 3-2. Of

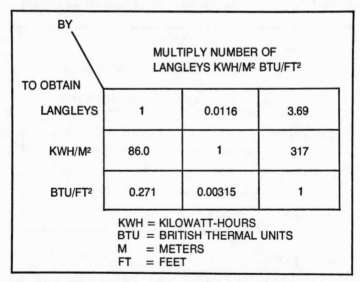

TO OBTAIN	MULTIPLY NUMBER OF		
	LANGLEYS	KWH/M²	BTU/FT²
LANGLEYS	1	0.0116	3.69
KWH/M²	86.0	1	317
BTU/FT²	0.271	0.00315	1

KWH = KILOWATT-HOURS
BTU = BRITISH THERMAL UNITS
M   = METERS
FT = FEET

Fig. 3-2. Relations for conversions between the commonly used solar energy scales. The quantity, Langleys, is sometimes found, but the values in kWh/m² is more common. For practical work BTU/ft² is most common.

these, the most commonly needed is the *watt hour* (Wh)-BTU conversion.

Another set of units we will need is for *power,* which is the time rate of change of energy. Thus, there is another set of equivalents, one corresponding to each of the units of energy, as shown in Fig. 3-3. Note that if the energy unit includes time, it disappears in the corresponding power unit, as in watt-hours and watts. If time does not appear in the quantity of power, it appears as a divisor, as in BTU and BTU per hour.

We will also have to work with other common units, for weight mass, length, area, and so on. The conversions commonly encountered are given in Table 3-1.

To save time and space, a symbol is customarily assigned to each unit. Some of these have been given already. In the following material the symbols of Table 3-2 will be used unless otherwise stated. In using these it is often necessary to keep track of the quantity relating to two or more objects. This is done by subscripts, such as T_W, T_A for the temperature of water and air, or A_1, A_2 . . . A_n for areas one, two, and so on up to some larger number.

In addition to these three quantities, energy, power and temperature, plus the basic ones of length, area, volume, and time, we will need two others. Their definition can be seen from Fig. 3-4. At the top, heat is being applied to a unit cube of material, say a

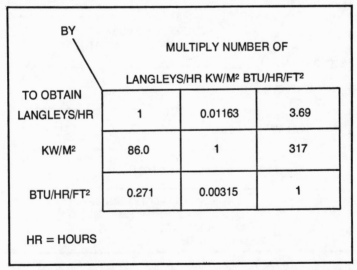

BY TO OBTAIN	MULTIPLY NUMBER OF		
	LANGLEYS/HR	KW/M²	BTU/HR/FT²
LANGLEYS/HR	1	0.01163	3.69
KW/M²	86.0	1	317
BTU/HR/FT²	0.271	0.00315	1

HR = HOURS

Fig. 3-3. Power conversion. Equivalent of Fig. 3-2, but for power, or energy per unit of time.

Table 3-1. Common Unit Conversions.

These conversion factors are often encountered in solar heating work.

1 Meter = 3.28 ft
1 Square Meter = 10.76 square feet
1 Kilogram = 2.2 pounds
1 Gallon water = 8.336 pounds
1 Cubic foot water = 62.4 lbs
1 Cubic foot = 7.48 gallons
1 Horsepower = 746 watts
1 Liter = 0.264 gallons
1 Ton = 2000 lbs
1 Million = 10^6
1 Kilo = 10^3

one-foot cube of masonry. The heat flows across one face into the cube, and out the opposite face. As stated above, there must be a temperature difference between the two faces for this to occur, and this is taken in common units—Fahrenheit degrees when measurements are in feet, centigrade when they are in meters.

Table 3-2. Common Units and Symbols.

Many common quantities are designated by a single letter symbol. The table lists the most commonly encountered units and symbols. Watch the definitions in other places, as there are many variations.

A	Ampere, Area
a	Ambient
b	Breadth
C	Capacity
c	Specific Heat
°C	Degrees Centigrade
D,d	Diameter
E	Electric Potential, Potential
F( )	Function of ( )
°F	Degrees Fahrenheit
H	Heat
J	Joules
I, i	current
k, K	A Constant
°K	Degrees Kelvin
l	Length
M	Meter
m	Mass
P	Power
Q	A quantity
R	Resistance
S, s	Speed
T	Temperature
t	Time, Thickness
U	Conductivity
V, v	Voltage
W	Weight, Wall
w	Width
X, Y, Z	Unknowns

Multipliers

k	kilo or 1000
M	Mega or 1,000,000
m	milli or 1/1000

Greek Letters

α	(alpha) Absorbtivity
Δ	(Delta) Difference
ϵ	(epsilon) Emissivity
π	(Pi) 3.14159

Because materials vary in the amount of heat flow, we will need to use the quantity, *heat conductivity,* or simply, *conductivity.* It is defined as the amount of heat flowing across the unit area, through unit distance, per unit degree of temperature difference between faces. Thus:

$$\text{Conductivity} = \frac{\text{BTU} - \text{ft}}{\text{ft}^2 - {}^\circ\text{F}}$$

or alternately:

$$\text{Conductivity} = \frac{\text{Cal} - \text{cm}}{\text{cm}^2 - {}^\circ\text{C}}$$

Occasionally one will find:

$$\text{Conductivity} = \frac{\text{Watts} - \text{Meter}}{\text{Meter}^2 - {}^\circ\text{C}}$$

Quite often, the item of distance above the line will be omitted, being understood. Conductivity is usually designated by the symbol U.

The second item shown in Fig. 3-4 arises from the fact that the temperature of a body increases as heat flows into it. It thus acts as a storage element. Strictly, this *thermal capacity* or *specific heat* is defined as the amount of heat energy stored in unit mass per unit of temperature rise, or:

$$C_p = \frac{\text{BTU}}{\text{lb}} \text{ or } \frac{\text{CAL}}{\text{gm}}$$

The unit of temperature being understood. However, in practical work, the quantity is not commonly used—instead, a derived quantity, the heat stored per unit volume per degree of temperature rise, is preferred. This is often called *storage* capacity, and is most commonly seen as:

$$C = \frac{\text{BTU}}{\text{ft}^3}$$

But, for liquids, may be represented as:

$$C = \frac{\text{BTU}}{\text{gal}}$$

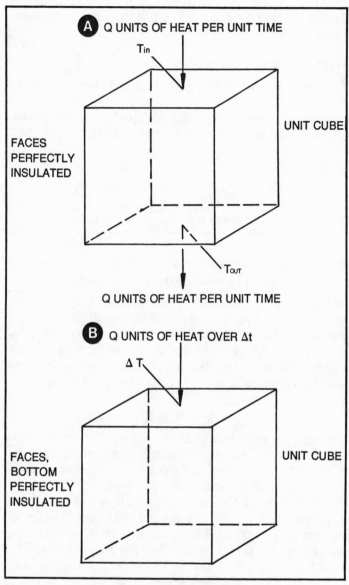

Fig. 3-4. Definition of thermal quantities. (A) Definition of thermal conductivity, the quantity of heat flowing through a unit cube for unit temperature difference in unit time. The common practical unit is the BTU/° F/hour. Resistivity is the reciprocal of conductivity. (B) Definition of specific heat, or heat storage capacity, the quantity of heat required to raise the temperature of a unit cube of material by one unit of temperature. The common practical unit is BTU/ft³/° F, but quantities in pounds or gallons will also be encountered.

The metric units are also found. Note that the unit of temperatures is understood.

EFFECT OF PHYSICAL CONDITIONS

The way in which heat energy transfer and storage vary with physical conditions is important. For heat transfer, the two basic situations are shown in Fig. 3-5. In the upper part, representing, say, two wall areas of different materials and thickness, the total heat flow is the sum of the two flows.
Thus:

$$\text{Heat flow}_{total} = \text{heat flow}_1 + \text{heat flow}_2$$

or:

$$BTU_t = \frac{\text{Conductivity}_2 \times \text{Area}_1}{\Delta t1} + \frac{\text{Conductivity}_2 \times \text{Area}_2}{\Delta t2}$$

and if areas and temperature drops are the same:

$$\text{Conductivity}_{total} = \text{Conductivity}_1 + \text{Conductivity}_2.$$

For the situation in the lower half of the figure, the two conducting materials are touching and heat must flow through both. Here it is usually easier to use a quantity which is equal to one, divided by the conductivity, times the thickness of each material, which is a *resistance* (R). The reason for this preference becomes clear when more than two materials are being considered. Since the relation is R:

$$R_{total} = R_1 + R_2 + R_3 - - - - -$$

for as many materials as are present. (Be sure to keep the difference between resistance and *resistivity* clear: resistivity is the resistance per unit thickness and unit area, and resistance is equal to resistivity times thickness divided by area.)

The unit of resistance is not often used. Instead it is customary to speak of an *R value*. For example, six inches of rock wool insulation will be shown as having an R value of 19. Tables are usually given in terms of conductivity. The precise relation is:

$$R = \frac{1}{t \times A \times U}$$

with t being the thickness.

The thermal resistance/conductivity properties of materials may be tabulated in one of several units. The most common appears to be the conductivity, U, in BTU per hour per square foot per degree Fahrenheit per foot of thickness. Metric units may be

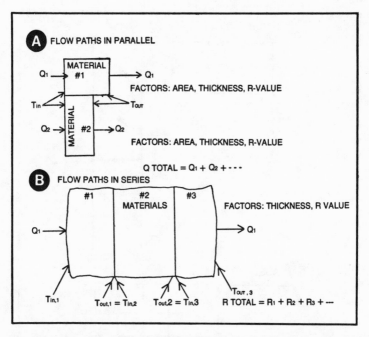

Fig. 3-5. Laws of heat flow. (A) Where insulation blocks are effectively in parallel, the total flow is the sum of the flow across each block. (B) Where the flow path is through successive layers of insulation, the total resistance to flow is the sum of the individual resistances.

found in technical papers. Sometimes the value for designated thickness is given. These units are commonly called *coefficients of transmission,* the values being given in BTU per hour per square foot per degree Fahrenheit. However, more commonly the reciprocal of this unit is given, usually called the *R value.* This is the easiest unit for design use, and it is suggested that all work be done with it.

While the basic elements of heat transfer are straightforward, the field can become complex. An example of this is illustrated in Fig. 3-6, which shows the heat flow at a wall corner. Instead of the heat flow being along straight lines, at right angles to the surface, it follows curved lines. This affects the transfer rate, partly due to the extra surface at the outside corner, partly due to the changes in path length.

In practical work, such fine detail is usually neglected. Heat flow is analyzed on the basis that the wall is straight, has an area equal to the area of the outside wall. The error introduced by this is negligible.

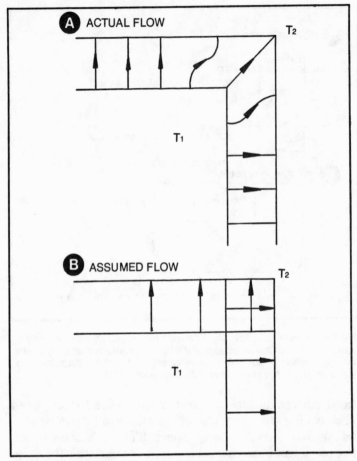

Fig. 3-6. The actual heat flow at a corner (or between two areas of different resistance) is complex, as shown at A, and is not easy to analyze. Calculations are made on the basis of the largest area, assuming the heat flow is in straight lines as shown at B. Error is minimal.

HEAT STORAGE: A COMMONLY NEGLECTED FACTOR

There is, however, one complexity commonly neglected in normal heating and air-conditioning work which is much too important to be neglected in solar heating. This is the combined effect of the heat storage capacity of materials and the presence of resistance to heat flow.

It is easiest to use some symbols from electrical work for this, as shown in Fig. 3-7. Here the symbol for an electrical capacitor is used to represent the heat capacity of a material; and the electrical symbol for resistance, the thermal resistance. Temperature at the input and output corresponds to electrical voltage, and the heat flow corresponds to electrical current.

Suppose the R-C circuit represents a wall, with the temperature raised suddenly on one side. Suppose also that the wall is very

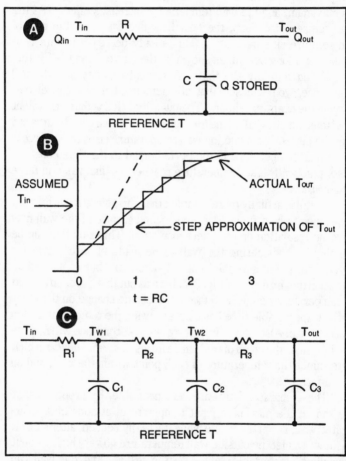

Fig. 3-7. The storage of heat is analyzed R-C electrical circuit as shown at A; R being the thermal resistance and C being the thermal capacity. The rise of temperature is sketched at B, for an assumed sudden temperature change at the face of the material. If temperature rise continues at initial rate, the final value would be reached in one "time constant," the product RC. Because the temperature difference is constantly reducing, the heat flow and temperature rise also reduce. Final temperature is reached practically in three time constants. Sketch C shows the series circuit used to represent a thick wall. T-out will not change for some time after T-in does—perhaps several hours.

conductive and is perfectly insulated on the rear side. In this case, the resistance is a film of stagnant air on the front surface of the wall, an item we will encounter many times.

The sudden change in temperature on the face of the wall is represented by the *step function* labeled T_{in}. At the first instant, the temperature difference is high, being T_{in}-$T_{w\phi}$. Thus, heat flow is at its maximum, and the wall temperature increases rapidly. As the wall temperature rises, the heat flow decreases, so the rate of temperature rise decreases. This steady decrease in rate continues for a long period, as shown by the curve T_w in the figure.

If you multiply the units of thermal capacity and thermal resistance, you will see that all elements but one cancel out, leaving the quantity 1/hours. The quantity 1/RC is thus equivalent to a time, which is called the *time constant* of the circuit. It turns out that the perfectly conducting wall temperature rises to 67 percent of its final temperature in the period equal to the time constant. Also, practically, the temperature reaches its final value in three *time constants*.

A wall is actually more complex than this, since it has internal resistance to heat flow. Also, the second surface of the wall may have no insulation or imperfect insulation. This situation can be handled by considering the wall to be made of successive thin layers, each acting as the simple R-C circuit, but connected as shown in the third part of Fig. 3-7. It turns out that a sudden change of temperature on one wall face produces no change on the other until an appreciable time has elapsed, when the temperature then starts to rise. Also, the temperature at the second face will not rise as high, since the chain of resistance forms a *potential divider* which determines the temperature of each point within the wall, and on its surface.

These characteristics are very desirable. By proper design, we can let the maximum input temperature, at noon on a solar-heated wall, reach the inside when it's really needed, after sunset. Also, we can let the outside wall temperature go very high without exceeding comfortable values on the inside. And the wall can continue to deliver heat long after the sun's energy is no longer there. These are the reasons behind many of the designs pictured in Chapter 2.

We can analyze these effects very simply by dividing the period of temperature change into short intervals, say about one-tenth of a time constant. Over the interval, we assume that the temperature does not change, so the heat flow can be calculated. At the end of the interval, the temperature rises, to an amount determined by the heat flow and the thermal capacity. This new temperature difference is used for the next calculation period, also shown in Fig. 3-7.

Because this process is tedious (unless a programmable calculator or a computer is available), our work can be based on simplifications, using guideline relations and results read from graphs of typical designs. For more data, see the Bibliography.

STEPS TO SYSTEM SIZING

With this review out of the way, let us turn to the matter of determining the size of the solar system needed. The general nature of the problem is shown in Fig. 3-8. At the inside of the house, conditions are relatively constant—a temperature in the comfort zone is needed. But the outside conditions are variable—changes in temperature, in wind, in cloud cover. Also variable over a period of time are the number of people in the house and the amount of cooking, lighting, and water heating energy added. These variables add up to a varying demand for heat input from a furnace in a conventional house. The detail solar design problem is how to cope with these variables, while still maintaining reasonable comfort conditions in the house.

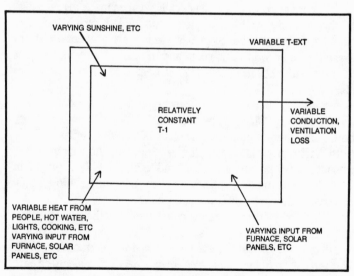

Fig. 3-8. This shows the major elements to be evaluated in a solar heating design. The goal is to keep the internal temperature (T_i) within the comfort range by employing the varying sunshine component.

If we want to avoid oversizing to keep from wasting money, and to avoid undersizing to eliminate unnecessary dependence on fossil fuels, we are going to have to come close to the best design. And to do this we will have to calculate, or to measure, preferably both. Of course, if it's a new house, we will have to calculate, but we will want to base our work on the measurements of others, or on our own work in models if we are trying something new. Let's go into techniques, starting with measurement of an existing home.

SIZING FROM FUEL BILLS

The first method of sizing by measurement depends on having fuel bills available for a season, or preferably for several seasons. If you haven't kept them, perhaps they can be reconstructed from your checkbook, or perhaps your supply company can give you copies. (Your bank keeps copies of your checks on microfilm and probably will supply lists for a small fee.) If you don't have them, start saving them at once if you want to use this method.

The first step in using these bills as data is to tabulate the amount of fuel covered by each and the date it was delivered, as shown in Table 3-3. In the third column place the running sum of the fuel use, the sum of all use up to the date shown. Fill out the table with all of your bill data.

Record also any changes which have been made in the house. In this example a "Florida room" was added during the 1977 summer. Because of the large increase in fuel consumption, storm sashes were added to this room and to other large windows just before the 1979 heating season. The benefit of the change shows clearly.

For the mobile home of this example, LPG is used in cooking and for heating. Thus, there is a small steady demand, cooking, during the summer months. The slope of the "by eye best fit" line to the summer points gives this demand. For the example, this amounts to 4.5 gal./month in 1977 and 1978, and 6.5 gal./month in 1979. Because the tank appeared to have been filled before really necessary, the last figure was ignored.

The slope of the line for the cold winter months gives the total fuel consumption during this period. This amounts to 80 gal./ month in 1977, 126 gal./month in 1978, and 70 gal./month in 1979. This is total input, but a solar system only needs to replace the heat energy coming out of the furnace. Accordingly, the cooking component is first subtracted, giving average furnace inputs of 75, 120,

Table 3-3. System Sizing by Fuel-Use Evaluation-I.

As a first step to system sizing, the fuel use (of an existing house) is tabulated chronologically and the cumulative use obtained by successive addition.

Date	Fuel Delivered (gallons)	Cumulative Use (gallons)
1/19/77	80	0
2/19/77	70	80
12/27/77	60	140
1/18/78	85	210
1/27/78	50	295
2/21/78	70	345
5/5/78	65	415
10/17/78	25	480
12/8/78	35	505
1/20/79	75	540
2/21/79	70	615
3/4/79	60	685
8/7/79	25	745
Delivered	770	

and 65 gal./month for the three years respectively, and an average input of 87 gal./month.

These consumption rates are now converted in BTU by multiplying by the heat content of the fuel, from Fig. 3-9. This gives:

Year	Monthly Use	Monthly Furnace Input
1977	75 gal.	6.98 MBTU
1978	120 gal.	11.16 MBTU
1979	65 gal.	6.05 MBTU

These, however, are inputs to the furnace. An appreciable amount escapes up the furnace flue. According to its nameplate, the particular furnace used is rated at 60,000 BTU/hr. input, 48,000 BTU/hr. output, for an efficiency of 80 percent. The monthly figures thus are:

Year	Fuel Used	Furnace Input	Furnace Output
1977	75 gal./mo.	6.98 MBTU/mo.	5.58 MBTU/mo.
1978	120 gal./mo.	11.16 MBTU/mo.	8.81 MBTU/mo.
1979	65 gal./mo.	6.05 MBTU/mo.	4.84 MBTU/mo.

We will use these figures later.

As an alternative to the above, we can work on an annual basis, using the total fuel used in a year. The estimated fuel used for cooking (12 times monthly use) is subtracted from this, and the furnace efficiency applied. For the data above, only two complete years are covered. Using the year from June to June, we get:

			Gal./Year
Period		Fuel	Cooking
June, 1977-June, 1978		262	54
June, 1978-June, 1979		320	54

	Million BTU/Year		
Period	Net	Furnace In	Furnace Out
June, 1977-June, 1978	208	19.34	15.42
June, 1978-June, 1979	266	24.74	19.79

We shall also use these values later. (However, we must be careful in doing this, because of the physical changes mentioned above.)

SIZING BY TEST DATA

For a second method of measuring heat loss, we need to consider the way in which a furnace works. Suppose that the thermostat has just closed and the furnace comes on. Heat starts pouring into the house and the internal temperature starts to rise. After a time interval (let's call it t_{on}), the temperature reaches the upper limit on the thermostat, T_{HI}, and the furnace goes off. Internal temperature starts to drop, and when it reaches the lower thermostat setting, T_{LO} (after an interval, t_{off}) the cycle repeats.

Figure 3-10 is a sketch of the heat flow and temperature situation during one of the cycles. While the furnace is on, it is feeding heat to the house at its design rate, shown by the block labeled GAIN, above the zero line. However, the house is losing heat all of the time, as shown by the block labeled LOSS, below the zero line. The temperature behavior is shown just below these blocks, T_a being the outdoor or *ambient* temperature.

Now, on the average, we expect the heat gain block to just compensate for the heat loss block, i.e., to be equal in heat content. As long as the indoor and outdoor temperatures are constant and someone doesn't upset the normal heating by leaving a door open, the relation will hold, even over short periods. Thus we can write:

$$\text{Heat Loss} = \text{Heat Gain}$$

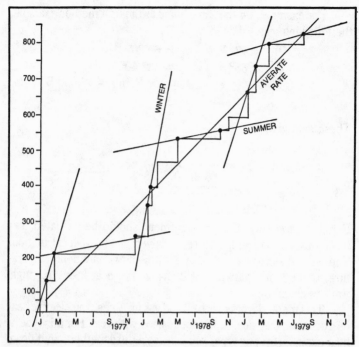

Fig. 3-9. System sizing by fuel use evaluation-II. The cumulative use is plotted against time, and lines drawn to indicate average use rate, peak rate during winter, and average rate during summer, if fuel is used at this time. Various methods of estimating are given in the text.

The heat gain is the furnace rating in BTU/hr. multiplied by the length of the on period, and the heat loss is the loss per hour multiplied by the sum of the two periods. Thus:

$$\text{Heat Loss} = \text{Furnace Rating} \times \frac{t_{on}}{t_{off} + t_{on}}$$

where we can measure the times in convenient units—minutes and tenths are good.

This loss applies only to the temperature differential between average indoor and outdoor temperature. To get the unit loss, in BTU/hr/° F, we divide the above relation by the differential, and get:

Heat Loss, BTU/hr/°

$$F = \text{Furnace Rating, BTU/hr} \times \frac{1}{\dfrac{T_{LO} + T_{HI} - T_a}{2}} \times \frac{t_{on}}{t_{off} + t_{on}}$$

For example, for the same home as the first method example, the following was obtained:

$$T_{HI} = 72° \text{ F} \qquad t_{on} = 6^m\ 20^s$$
$$T_{LO} = 68° \text{ F} \qquad t_{off} = 13^m\ 40^s$$
$$T_a = 48° \text{ F} \qquad \text{Furnace Rating} = 48{,}000 \text{ BTU/hr.}$$

These data give:

$$\text{Loss} = 48{,}000 \times \frac{1}{\dfrac{68 + 70 - 48}{2}} \times \frac{6.33}{13.66 + 6.33}$$

$$= 691 \text{ BTU/hr.}$$

For good accuracy, this measurement should be repeated, say three times at one temperature, and averages used in calculation. These results can be checked by a run at another ambient temperature. (Note that high winds will change the heat loss; you might want to check this.)

This method works with oil and gas furnaces, and electric heat on a common thermostat. It's not so good with coal. For this type of heat (actually for any type) you can use a third method. Shut down the heating system, turn off all lights, and note the temperature drop in a period of, say, one hour. Now bring the heat back up, and again shut down the furnace, but leave all of the lights on. Note the temperature drop in the same time period. It will be less, due to the heat input of the lights. Add up the wattage of all bulbs. The relations given will allow an estimate of the heat loss. With care, these results will be accurate.

COMPARISON OF HISTORICAL SIZING DATA

We now need a way to relate the two or three results of measurement and also to permit evaluation of the differences which occur from one year to another. To do this, we need another concept, the *degree-day*. To see the definition of this, let us take a reference temperature, which is usually 65° F. Suppose the outdoor temperature is exactly one degree lower than the reference for a period of 24 hours. This is called a heating load of one degree-day. If the temperature was 60° for the 24 hours, it would be a load of five degree-days and so on. The outdoor temperature is actually varying. We could allow for this by calculating for each hour, then summing over the day, but the results are just the same if we calculate the average temperature each day, and use this.

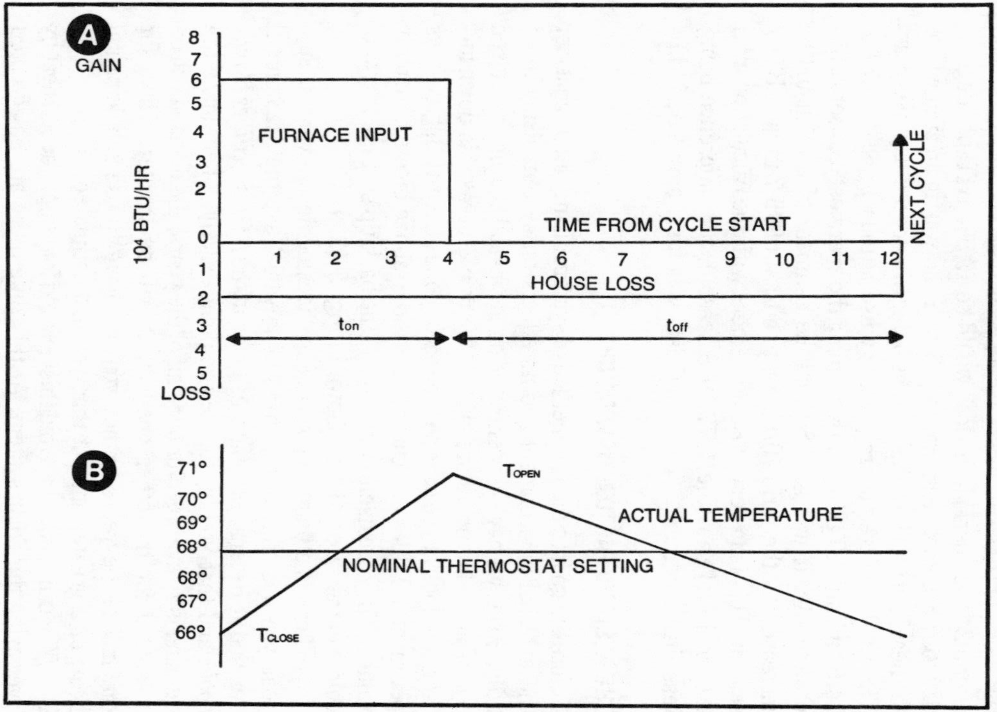

Fig. 3-10. System sizing by furnace cycle timing. The heat loss from the house between two successive furnace starts must equal the heat input by the furnace for the period it was on, as at A. The heat loss is only one-third of the furnace input. Accuracy is greater if several cycles are measured, and results averaged.

Values of these degree-day heating loads are made up by each Weather Service office. Tables of past years are available in many places, for example, in the *Weather Almanac*, in the *DOE Facilities Solar Design Handbook*, in Edward Mazria's book (1979), and others. A map showing the expected annual values for all of the U.S.A. is shown in Fig. 3-11. Figure 3-12 shows the contours for January, the coldest month. Interpolation between the contours will give an estimate for your locality, but it is better to use data for the city closest to you. Check the nearest Weather Service office, or see your library.

As an example of the use of the degree-day concept, consider the timed period test. This gave a loss of 691 BTU/hr. Continued over a 24 hour period, the loss would be 16,584 BTU per degree-day ($65°$ F indoor temperature). The home was in an area where the heat load was low, the average being 879 degree-days per year. The total expected average energy use is thus $16,584 \times 879$ or 14.58 million BTU/season, assuming the thermostat is set at $65°$ F. Actually, it was at $70°$ F, so the estimate of load should be increased by the ratio 70/65, or to a total of 15.7 million BTU/season. This is in very close agreement with the calculation from the total fuel use (the 1977-1978 season), the difference being less than 2 percent. (The timed data was for a single period.)

THE RESERVE FACTOR: HOW MUCH?

Before we go into the last method of system sizing, let us consider the external environment and its effects on system sizing more fully. So far we have concentrated on the annual heating, as caused by the annual temperature cycle. We would break this down further, and look at the heat needed each month, i.e., the degree-days per month. Tables and curves referred to above give the monthly values. They are useful when sizing the back-up system. A typical cold weather area plot is shown in Fig. 3-13.

There is a point to consider in choosing design values. Suppose you design a system for a table value, say the 8129 annual demand at Helena, Montana, as given in the *DOE Facilities Handbook*, and that you hit the design point exactly. Then, since the demand is an average, for one-half of the years, the demand will be less, and for the other one-half, it will be greater. Thus, for one-half of the years, either you will have to use supplemental heat, or a greater amount than you had estimated.

You can reduce or avoid this demand for supplemental heat by oversizing the solar system. At this time there are no accepted

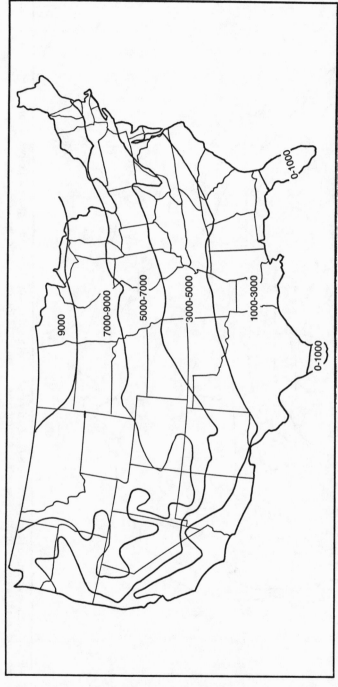

Fig. 3-11. Chart giving the average heating requirement for homes in the U.S.A., in degree-days. These are for average locations and will vary depending on lay-of-the-land, trees, and from year to year.

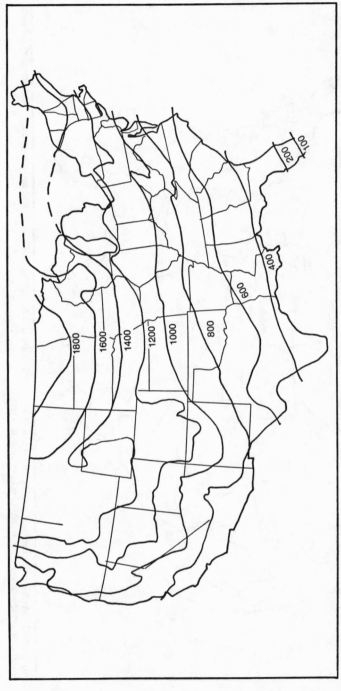

Fig. 3-12. January heating requirement, U.S.A., usually the coldest month. A system sized to give 100 percent solar heat in this month will be satisfactory in other months. See references for other months and for your particular area.

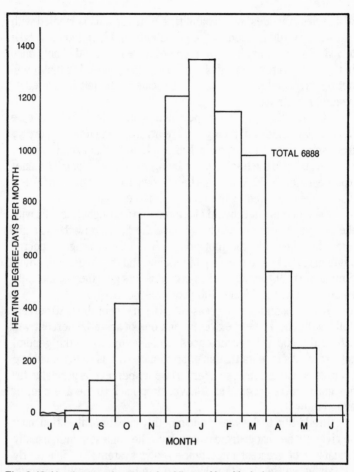

Fig. 3-13. Heating requirements for Albany, New York, for average years. Note that the temperature goes below 65° F every month of the year. These curves are used to estimate heating requirements in systems sized at less than 100 percent solar heating. For example, a solar system capable of providing only 1000 degree-days of heating per month will certainly require supplemental heat in December, January, and February. Because of weather variations, supplemental heat will be required in March for about one-half of the years.

guidelines for doing this. You will have to make your own choice of size, remembering that increasing size will cost installation money, whereas not doing it will increase fuel costs.

For those who want to investigate the extra costs, the method illustrated in Fig. 3-14 is suggested. This is based on the use of a special graph paper, called *extreme value paper*. The bottom axis is labeled in percent, the scale being warped to emphasize the "tails" of a series of values, or probabilities. The top axis is labeled with the quantity 100 divided by the probability and is called the *return period*. For example, if a given temperature is exceeded only once in ten years (return period of ten years), the probability that it will not be exceeded is 90 percent. The scale to the left is labeled as needed for the data.

To use this paper the pertinent data values, in this case degree-day values for each year, are arranged in numerical order, from smallest to largest, as in Table 3-4. Note that each is given a number, n, with the total number being equal to N. For each value, a percentage is calculated, this being equal to the quantity $n/N + 1$. The value is plotted at the indicated percentage.

Data of this kind should plot almost in a straight line, but with the last point sometimes being above the line. Draw the straight line which best fits the plot points. Then the average expected value is given by the crossing of this line and the 50 percent point. Similarly, the 90 percent or 99 percent points give the values likely to be exceeded in 10 and 100 years, respectively.

In this example, an increase of system size of about 10 percent will handle the 10-year extreme, and one of about 20 percent will handle the 100 year occurrences. This seems to be the general pattern, and suggests that an approximate rule is to mark out the average demand, then use a ten to twenty percent larger value for design. If costs become excessive, drop back to the average, or even below it.

In addition to the yearly and monthly variation, attention must be given to the change from day to day. The coldest month, usually January is of greatest importance. Solar systems are inherently averaging, so the design value used can be the monthly average temperature. For Helena, this is 18° F for January. Alternately, the average low temperature can be used, which is 7.8° F for January. The extreme value technique can be used to obtain temperatures not likely to be exceeded in a given number of years.

The lowest temperature of the day varies greatly in a given year, and from year to year. It is much more difficult and expensive to size a solar system to handle these swings. Thus, it is common practice to design for average temperature in the coldest month, and to depend on one of the following for comfort on cold nights:

Supplemental heat
Zoned heating, i.e., shutting off some rooms
Aids, such as insulating shutters
More clothing

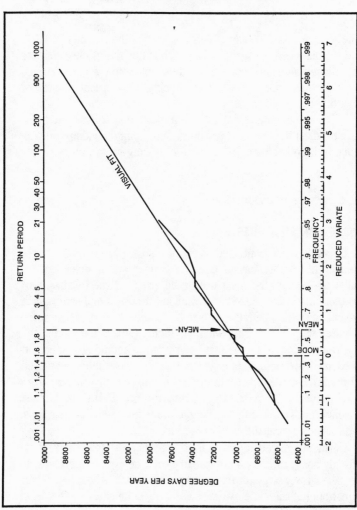

Fig. 3-14. Annual degree-days per year for Helena, Montana, plotted to emphasize the high demand years, sometimes called a Gumbel plot. A system sized to 7160 degree-days will require supplemental heat one year in two. If the system is sized at 7560 degree-days, it will only need supplemental heat one year in ten, and at 8340, one year in one hundred (assuming sufficient storage—a daily study is needed to size this.) Below 6600 degree-days, supplemental heat will be needed every year.

Or perhaps you can give a party, and have more people in the house.

Let us return a moment to the first method of heat loss measurement, and consider it with respect to annual degree-day values. Annual values can be obtained from the local weather office or from the *Weather Almanac*. For the calendar used in preparing Fig. 3-9, the data are:

Year	Heating per gallon	Output Heating MBTU	Annual Deg-Days	BTU Deg-Days
1977	280 (est)	16.8	1117	15,040
1978	330	20.5	920	22,260
1979	230 (est	13.1	865	15,140

The influence of increasing the floor area in the summer of 1977, and the use of storm sashes in 1979 and after shows clearly. Note that these values are not greatly different from the ones derived above, considering the effect of keeping the home at 70° rather than 65° F.

These examples point out two important factors to watch. Be sure to adjust the degree-day values if you want the indoor temperature to be other than 65° F, by multiplying by the ratio:

$$\frac{\text{Desired T}}{650}$$

Also, be sure to use furnace output when calculating fuel use.

SYSTEM BALANCE QUESTIONS

So far we have concentrated on sizing a solar system by measurement. This works for an existing house, but it does leave a question—should the solar design be sized for the existing heat loss, or should the house be worked on, first by simple steps such as sealing cracks, installing storm sash, and so on, or by the more complex step of changing windows, adding insulation, and such.

As a guide, it seems that solar heating should not be considered until after simple energy saving steps have been completed. There is a useful guide for this, the *Home Energy Savers Work Book*, available from the Government Printing Office, Washington, DC. This gives suggestions for reducing heat loss, and for estimating the fuel reduction.

The suggested approach is to take these simple steps, if not already done, then try a preliminary solar design. If this seems to be excessively large, or expensive, then return to heat loss determination, but this time by the calculation techniques which follow.

BASIC DATA		PREPARED DATA		
Season	Degree-Days	Serial No (n)	Value	Plot at
55-56	7395	1	6641	.0476
56-57	6795	2	6666	.0952
57-58	6724	3	6708	.1429
58-59	7720	4	6724	.1905
59-60	6641	5	6795	.2381
60-61	7243	6	6872	.2857
61-62	6666	7	6936	.3333
62-63	7452	8	6937	.3810
63-64	6872	9	6948	.4286
64-65	7172	10	7057	.4762
65-66	6948	11	7079	.5238
66-67	7251	12	7123	.5714
67-68	7057	13	7172	.6190
68-69	6937	14	7243	.6667
69-70	7328	15	7251	.7143
70-71	7316	16	7316	.7619
71-72	7079	17	7378	.8095
72-73	6708	18	7395	.8571
73-74	6936	19	7452	.9048
74-75	7123	20 = N	7720	.9524

$$\text{Plot at} = \frac{n}{N+1}$$

Table 3-4. Plotting Data.

Steps in preparing an extreme value plot. The data is first ordered from smallest to largest. For each, a plotting position is calculated. After plotting, a "by eye" line is usually sufficiently accurate to give desired estimates.

Using these will tell where to put the heat loss reduction effort to best advantage.

SIZING BY CALCULATION

The problems we face in calculating heat loss are shown in Figs. 3-15 and 3-16. At the top of Fig. 3-15, a house is represented by its outside walls, seen from above. Each wall loses heat, the paths being represented by the resistances T_{W1}, T_{W2}, and so on. There is also heat loss through the doors and windows, represented by T_ϕ and T_{WW}. For each of these paths, the temperature difference is $T_i - T_a$.

We must also be concerned with the flow through the ceiling, attic and roof, and through the floor, basement (if present), or floor slab (if used), as sketched in the lower half of Fig. 3-15. A further loss is due to air leakage, also as sketched.

The walls of houses are composed of several materials, and vary widely in design. Three typical constructions are shown in Fig. 3-16. At the top is a warm climate, concrete block type; in the

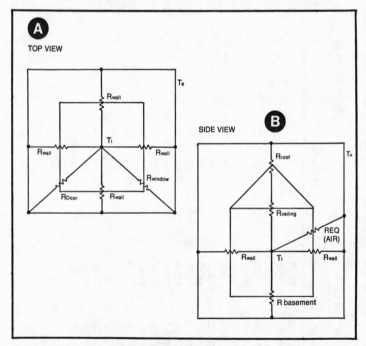

Fig. 3-15. These sketches represent the heat loss paths for a house, seen from the top at A and the side at B. For system sizing by calculation, each of these loss elements must be evaluated.

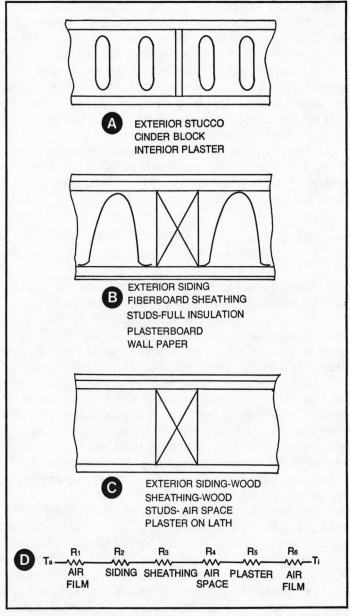

Fig. 3-16. For the evaluation of the loss path of an element the construction must be determined. A, B, and C show typical construction for a southern cinder-block house, a well insulated 1950 house, and an older house. For each, the thickness and R-value of material are used to calculate the overall R-value at D.

center a recent "well insulated" design; and at the bottom, an old, uninsulated wall. The analysis of these are similar, however. We must take the resistivity per unit area and add these together, as indicated by the bottom picture of series resistances in Fig. 3-16.

In doing this, we must take into account the presence of the resistive air film on the inner wall surface, and the second film on the outside. The outside film is affected by wind and is normally less than the indoor one. It may disappear completely with high winds, making a house appreciably colder.

The air film is also different for horizontal surfaces, as in attic floors. For these, the total resistance to outdoors is determined by adding the values for the entire path. If the attic temperature is needed, it can be calculated from the relation:

$$T_{attic} - T_a = T_i - T_a \; \frac{(\text{Resistance, attic} - \text{outside})}{(\text{Resistance, inside} - \text{outside})}$$

The same procedure is used for attached garages, shelter sheds, and shut-off rooms. While a calculation can be done for basements, it is often assumed that the basement temperature is equal to $(T_i - 45)$. Common material R values are given in Table 3-5. This also gives air film coefficients. Note that air spaces of four inches and less are handled as a single resistance, rather than two in series.

Loss values for doors and windows vary with type and also with the amount of glazing. Air-infiltration loss depends on the number of air changes per hour. It is a major loss factor, but remember that respiratory problems can occur if the air change is not sufficient. One change per hour is suggested. For slab floors, the heat loss is primarily controlled by the slab perimeter and by the amount of insulation. Typical values for these quantities are shown in Table 3-6.

Heat-loss evaluation of a building consists first in determining each of the effective R values for the surfaces, walls, ceilings, and so on. It may be easier to convert these to conductivity values by the relation $U = 1/R$. The conductivity value is then multiplied by the surface area and the temperature difference to get the heat loss for that surface. Don't forget to subtract the area of doors and windows from wall areas, since these are calculated separately. The loss due to air infiltration, and for a slab floor perimeter, if used, is also calculated (see Table 3-7).

The sum of these losses is the total design heat loss for the assumed outdoor temperature. It is often useful to take time to

	R
Air Film, Moving Air, Vertical Surface	1.2
Air Film, Stagnant Air, all	0.2
Air Film, at Floor	1.7
Air Film, at Ceiling	1.1
Air Space, 1/8"	2.5
Air Space, 1/4"	1.7
Air Space, 3/4" and more	1.2
Air Space, 3/4" and more, Aluminum foil one side	2.1
Air Spaces, (3), with two sheets Aluminum foil	6.8
Adobe, 1"	.28
Brick, 4"	.81
Concrete, 8"	.88
Concrete Block, 8"	1.93
Wood, typical	1.33
Plywood	2.0
Glass, 1/8"	.9
Plaster Board, 1/2"	.45
Mineral Wool, 6"	18.8
Fiberglas Batt, 1"	3.5
Polystyrene Board, typical	4.0
Vermiculite, 1"	2.5
Cellulose Fiber	4.7
Sawdust, 1"	2.2

Table 3-5. Insulation R-Values.

Typical R-Values for air films and spaces and for common construction materials. Extensive tables are available in standard references found in any public library.

Table 3-6. Air-Infiltration and Slab-Loss Factors.

(A) Air leakage for typical window and door construction. Loss can vary markedly with wind, especially if weatherstrip is not maintained. (B) Loss factors for slab on ground construction. Perimeter insulation is very important. For heated basements, calculate as for walls. For unheated basements, measure the temperature, or use 35° F as estimated value.

A. Air Infiltration, in cu ft/hr/inch of crack	Leakage
Wood Sash, Average	70
Wood Sash, Weatherstripped	24
Wood Sash, Air Sealed and Weatherstripped	6
Metal Sash, Industrial	175
Metal Sash, Average Home	55
Metal Sash, Weatherstripped	32
Doors, Plain	110
Doors, Weatherstripped	55
Doors, Air Sealed and Weatherstripped	12
B. Heat Transfer, Slab on Ground	
Bare Concrete Floor, on Ground	R = 1.0
Wood Floor over Concrete on Ground, 1″ insulation	R = 6.0

Note:
ΔT under floor is about $0.2 \times (T_i - T_a)$
ΔT at perimeter is about $0.9 \times (T_i - T_a)$

determine the contribution of each loss source in percent, by the relation 100 × Item loss/total loss. It seems to be easier to visualize the relative importance of each surface in the total picture. Finally, the heat loss per degree-day (Q/DD) and per average season (Q/season) are determined by the relations:

$$Q/DD = \frac{\text{Design loss} \times 24}{65 - T_i}$$

$$Q/\text{season} = Q_{DD} \times DD/\text{year}$$

Be sure to check all work.

This work is somewhat tedious, and it is easy to get confused. Generally, it is best to prepare a tabular form with quantities listed and blanks to fill in. This gives a permanent record which is easy to check. It is also easy to transfer data to a record form when calculating the effect of changes, as when checking whether to add more insulation.

While only arithmetic is needed, calculations are much faster if a small handheld calculator is used. In any event, the work is no

Table 3-7. Resistance Calculation Form.

A form for calculation of the R-Value of a house, providing for two types of walls and windows and up to five components for each element.

Walls, Type 1								
Area	___ + ___ + ___ + ___ + ___ + ___	= ___						
Resistances	___ + ___ + ___ + ___ + ___ + ___	= ___						
Walls, Type 2								
Area	___ + ___ + ___ + ___	= ___						
Resistances	___ + ___ + ___ + ___	= ___						
Ceiling								
Area	___ + ___ + ___ + ___	= ___						
Resistances	___ + ___ + ___	+ ___						
Floor								
Area	___ + ___ + ___ + ___	= ___						
Resistances	___ + ___ + ___	= ___						
Windows, Type 1								
Area	___ + ___ + ___ + ___	= ___						
Resistances	___ + ___ + ___ + ___	= ___						
Windows, Type 2								
Area	___ + ___ + ___	= ___						
Resistances	___ + ___ + ___	= ___						
Doors								
Areas	___ + ___ + ___	= ___						
Resistances	___ + ___ + ___	= ___						
Other								
Areas	___ + ___ + ___	= ___						
Resistances	___ + ___ + ___	= ___						

Table 3-8. Heat-Loss Calculation Form.

Form for calculating the heat loss of a house, in BTU, BTU/degree-day, and BTU total (worst month). Recommendation: keep all data in a notebook for future reference.

Element	Area	×	ΔT	÷	Resistance	=	Loss
Wall 1	——	×	——	÷	——	=	——
Wall 2	——	×	——	÷	——	=	——
Ceiling	——	×	——	÷	——	=	——
Floor	——	×	——	÷	——	=	——
Window 1	——	×	——	÷	——	=	——
Window 2	——	×	——	÷	——	=	——
Doors	——	×	——	÷	——	=	——
Other	——	×	——	÷	——	=	——

Conduction Loss Subtotal —————

Infiltration $0.018 \times$ —— (ft^3) $\times$ —— (T) = ——

Design Heating Load, BTU/hr ——

$\times$ 24 = Load, BTU/day ——

$-$ Design Degree-Days = BTU/D-D ——

$\times$ Jan. D-D = Worst Month Load ——

82

Table 3-9. Typical Heat-Loss Experience.

Table showing heat loss of a "well constructed" 1950 house before and after reinsulation and for a 1976 HUD recommended design house. Unless well designed, windows are likely to be the largest loss item; otherwise, air leakage. See cautions in the text before attempting to reduce air infiltration.

| | TYPICAL LOSS PERCENTAGES | | |
Type	1950 House	Reinsulated 1950 House	1976 House
Element			
Walls	28%	15.6%	13%
Ceiling	11.7%	9.8%	10%
Floor/Basement	10.2%	5.1%	17%
Door/Windows	32.6%	32.9%	18%
Infiltration	17.5	36.5%	35%

Data from HUD, NBS

more difficult than balancing a check book. (Of course, if you expect to do the work many times, say for friends, or for a business, it is worthwhile to use a programmable calculator.)

The form of Table 3-8 has been kept as simple as possible, while retaining adequate information. Other forms may be found in the *Solar Energy Handbook* (1979) and the *DOE Facilities Handbook*. The last also gives an alternate method of heat loss analysis.

REDUCING HEATING DEMAND

Before proceeding with design of a solar system, it is well to consider possible ways to reduce the heating demand. A guide for this is shown in Table 3-9, which gives the expected heat loss percentages for homes built to 1976 HUD standards. If your calculations show a great variation from these, improvements would be in order.

In these figures, infiltration is the major item and the air exchange rate might be reduced. This can be bad, especially if there are any open fires, such as a gas range, or if there are a lot of plastics in the house—they give off gasses which can be unpleasant, or dangerous. Doors and windows are the next largest item, and the effect of storm sashes or double glazing should be checked. Floor-basement insulation could be improved, as can that of other surfaces, but probably a general increase in insulation amount will be needed to secure marked reduction in heat loss.

If you have been complaining about fuel bills, or find high fuel consumption in test, follow the steps given in *The Home Energy*

Savers Workbook. Consider also the area around the outside of your home. For example, trees or fences on the windward side can reduce heat loss appreciably.

When you are sure that there are no untoward losses present, the heat loss remaining represents the demand on the solar system, or on the solar plus back-up systems. This heat loss determines the system size needed.

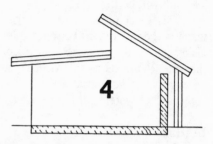

Sizing the Components

The sun is a nuclearly fueled heat engine of great complexity. For the purposes of solar heating, its most important characteristic is that it radiates energy as a heated body of nearly perfect emissivity, one having a temperature of 5760° Absolute, or nearly 10,000° F. The total amount of energy radiated is nearly constant, the variation being about 1 percent over a period of years. An appreciable fraction of the energy is in the band of visible light, with a small fraction as short-wave ultraviolet, and the largest as infrared, or "long-wave" heat energy.

At the average distance of the earth from the sun, the energy radiated amounts to 1350 watts per square meter of surface at right angles to the rays (preferred units). This quantity is called the solar constant, and can also be expressed as:

Solar constant = 1350 watts/meter^2
= 430 BTU/ft^2/hr.
= 125.7 watts/ft^2
= 1.8 horsepower/meter^2
= 1.94 gm.cal./cm^2/min.

The rate of heat flow is sometimes expressed in *Langleys*, or gm.cal./cm^2, so the solar constant can also be expressed as 1.94 Langleys/min.

While this amount of energy flow is appreciable, it is very small compared to many heating sources. An electric iron, for example, will release about 1250 watts over an area of 10 × 15 cm, corresponding to an energy density 60 times greater than that of the sun. A typical small gas furnace flame will release about 70,000 BTU/hr over an area of about one square foot, over 150 times greater. In a small rocket engine, just the heat leakage across the engine wall at the throat may reach 1 HP per square inch, some 800 times greater than solar energy density. The energy in the rocket jet itself will be thousands of times greater.

This great difference in energy density is responsible for many of the differences between solar and conventional heating. Using solar energy requires appreciable area properly exposed to the sun. Remember—this doesn't necessarily mean that solar energy use is better or worse or easier or harder than using conventional systems. It just means that there will be differences.

EARTH/SUN RELATIONS

The earth does not maintain a constant distance from the sun. Accordingly, as a result of the inverse square radiation law, the intensity of the solar radiation just above the atmosphere also varies, by about plus or minus 3.5 percent from the mean value. The greatest amount is received during the winter months for places in the northern hemisphere.

The earth's atmosphere modifies the amount of solar energy received and also the distribution of energy wavelengths. Most of the shortwave, or ultraviolet, radiation is absorbed. Part of the longwave, or infrared, radiation is also absorbed. At some wavelengths, which correspond to characteristics of water vapor, oxygen, and carbon dioxide, the absorption is high, essentially complete. On a typical clear day, with the sun directly overhead, the solar intensity will be about 70 percent as strong as it is just outside the atmosphere.

Clouds of condensed water vapor affect the solar energy further. First, they reflect a good part of the energy back into space. The amount which passes through the cloud is reduced by absorption. The direction of radiation is also changed by reflection and refraction due to the water droplets which make up the cloud. One can observe this effect by looking through polarizing sunglasses on a fully cloudy day. When looking at the position of the sun, rotation of the glasses makes no change in the light intensity, but away from the sun there is a noticeable to marked change as the glasses are rotated. In fact, a sun seeker for cloudy days can be made with a mechanism using this technique.

While these effects are important, other effects caused by the rotation of the earth on its axis and the tilt of the axis are the dominant ones. These give the apparent motion of the sun shown in Fig. 4-1. In addition to the day-night cycle, absorption increases as the sun gets lower and lower in the sky, due to the increased amount of atmosphere which the rays must traverse. The effect is further compounded if we are dealing with fixed surfaces, such as a window or solar absorber. As can be seen from Fig. 4-2, the area projected towards the sun decreases as the angle away from the perpendicular to the surface increases. Also, if we are dealing with transparent surfaces, such as windows, the amount of energy lost increases as the arrival angle of the rays becomes more grazing. The complications of this increase when we also consider the effect of solar altitude changes due to the tilt of the earth's axis. Again the effects are not necessarily bad—Fig. 1-3 shows how the effect of axis tilt can be used to give seasonal control of solar input.

However, since the human comfort zone is a relatively narrow temperature range, we are going to have a major problem matching the varying solar input to the needed relatively constant temperature. To see how to do this, we need to look at the varying solar components in more detail, then look at the various concepts of Chapter 2 to see what design values must be used to achieve close

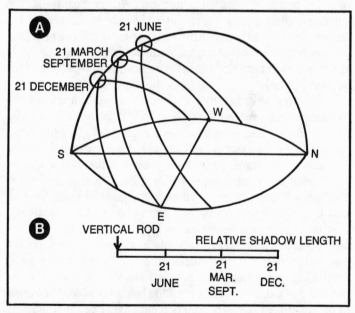

Fig. 4-1. Apparent solar position. *A* shows apparent path of the sun and noon position for four dates, for a location about 30° N. At *B*, relative shadow length from a vertical rod for the four dates.

to comfort zone temperatures. These steps are the heart of solar heating component sizing.

SOLAR DATA FOR SOLAR SYSTEM DESIGN

Because of the variation in solar energy availability with angle of incidence on the absorber, we need numerical data, rather than the visualization of Fig. 4-1. A typical plot of the needed data is shown in Fig. 4-2. This gives the sun's elevation above the horizon and the relative bearing from due south for an observer located between 28° N and 52° N latitudes. The times shown are sun time, and the plot is for the dates of November 21 and January 21, that is, one month before and after the winter solstice of December 21. Similar plots can be prepared for other dates, but this is usually not necessary for system sizing. If a system gives satisfactory heating on January 21, it will usually be satisfactory in other seasons.

The combined effects of solar angle and absorption cause the solar input to vary with geographic location. The major elements of this variation can be seen from Fig. 4-3, which shows the mean annual clear day solar radiation at the surface. The angle effect, in reducing northern radiation is dominant. In the Southwest, the combined effect of dry climate and high elevations reduce the absorption. This is the area where it is easiest to use solar heating. The poorest areas are in Oregon, Vermont, and upstate New York. However, even here the solar energy is within 60 percent of the best-area values.

This total solar radiation is the sum of two components: the radiation directly received and the diffuse radiation, scattered by the air, clouds, and suspended dust. Figure 4-4 gives the direct component for a surface at right angles to the solar rays. Note that this direct term shows greater variation than the total value.

The diffuse component is shown in Fig. 4-5. It is the least in the high, dry areas of the Southwest and greatest along the Gulf Coast. This diffuse term is the reason solar systems contribute heat on cloudy days—radiation is still received until the cloud layers become very thick, almost black, as seen from below. The fraction of time that this diffuse term is of special importance can be seen in Fig. 4-6, which gives the mean annual hours of sunshine for the U.S.A. Of the approximately 4400 hours possible, large areas of the Southwest have 75 to 80 percent cloud-free time, whereas direct sunshine may occur less than 50 percent of possible hours in the coastal areas of New England and the Pacific Northwest.

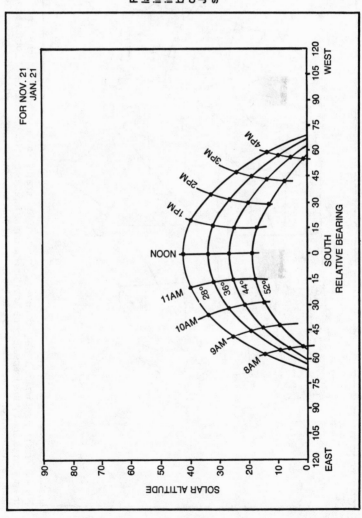

Fig. 4-2. Apparent solar position for latitudes from 28° to 52° N, with time indicated. Charts such as this are important for determining the possible shadowing of an absorber. This chart is for the critical month, January. Charts for all months are shown in the references.

89

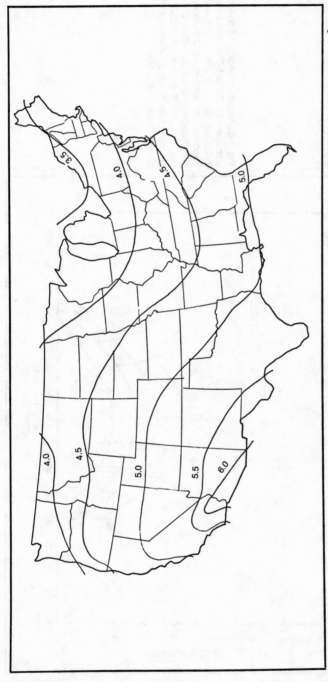

Fig. 4-3. This map shows the average day solar energy received on a horizontal surface, both direct and diffuse. The units are kWh/m²/day, the preferred unit for this measurement. Note that maximum input occurs for the clear air of Southwest U.S.A. Note also that these values include the effect of cloudiness. This and the following data are not recommended for design-see references for this data.

90

Fig. 4-4. This map shows the average day solar energy received directly from the sun on a surface at right angles to the sun's rays. The effect of clear air in the Southwest, and clouds and haze in the Northwest and Northeast are very marked.

91

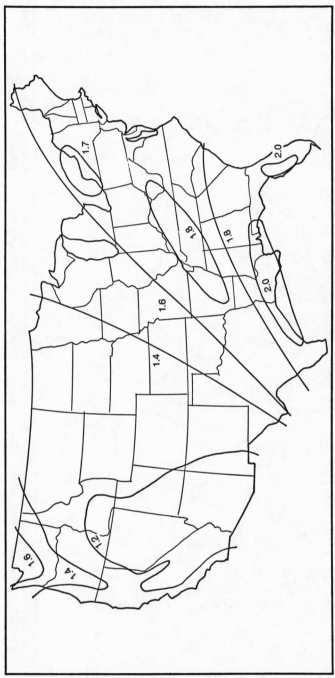

Fig. 4-5. The average day solar energy received on a horizontal surface from rays diffusely scattered in the atmosphere. Caused mostly by clouds, diffusion is least in the clear air of the Southwest.

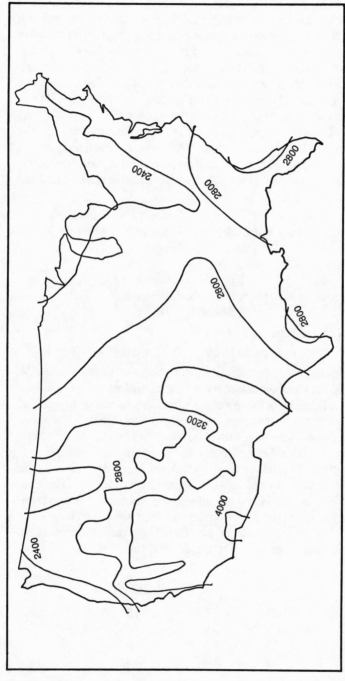

Fig. 4-6. Average annual hours of sunshine for the U.S.A. (Maximum hours is 4390 per year.) The geographic effects are very clear.

93

The way the available solar energy varies with the sun's position can be seen from Fig. 4-7. The upper curves give the direct solar component values for each midmonth, as a function of solar altitude. The variation is due to absorption. The lower set of curves gives, approximately, the variation in diffuse radiation. Note that this is for specific surface orientations. The diffuse term has components for any direction and elevation angle but is greatest for angles close to the sun's position.

The effect of angle between the solar collector surface and the solar ray line has been mentioned several times. For perfect absorbers and the direct component, the effect is purely geometric and varies only with the angle of incidence. This can be calculated from the relation:

$$\text{Cosine of Incidence Angle} = \left\{ \begin{array}{ccc} \text{Cosine} & \text{Cosine of} & \text{Sine of} \\ \text{of Solar} \times & \text{Absorber} \times & \text{Absorber} \\ \text{Altitude} & \text{Azimuth} & \text{Tilt} \end{array} \right\} +$$

$$\left\{ \begin{array}{cc} \text{Sine of} & \text{Cosine of} \\ \text{Solar} \times & \text{Absorber} \\ \text{Altitude} & \text{Tilt} \end{array} \right\}$$

Written mathematically as:

$$\text{Cos } i = \text{Cos } H \text{ Cos } Z \text{ Sin } T = \text{Sin } H \text{ Cos } T$$

Which can easily be calculated on a pocket calculator such as the TI-30 "student" or any of the larger calculators.

The effect of these various conditions is best understood by varying one element while holding the others constant. For example, Fig. 4-8 shows the hourly variation for a horizontal, a vertical, and a tilted absorber for latitude 40° N and a tilt angle of 40° in July. Note that all values are less than that which would be secured if the reflector always faces the sun, the upper curve shown. (The complexities of a tracking solar collector works against its use in home heating, but it is the best if maximum energy absorption is needed.)

The energy absorbed per day is derived by summing the energy input per hour. For the 40° tilt, this gives:

Period		
AM	PM	(July 21) BTU/ft²
5-6	6-7	5
6-7	5-6	40
7-8	4-5	105
8-9	3-4	180

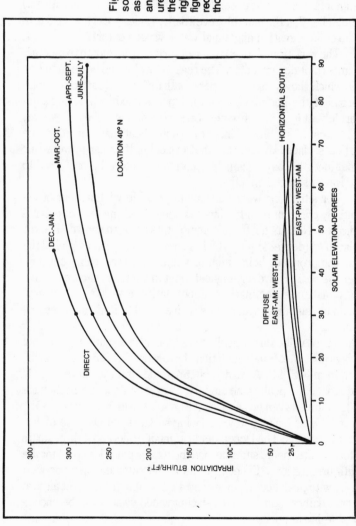

Fig. 4-7. The average clear day solar energy received by a surface as a function of solar elevation angle in degrees. The upper figures give the energy received from the sun, measured on a surface at right angles to its rays. The lower figures give the diffuse radiation, as received on horizontal surfaces, or those facing East, West, and South.

Period			
AM	PM	(July 21)	BTU/ft²
9-10	2-3	220	
10-11	1-2	270	
11-12	12-1	290	

for a total of 2200 BTU/ft²/day.

The monthly input is obtained by summing the daily inputs. Alternately, the input at the midmonth date can be calculated and multiplied by the number of days in the month. For July, this would amount to about 68,800 BTU. (The 21st is often used as the midmonth point, corresponding to the dates of the solstices.) Remember that the monthly, even daily, values are changing due to changes in elevation angle and water vapor content.

The variation of solar input to a surface from month to month is an important design factor. The reason for this can be seen in Fig. 4-9, which shows solar input per month for several surface orientations. For the horizontal surface, input is maximum during summer, lowest in winter. For vertical surfaces, it is highest in winter, and lowest in summer. Since it is winter heat that is needed, the vertical surface is better than the horizontal. If a solar-powered air conditioner becomes available, horizontal would be preferred to vertical in summer months.

For situations where maximum possible winter input or essentially constant monthly input is needed, tilting the collector is indicated. Results for three common tilts are also shown. The tilt of latitude (degrees) plus 10° is generally accepted as giving the best compromise, being high in winter and reasonably constant over the year. However, highest input in winter is secured with a tilt of latitude-declination, about latitude −20° in January. Maximum summer input occurs with a tilt of latitude plus declination.

These values are for collectors looking due south, which is not always possible. Small deviations have very little effect, as can be seen from Fig. 4-8. A change of 15° would shift the curve slightly and reduce the peak value slightly. Larger shifts in orientation are undesirable, as can be seen from Fig. 4-10, which shows the solar input for east-facing and west-facing surfaces versus time of day, for two seasons. The December heat input peaks about three hours before or after noon, suntime, and the total is much less than for the south orientations. Especially bad is the summer input for west walls, with peak heat input around 4 PM when the ambient air is at or near daily maximum. West-facing window walls will be uncomfortable in summer.

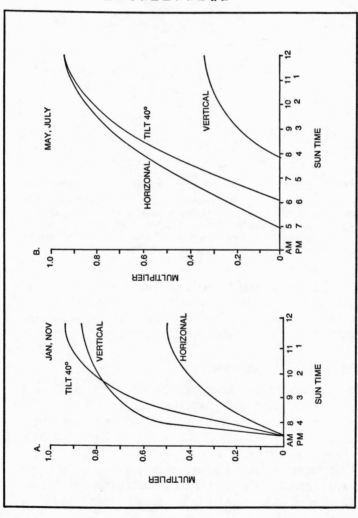

Fig. 4-8. Time of day correction. Multipliers for incoming solar energy received on a fixed surface, to the direct normal term of Fig. 4-4. These curves are for 40° N, and must be recalculated from the equations in the text, or obtained from references for other latitudes. The vertical and tilted surface values are for south-facing surfaces.

97

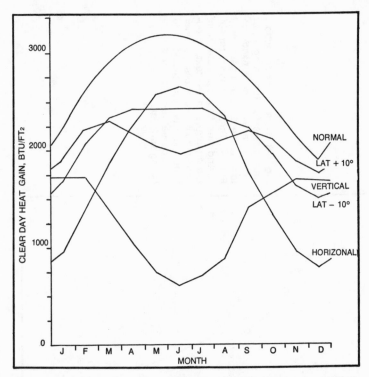

Fig. 4-9. Curves giving monthly values of clear day heat gain at 40° N latitude for various tilt angles. The upper curve is for a moving surface, always at right angles to the sun; the others for fixed collectors, tilted or vertical, facing south. A tilt of Latitude + 10 ° is considered to be the best compromise for maximum average heat collection.

While the curves of Fig. 4-10 indicate that the east/west wall input ceases or starts at noon, there will be some input throughout the day. This is due to diffuse radiation, which also gives some input to north windows. (See Fig. 4-5 for values.)

EFFECT OF LOCAL CONDITIONS

The solar considerations above apply to all locations and sites. Let us now look at some strictly local conditions and their effects. Of these, the most important is shading. This can be a major drawback if it markedly reduces solar input in winter, but it can also give a major gain in summer comfort.

If there are trees or buildings around your proposed site, you should investigate the amount of loss these will cause. To do this, you will need to measure the height of each obstruction and its

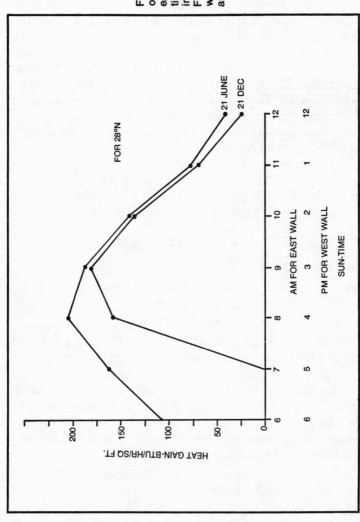

Fig. 4-10. Effects of vertical wall orientation. Direct solar input to east or west facing walls versus time of day. There will be some input at all times of sunshine, (see Fig. 4-7). Input for east facing walls will be less than shown for areas with morning haze.

azimuth from due south, as seen from the location and height of the solar absorber. These values are plotted on the curve of solar altitude versus time for your location. Figure 4-11 shows such a plot. Obviously, any time the sun is shaded, the direct solar input is zero. Diffuse input is still present, reduced somewhat by the shading.

There are several ways to measure the altitude and azimuth of these obstructions. If you or a friend have a sextant or a transit, either of these is ideal. Several books, such as Mazria's describe methods in detail. Residents of Florida can obtain, from the Florida Solar Energy Center, a transparent version of Fig. 4-2, called a Crome-Dome, which can be used to make the measurements and to determine the hours of shading.

If you have none of these methods available, satisfactory measurements can be made with a protractor. Figure 4-12 shows the principle for both the vertical and for horizontal, measured from some reference. The angle of this can be determined by a compass. Alternately, measure the angle from the reference to the position of the sun at sunrise and sunset. Half of the difference is the angle of the reference from due south.

In addition to this major factor, there is one which increases the solar input. This is reflection, usually that from the area close to the absorber. The magnitude of this is very variable, but if the area is essentially a flat surface, the additional input is:

$$I_R = I_H \cdot \frac{\rho}{2} (1 - \cos \Theta)$$

where

I_H = input to a horizontal surface
ρ = surface reflectivity
Θ = surface tilt angle

The reflectivity varies with surface, typical values being shown in Table 4-1. The values of 0.2 and 0.7 are often used for average ground and for average snow.

An additional local factor is the amount and type of cloud cover. The effect of this can be seen from the curves of Fig. 4-13. Estimates of cloud cover can be obtained from local weather data. Alternately, a *clearness adjustment factor* can be applied to the clear day input data. For estimates, there are:

Area	Multiplier
Gulf Coast	.9
Central U.S.A.	1.0

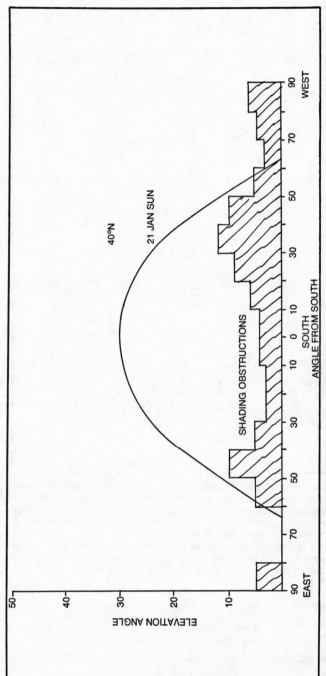

Fig. 4-11. Example shading chart, showing solar elevation and angle, and elevation angle of obstructions at angles from east to west. The shading loss for the example is negligible. However, if the obstructions between 40° and 50° east and west of south are trees, there will be appreciable energy input loss due to tree growth after a period of five to ten years.

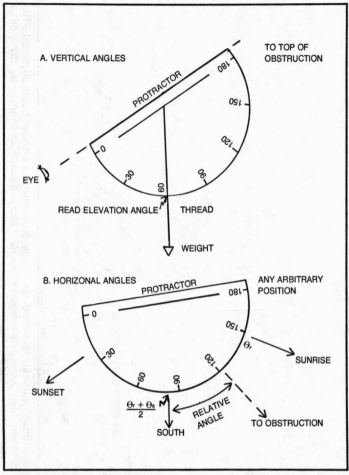

Fig. 4-12. While a transit or sextant is very convenient for angle measurement, satisfactory results can be secured with a "dime store" protractor. For vertical angles, as at A, a small weight on a thread is used to give the vertical. For horizontal angles, as at B, the protractor is fixed on a level surface. South is determined by the average of the angles of sunrise and sunset, and obstruction angles measured from this. It may be easier to measure angles if a small nail is placed in the center hole, and a second one moved along the angle scale to define the sighting line.

Area	Multiplier
Rocky Mountain	1.05
Pacific Northwest	.95
Northern U.S.A.	1.05

Tables and charts are given in several of the recommended references.

Table 4-1. Variable Input Factors.

Surface reflectivity factors for evaluating effect of grass, patio paving, and similar factors on the amount of sunlight reflected into a vertical solar absorber. Clean snow markedly increases the input. For marginal designs, a white patio surface, covered with "Astroturf" in summer might be used to avoid an increase in collector size. (Watch for glare.)

Surface	Solar Diffuse Reflectivity Factor, ρ
Bare Dry Ground	.1 - .25
Bare Wet Ground	.08 - .09
Sand, Dry	.18 - .3
Sand, Wet	.09 - .18
Dry Grass	.32
Green Grass	.03 - 15
Green Leaves	.25 - .32
Dark Forest	.05
Desert	.34 - .28
Salt Flats	.42
Brick	.23 - .48
Asphalt Drive	.15
General City Areas	.1
Snow	.05 - 0.9

$I_{reflected} = F \cdot \quad \cdot I_H$
I_H - Horizontal irradiation
F - From 4-13B

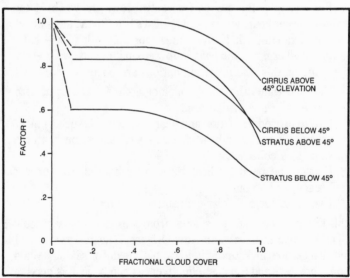

Fig. 4-13. Effect of varying cloud cover, the multiplier being applied to the direct normal term. Note that input is not especially sensitive to the amount of cloud cover until it becomes relatively high. (Some of this insensitivity is due to the geometry of cloud cover appearance from the earth's surface.)

For estimating, the following factors are sometimes used:

Clear weather periods	0.81
Average weather periods	0.70
Cloudy weather periods	0.62

These are applied to the solar radiation factor above the atmosphere (430 BTU/hr/ft^2) to obtain the direct input at the earth's surface.

GEOGRAPHY AND THE DIFFICULTY OF SOLAR HEATING

Because the winter climate gets colder as we go north, solar heating becomes inherently more difficult. The period of sunshine is shorter, with the sun lower in the sky, and the effect is further compounded by the fact that the amount of cloud cover may be higher.

A method of indicating the relative difficulty of solar heating is to divide the number of degree-days of required heating by the number of hours of sunshine available. The result is shown, in simplified form, in Fig. 4-14. The reason this is simplified lies mostly in the great variability of temperature and cloudiness, particularly in mountainous areas. Nevertheless, the plot is a useful guide.

For example, the curves for central Iowa shows about ten degree-days per hour, whereas for New Orleans the value is about two. Approximately, it is five times more difficult to use solar heating *for all heat requirements* in Iowa than it is in New Orleans. To expand on this, the following options are open:

Use five times the solar collector area, for the same size house and same insulations.

Use improved insulation and heat loss control, such as night shutters, ventilation heat interchangers, and so on, with the same size collector.

Reduce the need for heat by smaller houses, row or tier houses, and so on.

Use an integrated solar-conventional system.

If this last is used, the dollar savings from use of solar energy could be just as good in Iowa as in New Orleans. The first two would require a greater investment in Iowa, but the dollar savings would also be greater, and the cost effectiveness can be just as good in Iowa as in New Orleans.

In practice, a combination of the above four techniques would probably be used. The balance point is one of the factors to be sought in system sizing.

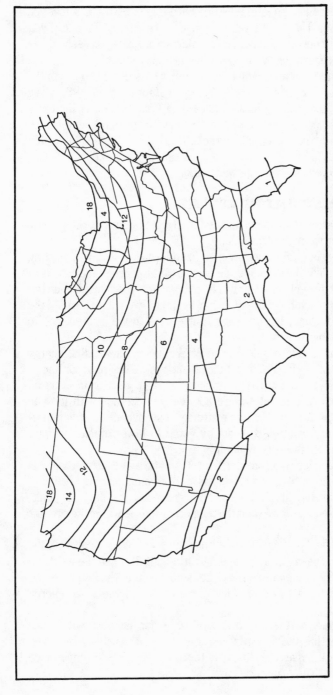

Fig. 4-14. Map showing the number of degree-days of heating needed divided by the number of hours of sunshine available; the ratio is a measure of solar heating difficulty. (Compare the ratios with those from Fig. 4-10) While the difficulty of solar heating is greater in the northern areas, the cost benefit is also greater.

There is a general message here. Don't let the fact that you are in a cold area steer you away from solar energy. Rather, if you are at all concerned about fuel problems, the cold climate should be a good reason for "going solar" as fast as you can.

While you are going to have to work harder if you are in the north, solar heating is perfectly practical for all of the U.S.A. and also for the densely inhabited areas of Canada. One of the early totally solar-heated homes is in Oregon. Boston has been a center for solar homes research, and solar heating has proven practical in England, at about the same north latitude as Labrador.

To repeat—solar power works.

GENERAL SYSTEM CONSIDERATIONS

In preparation for more detailed study, let us look at the general problem we must deal with.

Figure 4-15 shows a generalized heat flow diagram, starting with sunlight just outside the earth's atmosphere at the left, proceeding through our solar house, and going to the "ambient" on the right. At each point of our "solar system," we retain some of the energy for use, but let some of it escape to the ambient due to unavoidable losses.

Our design problem is to determine the amount of energy retained at each step, to get the conditions we desire in our home. Obviously, the ratio of energy retained to energy input is an important factor, but we are not really concerned with it as an efficiency. Rather, it is the matter of consequences that is important. If we can reduce costs by going to lower efficiency, fine. Remember, the energy itself is free.

We must also consider the temperature at each stage of this flow process. This is a closely associated element in determining energy availability, but we will find it important at only one point, the house, where we want the temperature to be within the comfort zone.

So far, we have looked at the matters of house heat loss (the items to the right of the line A-A in Fig. 4-15), and the available solar input, (at the line B-B). Let's now turn to the details of the area between those two lines, starting with the solar energy absorber.

Figure 4-16 shows a generalized solar absorber with a line representing the incoming solar energy. At each surface, and within each material element, there is a process of importance going on. The major ones are:

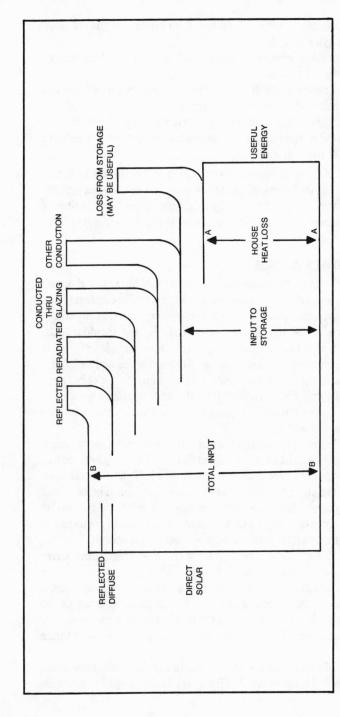

Fig. 4-15. Flow chart representing the inputs and losses which must be evaluated in designing a solar system. The relative values depend on materials, angles, temperature of operation, and so on, and vary widely from system to system. Use guidelines to select a system, then, preferably, confirm the choice by calculation.

107

Reflection, expressed as the fraction or amount of solar energy reflected.

Absorption, expressed as the fraction of solar radiant energy converted to heat.

Transmission, the fraction of radiant energy carried through the material in unchanged form.

Conduction, the heat energy carried through the material.

Emission, the energy of heat converted to radiation and sent out of the material.

While all of these processes go on, either at the surface or within the material, we can usually simplify our work by considering only the most important term. Usually this is the amount, or fraction, of energy delivered to the next step of the energy flow diagram of Fig. 4-15.

THE ABSORBER SURFACE

Let us start this simplification process by looking at the absorber surface. Here some of the incoming radiation is absorbed and some reflected. Concentrate on absorption; it is expressed as $E_a = E_{in} \cdot \alpha$, where E_a is the amount absorbed, E_{in} the incident solar energy, and α is a measurable quantity called the *absorptance*. It would be equal to zero if no energy were absorbed and to 1.0 if it were all absorbed. Practical materials have an α factor of between about 0.05 (polished silver) and 0.99 (lampblack). Since we want to design absorbers, we will be most interested in materials with high α factors: 0.8 and above.

While this approach has simplified the consideration of incoming energy, we must also think about the fact that energy can be lost from this surface. One way this can happen is by heat conduction. Usually, the absorber surface is in contact with air. The heat loss will be by conduction through the surface film, as studied in the last chapter. It can have an R-value of about 0.9, for still air, or as low as 0.2 for air moving over the surface at winter wind speeds. Keeping this loss factor low is one reason for having a transparent cover over the actual absorber surface (see Fig. 4-17).

The second way the surface can lose energy is by radiation. If the surface temperature is low, we can neglect this, but as the temperature increases the radiation lost increases very rapidly (by a factor of sixteen for a 2:1 temperature increase on the absolute scale).

In addition to the effect of temperature, surfaces vary in the amount of radiation emitted. This effect is measured by the emis-

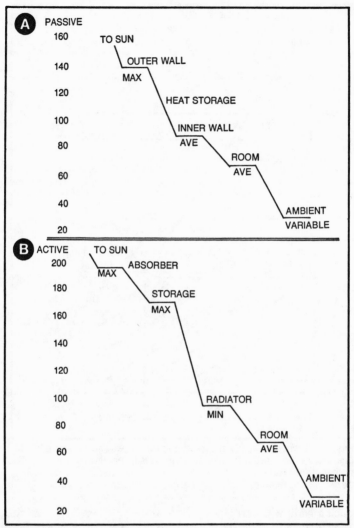

Fig. 4-16. Charts showing comparative heat loss of passive (A) and active (B) solar heating systems.

sivity, usually designated as ϵ, which has a value between zero and one, the last being a perfect emitter, and the first a surface with no radiation loss. Common materials have ϵ values between 0.1 and 0.98.

Since the absorbitivity factor and the emissivity factor are independent, a body may be a good absorber of solar energy and a poor radiator of the energy due to its own temperature. In sunlight

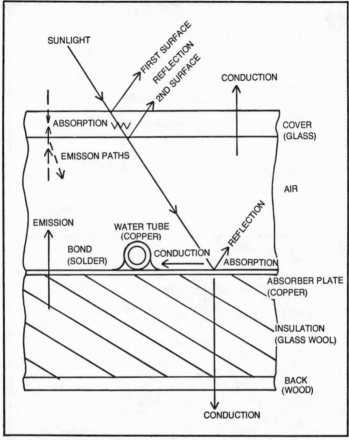

Fig. 4-17. Cross section of a flat-plate solar absorber, showing the paths of energy flow and loss. Emission from the absorber surface is low in low temperature designs, but a major factor in high temperature ones. The cover glass is used to trap energy and prevent conduction loss.

such a body will warm up (if there were no other loss) until its temperature is sufficient to reradiate the energy it receives. The degree of this depends on the ratio α/ϵ. For an otherwise loss-free body, the temperature it will reach is shown by Fig. 4-18. The variation is large—from 40° F to 250° F for α/ϵ of 0.5 and 2.0.

The values of α, ϵ and the α/ϵ ratio are tabulated in Table 4-2 for a number of materials. Most have α/ϵ near unity, but some have a relatively low value, about 0.2. Except for expensive metals or specially treated surfaces, α/ϵ values greater than one do not occur. This has many implications for solar heating. Actually, for common surfaces, it is easier to make a radiation cooler than a

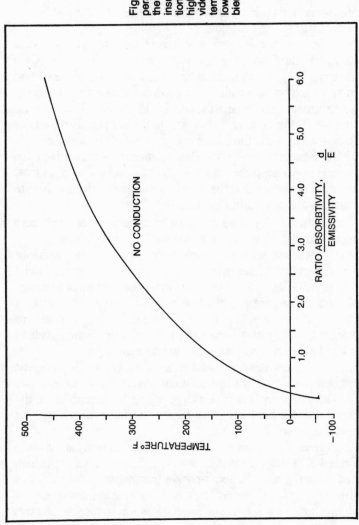

Fig. 4-18. The equilibrium temperature of a selective absorber is the temperature to which a perfectly insulated absorber will rise as a function of the ratio, absorption factor for high temperature solar radiation divided by the emission factor for body temperature radiation. If the ratio is low, the body will cool below ambient; if it is high, it will heat up.

111

radiation heater! (This is the reason a white boat or a white roof collects dew at night.) Fortunately, there is a compensating factor.

THE ABSORBER COVER

By now it is obvious that one reason for placing a cover over the absorber is to reduce the conductive heat. It does this by eliminating rapid air flow across the absorber surface and by interposing two additional surface films to the heat path. The cover material may be a heat insulator, although this is usually not an important item since cost dictates the use of thin films. However, we can always use two or more thin layers, obtaining the benefit of the additional film resistances to heat flow.

The absorber cover is a source of loss, however. At each surface, some of the incoming energy is reflected. Also, the body of the cover may absorb some solar energy. We can combine these two effects by considering the *transmittance*, the amount of energy which actually gets through the cover. This is affected by the angle with which the solar radiation strikes the surface. However, as shown in Fig. 4-19, the loss is not great for angles less than 60°. This is the second reason why fixed solar reflectors are oriented to the south—to keep the loss low when the solar energy is most available. (Note the collector surface absorption is also sensitive to angle, as also shown in Fig. 4-19.)

Transmissivity itself can vary from zero to one, with zero being completely opaque and one being perfectly transparent. Even opaque materials such as metal do have some transmissivity in very thin films. Interestingly, transmissivity of common "transparent" materials is found to vary with the wavelength of radiation. Many are transparent to short-wave solar energy, but opaque to long-wave heat energy. A few, Germanium, for example, are opaque to sunlight and transparent to infrared. Some, such as colored glass, are very selective in transparency.

This effect is very useful in solar absorbers, since it can compensate for the fact that most common materials have an α/ϵ ratio around unity. In addition to providing better insulation, the cover material can form a *heat trap*, admitting solar energy, but retaining the resulting heat.

Values of transmissivity for solar and heat energy are given in Table 4-3. Glass is found to be one of the best materials, with high transmissivity for solar and fairly low transmissivity for heat. It is also good for high temperatures, and has long life. But note that glass containing iron has considerable loss—a practical test for this

Table 4-2. Absorption/Emission Ratios.

The absorption/emission ratio for several classes of materials. Common materials are either good reflectors, or are neutral, with α/ϵ ratios around one. Some expensive metals and special surfaces are good absorbers, but their use is usually not necessary for home applications.

Material	α-Absortivity	ϵ-Emissivity	α/ϵ
Reflectors			
White Plaster	.07	.9	.08
Whitewash, New	.12	.9	.13
White Paint	.2	.91	.22
Low Absorbers			
Aluminum Foil, Bright	.05	.05	1.0
Aluminum Paint	.5	.5	1.0
Red Brick	.55	.92	.6
Concrete	.60	.88	.68
Dry Sand	.82	.91	.91
Green Roll Roofing	.88	.94	.94
Absorber-Emitters			
Lamp Black	.97	.97	1.0
Flat Black Paint	.97	.94	1.03
Tar Paper	.93	.93	1.0
Water	.94	.96	.98
Absorbers			
Tantalum	.59	.02	29
Black Chrome Over Nickel	.87	.06	14.5
Silver	.07	.01	7
Paint, "Meteor 7890"	.93	.47	2

is to look at the edge of the glass. If it is white or blue, it will be low loss, but if it is green, indicating the presence of iron, the loss will be high.

For absorber-only applications, several materials are good—glass, fiberglass, RFP, and polycarbonate are commonly used. For some combined uses, say a south wall of a home, only glass will do because of its freedom from visual distortion, strength, cost, and suitability for solar transmission. Even so, glass has some drawbacks, such as being breakage prone under impact, which might indicate use of one of the high-strength plastics. Where freedom from visual distortion is not a factor, some of the plastics serve very well, at relatively low cost. Greenhouses are often made from RFP sheets, and temporary heat storage systems using common polyethylene film are common. We'll look at specifics later.

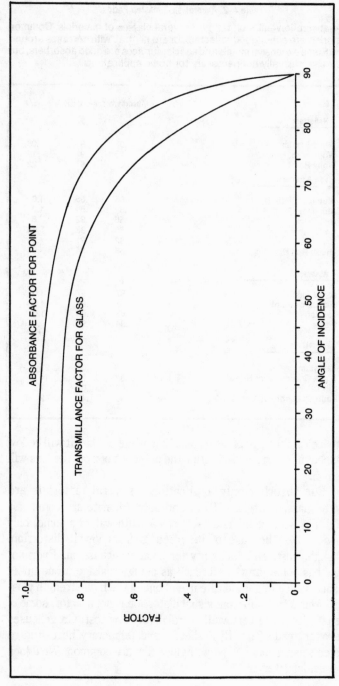

Fig. 4-19. Effect of incidence angles. Both absorption and transmission decrease as the angle of incidence of rays on the surface increases. Values shown are typical for common home use materials.

114

Table 4-3. Properties of Absorber Cover Materials.

Table of key properties of materials used for solar collector covers. An ideal material would have high solar transmission, low long-wave transmission, long life, and low cost. Heat conductivity is relatively unimportant in the thin layers used; air films on the surface are more important. Low-iron glass is very good, as are some modern plastics.

Material	Thickness	Solar Transmission Factor	Long Wave Transmission Factor	Max T°F	Life
Polyvinyl	4 mil	.93	.6	225	Low
"Mylar"	1 mil	.85	.2	220	Low
"Lenax"	⅛"	.85	.4	250	5 yr.
RFP	40 mil	.8	.07	200	7 yr.
"Plexiglass"	⅛"	.89	.02	180	5 yr.
Polyethylene	2 mil	.97	.25	240	Low
"Tedlar"	4 mil	.93	.2	225	5 yr.
Ordinary Glass	⅛"	.76	.02	400	Years
Low-Iron Glass	⅛"	.87	.02	400	Years
"Teflon"	1 mil	.96	.02	400	10 yrs.

HEAT-STORAGE AND HEAT-FLOW ANALYSIS

As mentioned in the preceding chapter, all materials can store energy as heat, with a resulting rise in temperature. The ability to do this is measured by the *specific heat,* for our purpose, the number of BTU's stored per pound or per cubic foot of material.

Specific heats of some common and a few uncommon materials are shown in Table 4-4. Note that water has a specific heat of 1.0, which is a consequence of the way a BTU is defined. Other common materials have lower heat storage capability, which is why water is used so often. Remember, the principle of trying to use material

Table 4-4 Heat Capacities.

In solar systems, heat must be stored in the daylight hours for release at night. Since high heat capacity and low cost are important, water is a good storage element. Common construction materials are quite good because of their low cost; storage may even be "free" if the material also has a structural use.

Material	Density lbs/ft³	Heat Capacity BTU/ft³/°F
Water	62.4	62.4
Wood, Oak Floor	47	27
Air	.075	.018
Brick	123	25
Concrete	144	22
Steel	489	59
Glass	150	30
Paraffin Wax	42	38
Sand	62	12

twice—water is not a good structural material! Even though brick and concrete store less energy per unit, they may be advantageous.

There are a few materials which store more heat than water, but they are expensive. However, a way of increasing the heat storage is to use a material which changes from a solid to a liquid at the upper temperature of the comfort zone. The solid melts due to solar heating, absorbing energy. During the night, the liquid freezes, giving off the stored *heat of fusion.* (The process is called a *phase change.*)

A common material, Glaubers Salts, is quite good, storing 108 BTU's per pound at a temperature of 90° F in going from solid to liquid. Some of the low melting-point paraffin waxes are good, storing about half as much. However, use of these materials cannot be considered perfected at this time. Glaubers Salts, in particular, tends to separate into a solid and a liquid, and all have problems with a phenomena called *super cooling,* whereby the material remains liquid well below the normal temperature of change, then becomes partly solid.

These materials have much promise in meeting comfort requirements. If you want to use them, keep up to date with developments and, preferably, get expert help. At present, it is generally best to stay with the simple materials—water, brick, concrete, or stone.

Heat flow in solar collectors and in storage is handled in exactly the same way as for houses. The one difference is that we must deal with constantly varying solar input to the absorber, whereas in houses we want to hold the house temperature reasonably constant.

For small collectors, the heat storage can be neglected. This is equivalent to assuming that the collector instantly comes to the steady state temperature which corresponds to the particular solar input. We can now easily make a heat gain/heat loss calculation, repeating this for each hour of sunlight. Summing the answers gives the total heat recovery.

CALCULATIONS FOR AN ABSORBER WITHOUT STORAGE

The basic nonstorage solar absorber is assumed to be as shown in Fig. 4-17. We must account for the following:

The solar input—if this collector is oriented to the sun as usual, we can neglect reflected solar energy

The loss in input due to reflectance and absorption

Heat loss through the cover

Thermal drop between the points of absorption and use, that is, to the water in this example.
Loss through the back of the absorber
Heat brought in by the water
Heat removed by the water
the last being the item of interest.

Using the electrical analogy, we can prepare an equivalent diagram, as shown in Fig. 4-20. The line slanting in from the upper left is the solar input. The *attenuator* crossing it is the reflectance and cover absorption loss. R1, R3, and R2 are the front and rear losses and the thermal resistance from surface to water. The second slant line represents the heat input due to inlet water temperature, and R4 the heat removed by the water. T_a, T_s and T_w are the ambient, absorber surface, and water temperatures.

Let's think about this a little. Suppose the water is initially at ambient, with the flow very high, so that $T_w = T_{in} = T_a$. R4 then is zero—all the heat is removed, or perfect conductivity. R3 has no effect since there is no temperature drop across it. If R2 is very small, as usual, $T_s = T_a$, very nearly. The temperature rise is zero, and the useful heat flow is just the solar input less the reflection loss, as seen in Fig. 4-20B.

Now suppose the water flow is shut off. The absorber temperature will rise until the heat loss through the front and back surfaces equals the solar heat input. At this point, the surface temperature has reached its maximum possible value, called *stagnation temperature*, or T_{STAG}. The schematic for this is shown in Fig. 4-20C. Knowing R1, R2 and R3, we can calculate T_{STAG} by the methods of the previous chapter.

Now, assume the water flow is started, but at a low rate. If one unit of heat is removed by the water, there will be one unit less flowing through the walls, and the temperature T_s will drop and T_w will increase. This relation is linear, which gives the plot of Fig. 4-21. This is a complete solution for the particular absorber.

If we have an absorber, we can measure its stagnation temperature and the water temperature rise for some known flow. Since the heat removed is $kQ\Delta T$, where k is the heat capacity and Q is the flow, we can plot the two resulting points on Fig. 4-21 and obtain the performance under any other flow.

CALCULATIONS FOR AN ABSORBER WITH STORAGE

For massive elements such as storage walls we cannot neglect heat storage. One way to include it is to calculate the temperature at the

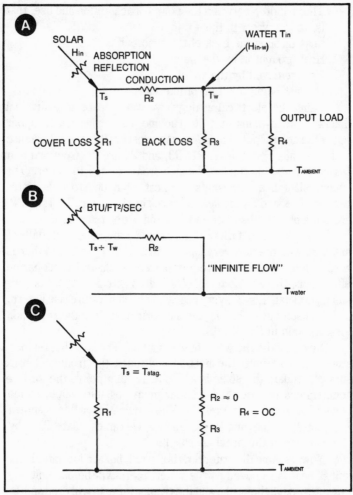

Fig. 4-20. Basic elements of absorber performance calculation. At *A* the absorber is represented as an analogue, an electrical circuit. Solar input is treated as a constant current source, not affected by absorber temperature. The same assumption is made for the energy of incoming water if its temperature is above ambient, as is usual. At *B* the circuit is simplified to show the high flow rate condition. Since energy is removed as fast as received, there is no temperature increase, except for the small thermal drop from absorber to liquid. At *C* is the simplified diagram for the no-flow condition. Here, the temperature rises until the loss is equal to the input.

start of an interval and at its end as if there were no storage. The average of the two is then used to calculate the temperature rise of the storage material. This value is then used as the starting point for the following interval, and so on. This method works well for

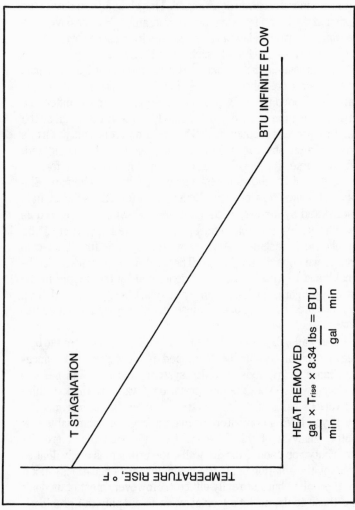

Fig. 4-21. Absorber performance curve. Given the two points, T-stagnation and BTU/minute at quasi-infinite flow, the entire performance curve of the absorber is defined. Actually, it is not necessary to use infinite flow. Any high flow-low temperature rise value can be plotted and used to define the relation. This relation is often shown as an "efficiency," obtained by dividing the measured or calculated heat removed by the solar input. At no flow, the "efficiency" is zero.

TEMPERATURE RISE, °F

T STAGNATION

BTU INFINITE FLOW

HEAT REMOVED

$$\frac{gal}{min} \times T_{rise} \times 8.34 \frac{lbs}{gal} = \frac{BTU}{min}$$

119

thin storage elements and also for thick ones if these are properly represented, as by the analogue of Fig. 3-7.

A second method is to take the average of the nighttime solar input (zero) and the peak input and to solve for the resulting temperature distribution as if there were no storage. This gives an expected average temperature for the entire house. If the daytime input period is short, a refinement of this equation is to determine the average daily input by calculating the input each hour, summing, then dividing by twenty-four hours.

The amount of heat which must be taken from storage to maintain house temperature is calculated separately, and the resulting temperature drop determined. This gives an estimate of the maximum deviation from average temperature. For massive storage walls, the time delay can be estimated from curves of transmission time versus thickness, such as in Fig. 3-7.

Let us assume that we want to examine the heat loss-heat gain situation for a greenhouse or solarium type of passive solar system, corresponding to Fig. 1-6. There is not much difference between this type and those of Figs. 1-1, 1-5, and 1-8, as far as the analytical process is concerned. The major difference between this and the simple absorber is that heat storage must be considered, and, of course, the general structure must be accounted for.

Figure 4-22 shows a resistance-capacitance schematic diagram of the heat flow of such a house. As before, the solar input is represented by arrows, with an attenuator symbol to remind us that this varies. Direct, diffuse, and reflected radiation to the greenhouse is included. Also, provision is made for direct gain through windows in the house. The final input is marked "additional," and represents the heat generated by the people in the house, by lights, cooking, and by auxiliary heat if needed. In a well-insulated house, none of these additional inputs can be neglected.

The walls, especially the heat trap walls, are represented by a special symbol, originally developed to represent inductance-capacitance delay lines in radar systems and modified here to represent walls. Note the interpretation if walls are thick or thin. The various parts of the house are listed below the schematic.

If you have a computer, or even a large programmable calculator, analysis of this is easy. Depending on the degree of complexity you choose for the walls, the problem is equivalent to obtaining the solution of six to ten simultaneous equations—not a trivial problem but not really difficult. However, most of us don't have these tools, so let's look at ways to simplify the problem.

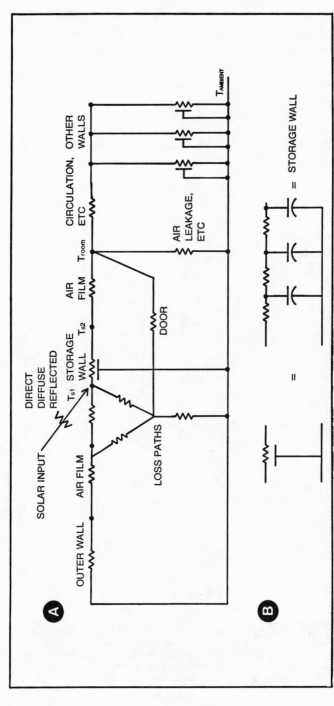

Fig. 4-22. Storage wall equivalent circuit. The electrical analogue of a passive storage wall system, showing major heat flow paths as labeled. *B* shows the special symbol used to represent massive walls where storage capacity and time constant are important. Calculator and computer programs are available to analyze this equivalent circuit.

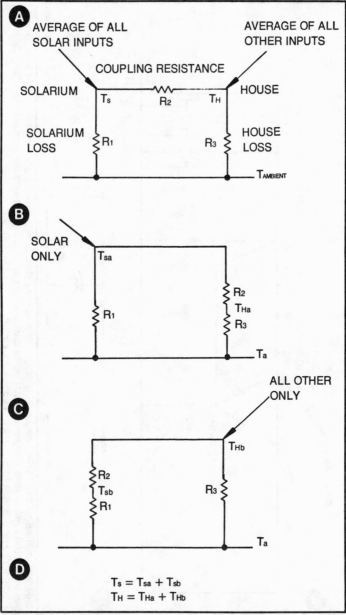

Fig. 4-23. Simplified equivalent circuit of a storage wall system using average solar input to obtain average temperatures. Successive steps of analysis are shown at B and C. The simplified circuit can be analyzed by elementary algebra, rather than by the solution of a set of simultaneous equations as required for Fig. 4-22.

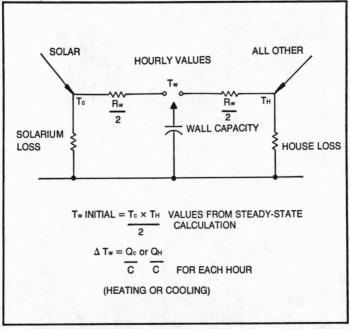

Fig. 4-24. Alternate method of analysis of a storage wall by a simple method of interval integration. The wall is assumed to remain at constant temperature over an hour, then instantly change to a new temperature. Subject to the flow path simplifications made to reduce the paths of Fig. 4-22 to this form, the errors are acceptable. The integration error can be checked by a few trials at thirty minute or fifteen minute intervals.

First, let's assume that the door between the solarium and the house is closed whenever the temperature difference is appreciable and that it is well insulated. Since it now has no effect, we can remove the element from the schematic.

Secondly, let's assume that the solar wall is really doing its job. Then the temperature of the center of the storage wall won't change much with time. Now we can neglect the storage capacity, and replace the various parallel and series heat conduction paths by single equivalent paths, one for the absorber and one for the house, just as we did for heat conduction alone. The heat inputs become the average input for the twenty-four hour day. The schematic diagram becomes that of Fig. 4-23, exactly the same as for the simple solar collector.

We can simplify this still further by using the principle of *super-position*. For this, we first calculate temperatures as if there were no input to the house, as shown in Fig. 4-23B, and then as if

Table 4-5. Calculation Techniques.

Table summarizing calculation techniques available, and a starting reference. Some proprietary programs also exist. Lists are sometimes found in computer journal ads.

Reference	System	Technique
Mazria	Passive, Several Types	Step-by-Step
		Guideline
HUD, 1977	Active, Hot Water	F-Chart
Solar Energy Handbook, 1979	Active, Air	Charts, Tables
ERDA, 1976	Passive, Several Types	Models
DOE, 1980	Solar Input	Maps
	Parameters	Guidelines
	Heat Loss	Bin-Hr
Sandia, 1979	Storage Wall	Semi-Empirical
	Direct Gain	Semi-Empirical
Design and Build, 1977	Heat Loss, Gain	Tables, Curve, Form
Solar Greenhouse, 1978	Loss, Gain	Tables, Relations
Hewlett-Packard 97/41	Loss, Gain, Input	Calculator

Note: See Solar Energy Research Institute Brochure SERI/SP-35-232R for a list of available computer programs. Others may be available.

there were no input to the solarium, Fig. 4-23C. The temperatures are then calculated as shown in Fig. 4-23D.

Suppose we are doubtful of our assumption as to the wall, and suspect that there will be too much temperature variation. Let's now assume that the temperature at the center of the wall doesn't change over a one-hour period, which is essentially true even for thin walls. Then we can split the wall into two parts, as shown schematically in Fig. 4-24. It is now easy to calculate the temperatures T_c and T_h for the first hour, say 9:00 AM. The wall center temperature is now changed by the change in its temperature due to the heat flow during the hour, and the process repeated for each of the twenty-four hours. If it appears that the variations in house temperature are excessive, the design should be changed and the analysis repeated.

As with heat transfers, it is best if this analytical work is organized, a form being helpful. Suitable forms are shown in later chapters, and specific designs are discussed. Also, guidelines are given for several system types.

There are many variations in analysis methods, with several different starting points. Several of these are tabulated in Table 4-5, together with a reference and a brief description. It is suggested that you review at least one or two of these, with a view to choosing the one which best suits your problem and your experience.

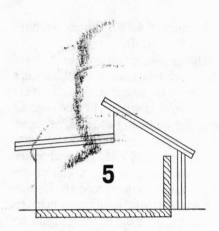

5

Solar Hot Water:
Most Return/Least Investment

Let us now turn to practical ways of using these solar heating ideas. For this, a convenient place to start is water heating—hot water for the kitchen, the bath, and the laundry. The installation can be small and simple, and its a good way to get some practical experience. It is also important—over the year, a good fraction of home energy use is to heat water. Major savings are available, and, because the design is simple and the components small, the installation cost is low. It's not uncommon for the savings to equal the total cost in two or three years. Thereafter, water heating is almost "for free." To use terms borrowed from the military, the "benefit/cost" ratio is high, and the "cost effectiveness", excellent.

THE TEN-CENT WATER HEATER

Actually, the ten-cent figure assumes that you, like most home-owners, have most of the required parts on hand. The parts are common, but even if you have to buy everything, you can get by for two or three dollars—even today.

To follow the idea flow, and to get a feel for the elements involved in all hot water systems, suppose you take an empty, cleaned, one-gallon milk jug, full of water, and set it outside where it will be in full sunlight from at least 9 AM to 3 PM. You measure the air and water temperatures. You will find that the water temperature rises as the air warms up but usually lags behind the air temperature increase. The difference will depend on the wind—air and water temperatures will be close when the wind is strong, further apart when there is no breeze.

If you leave the jug out continuously, you will find that the water tends to stay close to the average air temperature, with some lagging behind the air temperature changes.

Now suppose you paint the jug black, using a flat black paint. Immediately, a change appears. The water in the jug now warms up a little faster than the air, and, by midafternoon the temperature of the water will be above the temperature of the air—not by any great amount, perhaps only five or six degrees, but definitely warmer. The rise can be increased to perhaps eight or ten degrees by setting the jug on a piece of aluminum foil.

Since the wind is definitely affecting the rise, suppose the jug is now placed in a container: the bottom part of a Styrofoam ice chest or cooler. Now things start to happen. For example, on a sunny spring day, the following values were measured:

Dawn air temperature	37° F
2 PM air temperature	73° F
2 PM water in shade	50° F
2 PM black jug on foil reflector	83° F
2 PM black jug in cooler	95° F (open top)

This represents real progress.

Let's take another step and cover the cooler with a sheet of transparent plastic. Here are the results of a test run, again on a spring day:

Time	Air Temperature, ° F	Chest Temperature, ° F
0845	36	48
0940	39	55
1040	47	78
1145	54	90
1240	54	76
1334	54	112

The drop at 1240 was due to a short cloudy period. Water temperature would not be as high as chest temperature, but a temperature rise of 30 to 40 degrees could be expected by midafternoon.

Suppose we now combine all of the ideas. Line the cooler with aluminum foil. Cover the inside of the lid also, and set it where sunlight is reflected into the cooler. Change the position of the cooler every two hours so that it faces the sun. Now we will get a water temperature rise of 40 to 50 degrees above starting temperatures by midafternoon. During spring and fall, water temperature would run around 100° F, comfortable for washing. During the summer, water temperature will reach 120° or more.

This little demonstration is hardly more than a toy, but it's worth remembering. It is useful on a picnic to give some water to wash up with, and if there is a power outage, it can be pressed into service.

GROWING THE IDEA: THE BREAD-BOX

The chief fault of the little cooler type water heater is that it doesn't hold enough water. Also, the top area of the usual cooler is too small to collect much energy. But the basic ideas are sound, and there's no reason for not going to bigger sizes. The usual name for such a design is a *bread-box* water heater. This appears to have been coined by Steve Bayer or one of the others at Zomeworks, pioneers in low-cost solar systems in the Albuquerque area.

Figure 5-1 shows a version of such a bread-box type. This is designed around a 55-gallon steel drum and laid out to make maximum use of two sheets of plywood. The other structural elements are 1″ × 2″ or 1″ × 3″ furring strips.

Figure 5-2 shows the construction with the lid and the top plastic sheet removed. The box and top are lined with two layers of one-half inch rigid foam board. In the prototype, only the inner surfaces were covered with reflective foil, but slightly improved performance can be secured by using foil between the two layers of insulation.

The performance of these simple units is quite respectable. Figure 5-3 shows measured air temperatures outside and inside the box and water temperature at the top and bottom of the drum, for a one-week test. For this, the lid was raised each morning and closed when the sun became too low. Lid angle was set to give best reflective around noon. There was no water flow.

On a clear day in late spring, the water temperature reached 140° F at the top of the drum, and 116° F at the bottom, for a rise of 60° above ambient. There was some heating on cloudy days, about ten degrees rise above ambient. Note that the design is intended to cause some mixing of the top and bottom water, this being secured by shaping the box into an approximate parabola. The shape is clear in Fig. 5-1. Other shapes will allow stratification, causing a greater difference between top and bottom temperatures. (Sometimes it is better to have at least a small quantity of warmer water on the top layer.)

Fig. 5-1. A box-type water heater on test. The integral water-tank absorber is under the plastic cover. The insulated lid, foil covered on the underside, increases the amount of sunlight reaching absorber to approximately the area of the plastic if normal to the sun.

It is instructive to compare the calculated and measured performance. The heat loss, clear day and cloudy day inputs, and the resulting day and night average water temperature calculations are shown in Table 5-1. Comparing these results with Fig. 5-3 shows that the measured performance is somewhat lower than calculated. Part of this was traced to air leakage at the joint between the transparent cover and the box. This is a critical area, since temperature is maximum here. The rest appears to be due to neglected factors, principally conduction to box supports. However, the error in calculation is not serious.

The air leakage had another effect, which showed up after a heavy rain. Water got into the box and condensed on the plastic

Fig. 5-2. Removing the lid and plastic shows some interior detail. The 55 gallon drum absorber rests on bottom chocks. The box is lined with foam plastic board insulation covered with foil. Sloping sides reduce heat loss slightly and direct heat to all parts of the absorber.

130

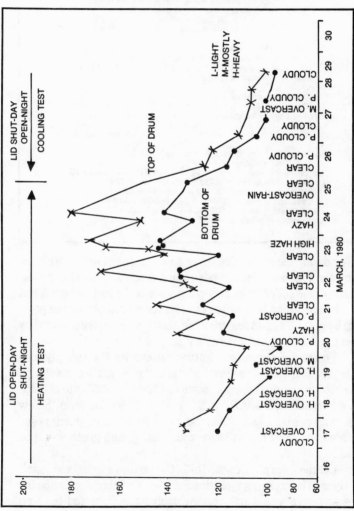

Fig. 5-3. Chart of water temperature at top and bottom of drum. General weather condition is indicated. On clear days, note that bottom temperature initially rises rapidly, then stays constant as circulation mixing occurs. The last third of the period is a test check of loss rates, conducted with no water flow, but performance is easily calculated for any flow rate. Generally, the data indicates that performance would be improved with a smaller drum, around 30 gallons, and with somewhat more insulation.

Table 5-1. Bread-Box Thermal Analysis.

Simplified analysis of box heatre performance, using successive approximation to secure estimated water temperature rise. The estimated value, around 37°F, shows that specific design is good year round for southern states when a large quantity of relatively low temperature water is needed, and for summer in northern areas.

```
Areas:  Top 4' × 4'                                        16 sq. ft.
        Bottom 2' × 4'                                      8 sq. ft.
        End 2 × 2' × 3.6' (average)                       14.4 sq. ft.
        Sides 2 × 4' × 2.5'                                20 sq. ft.

Insulation, Box:  Air Film + Plywood + Board + Air film
                  R = 0.2 + 2 × .375" + 4.7 + 0.2 = 6.3
                  Cover: 1 exterior, 3 other air films
                         R = 0.2 + 3(0.7)               2.3
                  Lid closed: R = 6.3 + 2.3 or          8.6

Los factor, L, in BTU/hr/deg
        Lid Open: 42.4 sq. ft. ÷ 6.3 + 16 sq. ft. ÷ 2.3 = 13.7
        Lid closed: 42.4 sq ft. ÷ 6.3 + 16 sq. ft. ÷8.6 = 8.6
        Assume lid closed 12 hrs per day        Lave = 11.1

Solar input, 0.95 effective area, BTU/day
        Direct term@0.8 absorbed: 16 × .95 × .8 × 5 × 316 = 19212
        Indirect term@0.4 absorbed: 16 × .95 × .4 × 2 × 316 =  3842
        Reflector@0.4 absorbed:   16 × .95 × .4 × 5 × 316 =  7685
                                        Total per day = 30733

First estimate of rise, 55 gal × 8.34 lbs/gal = 458 lbs
        Rise = 30733/458 = 67°F
First estimate of loss    = 67° × 24 hr × 11.1 BTU/hr = 17848 BTU
Second estimate of rise = (30733 ÷ 17848) − 458 = 28°F
Second estimate of loss = 28 × 24 × 11.1 = 7459 BTU
Third estimate of rise  = (30733 − 7459) ÷ 458 = 50.8°F
Third estimate of loss  = 50.8 × 24 × 11.1 = 13537 BTU
Fourth estimate of rise = (30733 − 13535) ÷ 458 = 37.5°F
```

cover during the night. The cover appearance the next morning is shown in Fig. 5-4. These condensation drops decrease the performance of the collector by reflecting some of the incident light, and also by absorbing heat which can't be recovered. Avoid the problem by getting a good seal from the plastic sheet to the plywood by overlapping or by using a rubber sealant.

Figure 5-5 shows the cutting pattern for the two plywood sheets which form the box body and the layout for the strips fastened to the ends and for joints to the sides and bottom. Each joint is reinforced with 1" × 2" or 1" × 3" furring strip. Screw fastening is suggested. When the woodwork is completed, prime with a good wood preservative and paint. A dark green would be suitable.

Cut the foam plastic board to fit the various spaces, and install it, layer on layer, using a mastic adhesive. Test the adhesive on the plastic before you start—many dissolve the foam and have no adhesive value. As noted before, the unit shown used aluminum foil only on the inside layer of foam board. Slightly better insulation is secured with foil between the insulation layers.

This design uses a 55-gallon drum for water storage. These are readily available in surplus, but make sure that the drum has been steam cleaned and is free from rust. It is best to be certain that the drum was not used for a toxic substance.

Water is often corrosive, and the use of steel drums will certainly result in a short life. It may be better to use a glass-lined or galvanized storage tank. Alternately, at some expense, the drum can be hot-dip galvanized. Anticorrosion chemicals can be used for some purposes.

The outside of the drum must be painted flat black, Rustoleum 412 rust preventative paint is good. The special "selective absorber" paints now becoming available are not worthwhile in this low temperature application.

This type of collector is intended for use where it is readily accessible—it should be opened each morning and closed each night. Pick the place, remembering that the hot water from the drum must be used directly or the lines to the point of use must be well insulated. In installing, remember that water is heavy—the completed unit, filled, weighs nearly a quarter of a ton.

Take special pains with the piping. A small leak wastes a lot of water can lead to poor performance due to water in the insulation

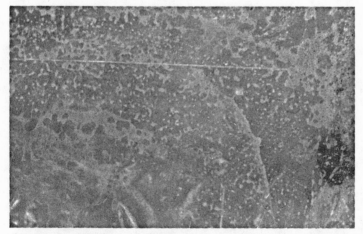

Fig. 5-4. Condensation on the inner surface of a collector due to water accumulation. The moisture will deteriorate wood, produces a reflection loss, and further heat loss as moisture heats up and evaporates. Seal the upper surface of the collector thoroughly.

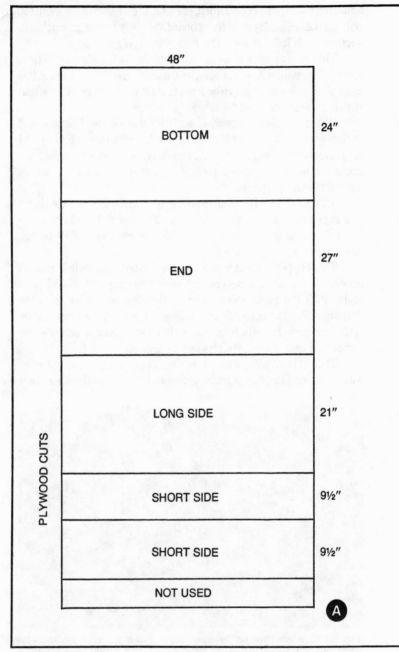

48″

BOTTOM — 24″

END — 27″

LONG SIDE — 21″

SHORT SIDE — 9½″

SHORT SIDE — 9½″

NOT USED

PLYWOOD CUTS

A

Fig. 5-5. Construction of a bread-box water heater. (A) Plywood cuts, top, sides and bottom.

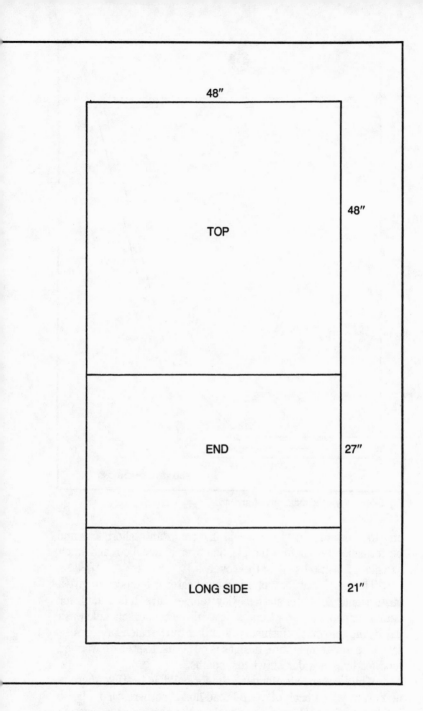

48″

48″

TOP

27″

END

21″

LONG SIDE

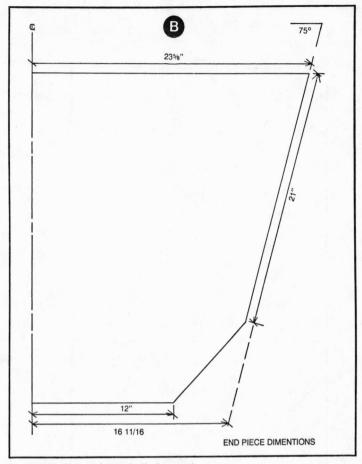

Fig. 5-5(B). Plywood cuts, half of an end.

and to short life due to rust and dry rot. Run a short leak and performance test before the plastic cover is installed, and when satisfied, finish by sealing the cover.

This particular form of bread-box heater is intended to give a large quantity of water at a fairly low temperature. It is suitable for bathing or showers—for laundry, it would be best to schedule wash day by the amount of sunshine, rather than by the calendar. One use for these low-temperature designs is on farms, to prepare warmed food for livestock during winter months.

While not specifically designed for building heating, there is no reason why a bank of these bread-box absorbers cannot be so used. A bank could be used to replace the furnace of an existing hot-water system, or better, to serve as its replacement during most periods and as a preheater during very cold periods. For new installations, the basic idea might be used in the form of a combined solid-liquid storage system. The bread box could take the form of a window seat, open to the sun in the day and closed to form the seat at night.

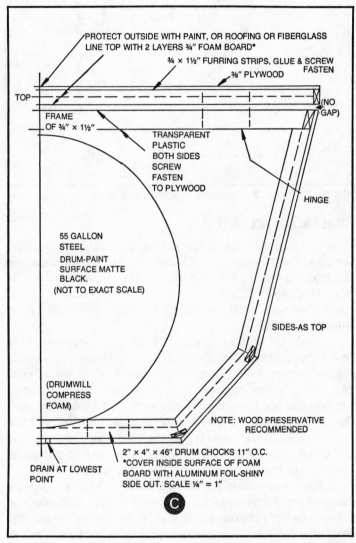

Fig. 5-5(C). Assembly, showing 1″ – 2″ fastening strips. Screw fastening is recommended.

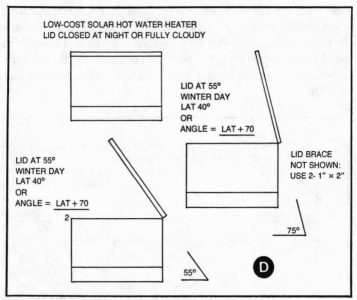

LID AT 55°
WINTER DAY
LAT 40°
OR
ANGLE = $\dfrac{LAT + 70}{}$

LID AT 55°
WINTER DAY
LAT 40°
OR
ANGLE = $\dfrac{LAT + 70}{2}$

LID BRACE
NOT SHOWN:
USE 2- 1″ × 2″

75°

55°

D

Fig. 5-5(D). Sketch of lid positions in summer and winter.

OTHER BREAD-BOX DESIGNS

There is no great magic in the size or shape of bread-box water heaters. About the only rule to follow is that they should not get too far away from a cube, or the heat loss will be too great compared to the storage volume. Ratios of two to one or three to one in longest to shortest dimensions are all right. Keep the largest area surface towards the sun.

Figure 5-6 shows such a rectangular heater, mounted at the optimum tilt angle for the location. Sides of this unit are straight, like a shoe box. Water is contained in a 30-gallon, glass-lined tank. An unusual feature is a dual solar heating mode—the first is direct to the tank, and the second is to a section of finned, hot water baseboard radiator, the length of the tank, painted black, and also inside the box. This connects from the lowest point of the tank to the center of the top end and is intended to give a circulation path to equalize the temperature at the top and bottom of the tank.

Another bread-box design is shown in Fig. 5-7. This opens the side and top of the box, for use as reflectors. The plastic heat trap cover is formed to be one-fourth of a cylinder, giving the minimum heat loss. The storage tank is a 30-gallon galvanized unit, some 12 inches in diameter by 5 feet long. At one time these were commonly used with a separate "side arm" water heater.

Both of these units are being tested at the Florida Solar Energy Center.

FLAT-PLATE COLLECTORS

While the integral storage design of the bread-box water heater is good, by far the largest number of solar water heaters separate the functions of collection and storage. One reason for this is that most solar collectors are add-ons to existing systems which already have storage. A further reason is that the logical place for collectors is on the roof, out of the way and well located for sunlight; the weight of stored water on the roof is undesirable.

Fig. 5-6. Bread-box heater on test at the Florida Energy Center. The box is tilted to the south to increase input. The two top lid halves fold back during the day.

Fig. 5-7. Open top and side water heater on test. The glazing is RFP, curved to one-fourth of a circle. The inside of top and open side are reflective.

The basic design optimization of separate storage collectors was worked out 50 or more years ago. What emerged was a thin box, roughly the shape of a shoe-box lid with a transparent cover for the open side. Experimentally, it was found that best results were obtained with water tubes completely bonded to a metal sheet, painted black, and installed over a layer of insulation. While there have been thousands of design variations, the basic principles are unchanged.

Figures 5-8 through 5-11 show a design intented for home construction. This extremely simple approach is a minor modification of a design worked out at the University of Florida Solar Energy Center. While details of joint construction, fastenings, and finishes are not shown, any good construction techniques are satisfactory.

There are a few points to watch. The design is based on the use of soft copper tubing, the type which comes in rolls. Hard tubing will require ells and short lengths to form the flow pattern. If you use this, be extra careful with joints. Figure 5-12 shows what can happen if the joints are poorly made. Also, be prepared for more trouble in soldering the tubing to the absorber plate because of the spaces introduced at the joints.

Inorganic insulation is recommended. The collector will become hot on a clear summer day with no water flow. Plastic insulation, in particular, is likely to soften and distort.

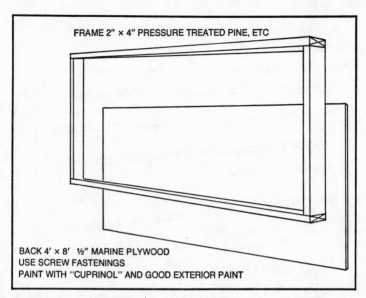

Fig. 5-8. Wood for a flat plate heater. Frame and back for a simple effective low-cost heater designed at the University of Florida.

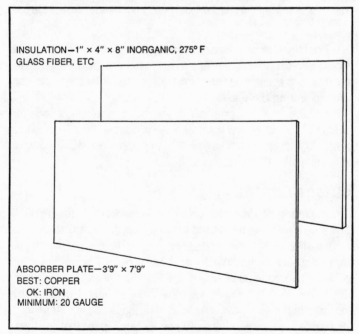

Fig. 5-9. Sheet material for a flat plate heater. Metal absorber plate and insulation for the collector.

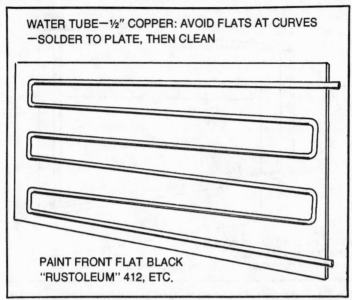

WATER TUBE—½" COPPER: AVOID FLATS AT CURVES
—SOLDER TO PLATE, THEN CLEAN

PAINT FRONT FLAT BLACK
"RUSTOLEUM" 412, ETC.

Fig. 5-10. Location of tubing on the absorber plate. Slightly improved performance can be secured with another "zig" of tubing, and still another small improvement by using a selective absorber. These niceties are not justified from a cost view.

For long life and maximum temperature rise, use glass for the cover. Be sure to get the low-iron type—look at the edge, and reject it if it appears green. Don't forget to allow for expansion when mounting the glass.

If there is a hail problem in your area, you might look for surplus plate glass—even automobile windows. Alternately, use Lexan, Mylar, or even fiberglass. The performance will go down a little but will still be adequate.

COLLECTOR MOUNTING

The mounting of the solar collector is important. Figure 5-13 shows a large panel supported by posts on the north, to get the optimum tilt angle (latitude plus ten degrees for year around use). These supports must be strong. A wind of 70.7 miles per hour produces a force of 20 pounds per square foot of exposed surface. This increases to 40 pounds per square foot at 100 miles per hour. For most of the U.S.A., recommended design loads are 30 pounds per square foot, increasing to 40 pounds per square foot in storm areas and to 50 pounds per square foot in South Florida and near Cape Hatteras.

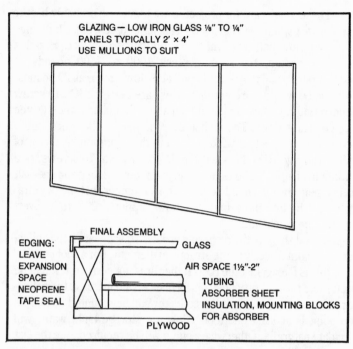

GLAZING — LOW IRON GLASS ⅛" TO ¼"
PANELS TYPICALLY 2' × 4'
USE MULLIONS TO SUIT

FINAL ASSEMBLY

EDGING:
LEAVE
EXPANSION
SPACE
NEOPRENE
TAPE SEAL

GLASS

AIR SPACE 1½"-2"

TUBING
ABSORBER SHEET
INSULATION, MOUNTING BLOCKS
FOR ABSORBER

PLYWOOD

Fig. 5-11. Glazing and assembly of an absorber. Consider surplus glass, if of low-iron type, or even increase collector area if glass cost is very low but quality is poor. See text for low-iron test. Don't forget glass expansion space.

Fig. 5-12. Leakage in a collector resulting from poor soldering of pipe joints (see Fig. 5-5). If possible, use a single length of tubing with all joints outside the collector. If joints are necessary, test under pressure before final assembly.

143

These values are for projected area, but it is probably best to use full area when considering the resistant forces, since buildings cause air flow patterns which are difficult to predict. For this collector design, forces may reach 1000 to 1500 pounds. A sixteen-penny nail may start to pull at as low a force as 20 pounds, so some 50 would be required. Screws are better; a No. 10 screw penetrating two inches should hold about 60 pounds when driven into good new wood. There should be a generous allowance for the accumulative effect of wind gusts and deterioration. A factor of safety as large as eight is indicated. Twenty No. 10 screws, or a minimum of eight lag bolts ⅜ inch in diameter with two and one-half inches penetration would be normal. Remember that the penetration must be into the actual structural support, not into an overlayer, such as sheathing.

A good share of the mounting problem disappears if the collector can mount directly to the structural element. For a roof installation, this is flat against the roof. If the tilt is not correct, it might be preferable to accept reduced performance, and increase the collector area to compensate. If the collector can be mounted so that its top point is at least one foot below the storage tank, water will circulate naturally. Otherwise a pump will be required. See the last chapter for this.

In cold climates there is the problem of freezing to deal with. One way to handle this is to provide manual shutoff valves in the two lines, plus a drain in one and an air inlet in the other, and drain the collector at night. Be sure the lines are routed to drain easily—this may require a suction vent valve at the top of the collector.

This manual operation can be a nuisance. A way to avoid it is to provide a heat interchanger; for example, place a coil of pipe in the storage tank and filling this and the collector with antifreeze. This reduces collector corrosion problems, but also reduces performance and increases cost. It might be better to allow a small reverse flow, sufficient to keep the water above the freezing point on the coldest nights. Determine the amount by calculating the collector heat loss, and calculate the amount of flow needed. If it appears too high, consider a double or even triple layer collector cover. The inner layer, or layers, can be plastic film, since it is the insulating value of the air film which counts. Or consider a movable cover, as for the bread-box collectors.

Rules of thumb for these collection systems are:

Design on the basis of 20 gallons of hot water per person per day.

Fig. 5-13. A method of mounting a collector when roof tilt is not correct the unit being in the mountains of Arizona. See text for a discussion of wind forces.

145

Provide 12 square foot of collector for each person.
Tubing size, one-half inch to three-quarters inch.
Tube spacing, eight inches, less for maximum performance.
Absorber plate, 20 gauge, thicker for maximum performance.
Insulation, one inch, more for maximum performance.
Provide storage for at least one day's consumption, three day's storage is better.

PERFORMANCE CALCULATIONS

It is suggested that you work out performance calculations for the collector above, then vary the design assumptions and see the change in performance. The first step of this is shown in Table 5-2, for the infinite flow and no flow conditions. In the infinite flow condition, all input energy is removed by the water flow so there is no heat loss. In the no flow, or stagnation condition, the temperature rises until the loss equals the input. The temperature rise at other flow rates is calculated by the construction of Fig. 4-21 and Fig. 5-14.

Values for the surfaces of these collectors are tabulated in Table 5-3. These are typical, but remember that the reflectance values are for a clean surface and for low-iron glass.

Table 5-2. Performance Calculation for a Flat-Plate Collector.

Calculation for flat-plate collector performance, with assumptions shown. Summer stagnation temperatures are beyond the capability of plastics.

COLLECTOR CALCULATION

Glazing - R = .90, including air films
 - C = 32 sq. ft. ÷ 0.9 = 35.6 BTU/hr/deg

Back   - R = 1.0 + 3.3 + 0.6 + 0.17 = 5.1
 - C = 32 sq. ft. ÷ 5.1 = 6.4 BTU/hr/deg

Sides - Area = 2 × (4' + 8') × 4"/12" = 8 sq. ft.
 - R = 2.0
 - C = 8 sq. ft. ÷ 2 = 4 BTU/hr/deg

Total loss = 35.6 + 6.4 + 4 = 46 BTU/hr/deg
Heat input, noon, 290 BTU/ft^2 × 32 ft^2 × 0.845 = 7865 BTU/hr
Expected temperature rise, no flow = 7865/46 = 170°F
Stagnation temperature, winter day = 170 + 32 = 202°F
Stagnation temperature, summer day = 170 + 80 = 250°F
Assume flow of 10 gal/hr = 54 lbs/hr
 To remove 4000 BTU/hr, rise = 4000/54 = 74°
See part B for solution.

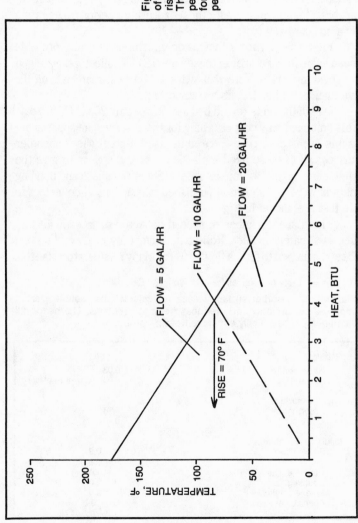

Fig. 5-14. Graphical construction of collector output-temperature rise and heat removed by water. The intersections are the expected rise. Performance is good for flows up to about 20 gallons per hour.

147

The *Bead-Wall* is a Zomeworks idea, which blows hollow plastic beads into the space between two transparent sheets at night and stores them in a container during the day. It is a convenient way to essentially eliminate freeze problems in cold climates, but a movable panel would do the same job at lower cost and would not be subject to power failure.

COMMERCIAL DESIGNS

Hundreds of designs for these solar collectors have been made, and a good number are now available commercially. Florida, in particular, has a testing program for these, securing a performance rating by a standardized test.

Figure 5-15 shows the maximum, minimum, and probable mean value for a number of these commercial collectors, arranged by cover material. Note that glass is the best material, on the average, but other factors are important.

One of the units tested had a rating of only 203 BTU/ft^2/day. This unit used only copper tubing for the absorber, an appreciable saving in material cost. Five units used a steel sheet absorber surface; all of these used a plastic cover and appear to give the same performance as copper sheet. (Sheet thickness and bonding method were not shown in published data.) Typical collectors in life test are shown in Fig. 5-16.

There are a number of special collector surfaces available. One is a material called Roll-bond, formed by cold welding two sheets, stamped to form a flow pattern. Many refrigerators use this

Table 5-3. Values for Solar-Collector Calculation.

Glazing and absorber surface values for calculations. Double glazing improves performance, and reduces freezing problems. The bead-wall technique will essentially eliminate freezing problems.

Glazing	
Reflection loss	0.08
Absorption	0.06 (Low-iron glass)
Absorber surface	
Absorptance	0.98
Emittance	0.98
Insulation R-Values	
Single glass	R = 0.9
Single RFP	R = 0.8
Double polyethylene	R = 1.4
Double glass	R = 2.0
Double acrylic, RFP	R = 2.0
Special, beadwall, 5″	R = 20.0

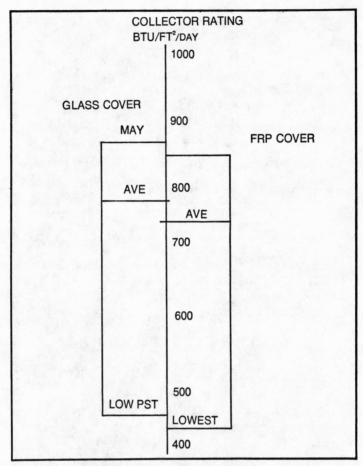

COLLECTOR RATING
BTU/FT²/DAY

1000

GLASS COVER

MAY   900   FRP COVER

AVE   800
             AVE

             700

             600

             500
LOW PST   LOWEST

             400

Fig. 5-15. Test data from the Flordia Energy Center.

design. Figure 5-17 shows a section of special extruded aluminum, made to snap over copper tubing. It would appear to be good with high temperature collectors using a selective absorber surface. The producing organization, Zomeworks, also offers a snap-on pipe collector-concentrator, intended to replace insulation on the hot-water line exposed to sunlight.

COST CUTTING WITH PLASTIC PIPE

It is tempting to reduce the cost of the collector by using plastic pipe. The general comment about this is—don't. The reason lies in the fact that the collector temperature under normal flow conditions will be close to the maximum recommended temperature for

Fig. 5-16. Various flat-plate collectors on test or after test at the Florida Solar Energy Center. Detail data on the units tested is available from the center.

150

Fig. 5-17. A proprietary collector by Zomeworks, an aluminum extrusion to clip on a copper tube. The technique is particularly useful in high temperature applications.

plastic pipe. With no flow, the collector and pipe temperature climb to the stagnation temperature. The pipe softens, and "cold flows" due to the stresses of the water pressure. The groups which test collectors advise that it is common to see a "mess of limp spaghetti" when plastic is used.

However, with care, it is possible to use plastic pipe in collectors. The requirements are:

Limited stagnation temperature rise

Guaranteed water flow

Low water pressure

Heavy duty piping

Later chapters will show how to take advantage of these in some special situations.

For general water heating, the two major factors would be:

Use a storage tank located above the collector (minimum of one foot higher), to guarantee fluid circulation.

Use a pressure reducer on the water line. However, if long life is needed, forget plastic and use copper tubing.

BANKED COLLECTORS

In addition to single collectors for homes, it is becoming common to see banks of collectors for special purposes. Figure 5-18 shows such a bank, as installed on the reception building at Yosemite National Park. Figure 5-19 shows an even larger installation at the University at Flagstaff, Arizona. This is essentially an industrial use, being installed at the maintenance garage.

Schools should be looking to these designs as a way of reducing operating costs. The same is true of any user of hot water at

Fig. 5-18. A sight becoming more common—banked collectors at Yosemite. Similar installations are now found at airports, school dormitories, and motels.

152

Fig. 5-19. An installation at the University, Flagstaff, Arizona, illustrating an add-on to an existing building for industrial purposes. Capture area is nearly 500 square feet, or nearly 50 kW at peak input.

153

medium temperatures. Car wash and food processing plants are examples of potential industrial users, and, of course, any office building, supermarket, and so on would be well advised to consider solar hot water heating immediately.

AN HISTORICAL NOTE

The fact that we must recover forgotten solar technology has been mentioned. An example of this is shown in Fig. 5-20. A solar collector was installed in Daytona Beach, Florida, in 1938, used for forty-two years, and removed when the house it was on was torn down. It is now on display at the Florida Solar Energy Center.

The design is interesting. The collector plate is covered with small, ell-shaped copper tabs soldered on to the front of the plate.

Fig. 5-20. A 1938 collector. Except in detail, this design is the same as any of the flat-plate collectors shown. The owner made an excellent trouble-free investment! See text for constructional data.

154

Fig. 5-21. A high temperature concentrating collector being prepared for test at the University of Florida. The near-parabolic mirror is made of narrow strips of window glass. Unless the absorber tube is a selective surface, the heat loss of these simple designs is very high. These collectors must be oriented to the sun.

155

These appear to be an attempt to increase the heat flow from air to collector and to reduce the reflection loss at low solar angles. The water tube is soldered to the back of the sheet.

The insulation is composed of seven layers of aluminum coated paper. This is currently used in space vehicles, in the form of *glass mat*—aluminized Mylar layers—and is sometimes called *superinsulation*. Foil-coated paper is also found in some types of batt insulation but does not appear to be as readily available as it once was.

The general construction of the collector resembles that of Figs. 5-9 through 5-12, with a wood frame and back and a glass cover. Performance could not be measured, as the collector was damaged in removal but should be at least as good as average glass absorbers.

The original owner should have been happy with the installation. Return on investment, in the form of savings, would have been about 50 percent per year. Compounded in an annuity, this amounts to a recovery of 26,000 percent!

SUPERPERFORMANCE COLLECTORS

The simple collectors shown here are reasonably "efficient" for low temperature rise and are so low in cost that their efficiency is really unimportant. Quite a different situation arises if really high temperatures are needed. Radiation loss becomes important, and the importance of heat transfer through the cover and back increases markedly. If these losses are not controlled properly, the collector will fail to reach the required temperature under any condition.

It is probably best to leave these superperformance designs to commercial outfits. They are doing a lot of work on such exotic items as vacuum insulated collector tubes, selective paints, superinsulation, rotating, and focusing collectors. Figure 5-20 shows such a superperformance collector on test.

It would be hard to do any work on this type without duplicating work already done. However, if you do find a need for this high performance, and wish to investigate low-cost approaches, it is suggested that you start with concentrating designs. These can produce spectacularly high temperatures—a solar furnace in France can melt firebrick. A bank of one-foot square mirrors aimed to a common point is the key to this design. The problem is in keeping the mirrors aligned to the sun, by moving the mirror and collection points as a body or by moving each mirror individually. See Fig. 5-21.

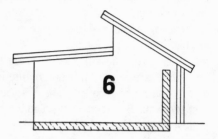

Solar Heat for Mobile Homes: Active Solar Systems

Although mobile homes are often regarded with scorn by architects, fear by builders, and derision by zoning commissions, the fact remains that they are among the most popular single form of housing. In some areas of the U.S.A., mobile homes represent the majority of new housing starts.

Traditionally, these mobile homes are very poor from the view of energy demand for heating and cooling. Partly, this stems from the original concept of mobility; this has led to minimum-weight designs, with a trend to minimum insulation, no storm sash, and so on.

Gradually, the good qualities of mobile homes became apparent, and they were increasingly used for semipermanent and permanent housing. This led to a demand for larger and larger units, with more features. For a time, installation practices improved, and many add-ons were developed in the nature of patios, carports, and storage walls. Many installations approached prefabricated housing in intent and use.

However, the increased demand led to the reinforcement of the original energy problem, due to weight. One of the attractive features of mobile homes was (and continues to be) the relatively low cost of production. Intense competition, and unscrupulous operators, led to many poor, even dangerous practices. While a number of these poor practices were corrected by industry standards and legislation, the element of energy demand was largely neglected. This was a natural and understandable result of cheap energy, the drive for low cost, and the availability of devices to give comfort at the expense of energy.

As a result of this history, the mobile home presents a real problem in these days of increasing energy costs. It's also a sizable problem—some 20 percent of the American people are affected. Unfortunately many of these people are at the upper end of age groups, and others are at the lower end of income groups. For many, the problem will mean real hardship.

The features which make mobile homes attractive are completely contrary to the easy use of solar energy to escape the fuel cost problem. But some things can be done for mobile homes. It's easiest to start this by looking at the specific elements which make mobile homes such "energy dogs."

TYPICAL MOBILE-HOME CHARACTERISTICS

Figure 6-1 shows the outline of a typical mobile home of the 1970s. They are still being built but in decreasing numbers.

The first factor in their energy use is their poor geometry, which contributes to high heat loss per unit of floor area or volume. Specifically:

The outside wall to floor area ratio is typically around 2.5, whereas for a small Cape Cod house this will be about 1.0, and a row house around 0.33.

The roof/floor area is 1.0, the same or less than a Cape Cod or Ranch House (1.0-1.25 typical), but less than a split level or two-story house, which range from 0.5-0.75. In row houses 0.33 to 0.5 is common.

The underfloor area exposed is generally 1.0 (usually skirting only, whereas conventional houses have, at most, small vents, for an effective exposure factor of 0.1 or so).

All of these factors indicate that a mobile home will lose or gain heat at a much higher rate than a conventional home.

These geometric factors are improving. Many states now allow 14-foot wide homes, and the number of "double wides" is increasing. These last approach the geometry of a Cape Cod, except for the underfloor exposure, which remains at 1.0. The "14-wides" are only a little better than older designs.

The second factor is the fenestration. The window/floor area is typically 0.3 in the south and 0.2 in the north. These are not greatly different from conventional houses but are larger than for row houses. However, the quality of window hardware in the mobile home tends to be poor, if not markedly inferior. Single

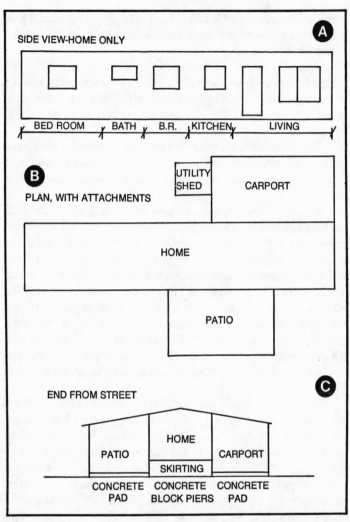

Fig. 6-1. Outline drawings showing a typical "12-wide" mobile home, and its add-ons. The energy deficiencies of these homes are covered in the text.

glazing is universal, jalousies and awning windows are difficult to seal against air leakage, and the weatherstrip provided is often poorly designed, of poor quality, not easily replaceable, and even impossible to obtain for replacement.

The door-floor area of mobile homes is not greatly different from conventional homes, but the weatherstrip is as poor as that on the windows. The problem is made worse by failure to get the home level and to keep it level, leading to gapping around doors. Windows and doors are often aluminum, with no provision for heat path control.

Primarily due to air leakage from windows and doors, the mobile home may have two to three times the ventilation loss of a conventional house. And remember, ventilation loss is appreciable in normal housing and the largest single loss in well-insulated houses.

This situation is also improving however. The current trend is to use double-track windows, which are appreciably better with respect to leakage, but high conduction due to aluminum frames remains.

Inefficient thermal insulation is the largest single cause of poor energy conservation in mobile homes. Figure 6-2 shows the cross-section of a typical mobile home wall intended for use in the south, and its resulting insulation factor. The design value of about R-8 is well below the current recommendation, R-19, and, unfortunately, even this R-8 value is rarely attained. Installation of the insulation is often sloppy, with gaps and voids. In transport, the insulation will settle unless properly fastened, again too rare a practice. The settling produces a gap at the top, leaving an area with an insulation value around R-2. Because of this, and other gaps and voids, the effective insulation value may be no greater than R-2.

The roof is usually not much better with a value of R-6 not uncommon. Settling is not a problem, but gaps and voids are likely.

Not only are these homes energy wasters, they are difficult to make comfortable because of the high wall radiation factor. It is hard to be comfortable inside the home when the outside walls are cold. A higher than normal thermostat setting is the result, further compounding the heat loss. In summer, the wall temperature will be above ambient, leading to air conditioning, and a lower than normal thermostat in an attempt to achieve a comfortable environment.

But this is not the end of the list. Other energy wasting factors are:

Minimum sized hot (and cold) air ducts, installed under the floor with minimum insulation to ambient.

Invariable use of "contractor grade" refrigerators, having at most two inches of rock wool insulation.

Invariable failure to provide a vent route for hot air from the refrigerator to outside in summer.

Inadequate kitchen air ventilation and cooling: if provided, it is likely to be electric motor driven.

Long runs of uninsulated hot water piping.

Failure to install air seals at top and bottom of exterior siding.

Invariable use of incandescent lighting.

Use of minimum insulation hot water heater-tanks, typically with one inch of fiberglass insulation compressed to one-half inch.

The sum of all these factors increases the problems of heating in winter and cooling in summer.

Corrective steps are often taken by owners of these homes, such as painting the roof with a white plastic, to reduce summer heat input. Awnings over windows, plus patios and carports to shade the building sides are common. In southern states, air conditioning is common. Some mobile homes have no heating system at all, being intended for use with an external bidirectional heat-pump package, heating in winter and cooling in summer.

Currently, there is a trend toward design improvements. Insulation is improving, and it is possible to find units with R-19 insulation. Hot water lines are routed more carefully. The factors relating to geometry and ventilation loss reduction mentioned above are usually present, but many of the other poor energy practices remain.

MOBILE HOMES AND SOLAR HEATING IN GENERAL

As we consider the energy efficiency drawbacks of mobile homes with respect to solar heating, it appears that either the solar heating system will have to be disproportionately large as compared to one for a conventional house of the same size, or substantial work on reducing the heat loss in winter will be necessary. Since such work can also reduce heat gain in summer, it seems the best approach. In the event that we may not be able to really correct the deficiencies, oversize heating may be necessary.

Let us look at the loss elements to see what can be done to correct the problem in an existing home and estimate the amount of correction which is reasonable. As a guide, remembering that a mobile home should be mobile and low in cost, let's define "reasonable" as:

Negligible increase in over-the-road weight

No more than 20 percent increase in cost

These findings should also be useful guides in buying a new home.

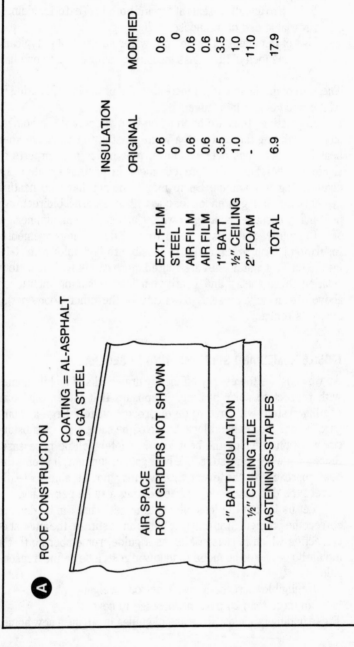

A ROOF CONSTRUCTION

COATING = AL-ASPHALT
16 GA STEEL

AIR SPACE
ROOF GIRDERS NOT SHOWN

1" BATT INSULATION
½" CEILING TILE

FASTENINGS-STAPLES

	INSULATION	
	ORIGINAL	MODIFIED
EXT. FILM	0.6	0.6
STEEL	0	0
AIR FILM	0.6	0.6
AIR FILM	0.6	0.6
1" BATT	3.5	3.5
½" CEILING	1.0	1.0
2" FOAM	-	11.0
TOTAL	6.9	17.9

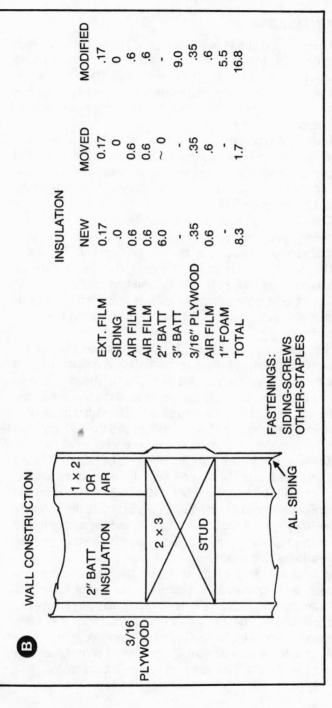

B WALL CONSTRUCTION

3/16 PLYWOOD

2" BATT INSULATION

1 × 2 OR AIR

2 × 3 STUD

AL. SIDING

INSULATION

	NEW	MOVED	MODIFIED
EXT. FILM	0.17	0.17	.17
SIDING	.0	0	0
AIR FILM	0.6	0.6	.6
AIR FILM	0.6	0.6	.6
2" BATT	6.0	~ 0	-
3" BATT	-	-	9.0
3/16" PLYWOOD	.35	.35	.35
AIR FILM	0.6	0.6	.6
1" FOAM	-	-	5.5
TOTAL	8.3	1.7	16.8

FASTENINGS:
SIDING-SCREWS
OTHER-STAPLES

Fig. 6-2. Cross sections of typical mobile home structural elements, showing design conditions. Tables give the design heat loss, typical loss factor after moving, and possible loss factor after modification.

WINDOW CHANGING

Since the ventilation loss is so much greater than needed, this is the first problem to solve. One solution is to replace the windows with dual track, or even triple track storm sash. This would be fine but expensive. Triple track storm sash are usually glass, also fine but heavy. Rigid plastic sheet would be lighter but would increase the expense.

Instead of replacing the windows completely, it would be better to keep the present ones and to use storm sash to do the dual job of reducing ventilation loss and reducing window heat transmission. For most mobile homes, this will mean fabrication of the seal and fastening devices.

Considering the goals of low cost and light weight, the use of thin, transparent plastic sheet is indicated. Vinyl is available with essentially no optical distortion, and no color change. Its life should be satisfactory if it is installed on the inside of the window. On most mobile homes this is easiest, since the windows are flush with the outside surface. Often the window space is simply a framed opening, lined with wall paneling, with the screen set against the inside wall surface.

Sash frames may be wood, but it is convenient to use the aluminum extrusion made for screens. Details in constructing and mounting such a sash are shown in Fig. 6-3. The sash is held against a batten permanently fastened around the window frame. Weatherstrip is used to give a good air seal. The sash is fastened to the batten by screws, which also serve to pull the sash frame in shape, keeping the plastic tight and wrinkle free.

The sash must be made in a jig, which can be battens fastened to the workbench or to a piece of plywood. If the jig is not used, the frame sides will bow in at the center, and wrinkles will develop. Do not use aluminum splines for holding the plastic into the fastening groove—they will cut the plastic. Instead, use the rubber tubing sold for this purpose. A spline roller is fast, but a scrap piece of thin plywood is also a satisfactory mounting tool.

It is possible to completely seal the windows by this technique, but be careful. Mobile homes contain a lot of plastic, and more than normal ventilation is needed to avoid odor, and even health problems. Allow at least two ventilation points, preferably near opposite ends of the home. One set may be associated with the heating system (inlet and exhaust), the second with the kitchen (exhaust); or, simply, two windows may be left openable.

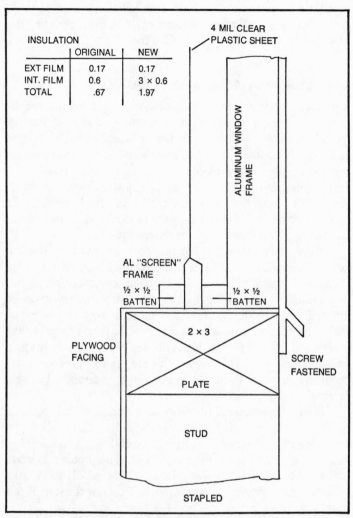

INSULATION	ORIGINAL	NEW
EXT FILM	0.17	0.17
INT. FILM	0.6	3 × 0.6
TOTAL	.67	1.97

4 MIL CLEAR PLASTIC SHEET

ALUMINUM WINDOW FRAME

AL "SCREEN" FRAME

½ × ½ BATTEN

½ × ½ BATTEN

2 × 3

PLYWOOD FACING

SCREW FASTENED

PLATE

STUD

STAPLED

Fig. 6-3. Cross section of a typical mobile home window, showing a method of adding a low-cost storm sash. Of course, glass could be used instead of plastic, but the weight is undesirable. Two or even three sashes could be added.

An alternative to this frame system is a sheet of clear, rigid plastic, cut to size. It will be more expensive, but should be longer lasting and have less optical distortion.

In addition to reducing ventilation loss, the storm sash reduces window conduction loss, due to the additional surfaces. Very nearly, the loss is cut to one-third its initial value. In northern areas, two or even three added sash could be used, reducing the heat loss to one-fourth or lower than that of a plain window.

WALL, ROOF, AND FLOOR INSULATION CHANGES

Correcting poor wall insulation is more difficult and will require some work and probably some investment. The least-cost approach is to correct any installation deficiencies in the original insulation. On most mobile homes, this can be done by removing the siding, one or two pieces at a time. Because of the use of self-tapping screws, this is not difficult, just tedious. Reposition and refasten insulation as needed to get a tight fit. You might take this opportunity to correct any deterioration found, to add electrical wiring, television lead-in, or other items.

If less than full-wall-thickness insulation has been used, it probably is worthwhile to install additional batt, to reach full thickness. Typically, this would give an improvement from R-8 to R-11. Consider also adding rigid insulating board at the outside of studs. Depending on the construction, from one-half inch to one inch should be possible without major work. (Don't forget to use longer fastening screws.) The last step would, typically, give insulation around R-17, not bad. This step can also reduce insect problems, although these can be reduced by a carefully fastened layer of 4 mil polyethylene at less cost.

Improving roof insulation is more of a problem. It is possible to detach one side of the roof panels and to blow pellet-type insulation into the space. The fiberboard ceiling may not like the extra weight and bow or even pull loose. The problem is made worse by the practice of staple fastening the panels to the roof girders and, especially, by carelessness in driving the staples too deep.

If the ceiling is not in the best of shape, it would be better to cover it with lightweight panels, say one-inch white foam. This can be independently supported by the frame made for the purpose or can be screw fastened to the girders, using trim battens for strength.

If the exterior roof is in poor condition or leaks, an exterior layer of insulation and a new roof can be added. Special material is now available for this step, but you might want to work along lines suggested later, to combine better insulation, new roofing, and solar absorption.

Insulation gain will depend on the amount added, of course. Typical values would be R-18 for two inches of foam or pellets, R-30 for four and one-half inches and R-13 for one inch inside a false ceiling. Any gain would be helpful.

Under-the-floor insulation improvement will be a dirty, tedious job at best. Examine construction and condition before making any decisions. If the tar-impregnated fiberboard has deteriorated badly, it may be best to replace it completely. In some designs, it is possible to lift out sections, which can be used as patterns to cut a replacement, or a doubler of rigid foam board. For other designs it will be necessary to add a frame, to which insulation can be nailed or screw fastened. Insulation of R-12 or more would be desirable.

While under here, look at the hot-water lines. It's probably worthwhile to wrap these, and, of course, check for deterioration, especially for signs of water leakage, which can destroy the fiberboard subflooring in short order. Do not make the mistake of totally enclosing the area between the floor and ground. Rot will almost certainly result.

In the south, the full treatment may not be necessary—just correction of installation faults to bring insulation up to design value. Run an estimate of the solar system size needed and decide, on the basis of added investment, whether to add more insulation or to oversize the solar system. In the north, it is likely that least cost will require improving insulation appreciably. In any event, comfort will be greater if this is done, due to elimination of cold spots and drafts.

A SOLAR CONCEPT FOR THE MOBILE HOME

Now let's look at the design of solar heating for mobile homes. Weight, space, and strength considerations mean that we don't want to add anything to the home itself (although we could modify existing structures). This rules out water and masonry storage walls, and heavy solar absorbers. We are also unable to cut large window areas to get energy capture. For existing mobile homes, solar heating must be external, thereby eliminating the "use what is there" adage—at least in the home itself. But what about the add-ons. Can they be used?

The most common add-ons, carports and patios, lend themselves to the active solar system we will discuss in this chapter. A passive or semipassive system resembling the atrium-greenhouse system for conventional homes can also be adapted to the mobile home. Its installation will be discussed in the next chapter.

A typical mobile home patio will be 10 to 12 feet wide and 16 to 25 feet long, with a roof overhang of 1 foot. Areas will be 175 to 300 square feet, with incident solar energy of up to 3kW, or nearly 100,000 BTU/hr. at the peak. Carports are usually larger—from a minimum of 25 feet long to usually 35 to 40 feet long, with areas around 450 square feet. Where both have been added, there may be 1600 or more square feet available.

If the add-on roof area is converted to an efficient solar absorber, say one producing 600 BTU/sq. ft. per day, the energy available would be much larger than is needed by a well-insulated mobile home and probably greater than that needed by a poorly insulated one, in milder climates. This indicates that we can make some compromises in efficiency, in the interest of cost. Let's see what is reasonable to expect.

Figure 6-4 summarizes the results of some measurements on a single aluminum panel of the type used for patio roofs. The panel was originally painted white on the top surface, and showed essentially no temperature rise when there was a breeze, but an appreciable rise in still air. Moving air convection is an important factor in keeping these roofs cool.

Painting the inside or upper surface of the panel black gave an immediate increase in temperature of over 30° F even with a fair breeze. Quite high temperatures have been observed on quiet days, especially with the sun high in the sky, as in summer months in the south. It is not uncommon for the panels to reach 120° F or so. This varies with air flow.

Further improvement as a solar collector was secured by stretching a sheet of 4 mil polyethylene across the top of the panel. Temperature rise now reached 49° F even in a good breeze. The plastic serves as a heat trap and also reduces the conduction loss.

Further improvement was secured by adding insulation to the sides and bottom of the panel. With only one-half inch of Styrofoam added, the rise reached 66° F with a light breeze. Interestingly, a fair rise, 25° above ambient, was found on an overcast day where the sun's disc could not be seen, although the clouds were somewhat brighter at the sun's position.

These tests were made with the panel tilted 8° from horizontal, to the south, on autumn afternoons. Solar angles would be typical of many installations, but others may have east-west or even north tilt. It is suggested that these experiments be repeated if you are considering such an installation, partly to gain experience

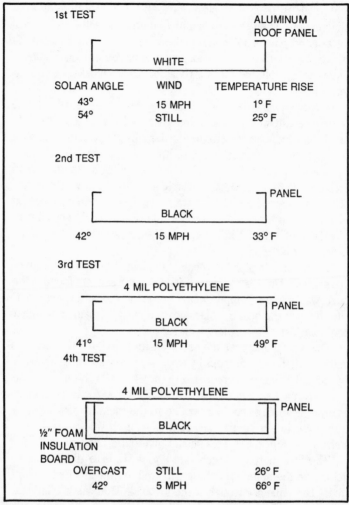

Fig. 6-4. Temperature measurements of an aluminum pan used for mobile home patio and carport roofs. Relatively low-cost additions give reasonable temperature rise suitable for many home uses. The insulation of the fourth test also improves home comfort, by reduction of re-radiation from roof to home.

and partly to obtain data representative of your installation problem.

Since the tests indicated the feasibility of using these panels, different ways were explored for capturing the energy. Several ideas are shown in Fig. 6-5. The first, and at first sight simplest, is

169

to blow air through the space between the pan bottom and the collector, but when the pan installation was inspected, this didn't look as good. The problem lies in the additional ducting needed, its insulation, and its weight. Also, air systems require a fair amount of storage mass in the form of rocks, concrete blocks, or equivalent.

What appears to be the least expensive system is to use plastic pipe laid loosely in the pans. Black polyethylene is available in coils and could be laid two or four lengths per pan for the entire roof, then the entire roof covered with plastic pulled tight. Installation would be quick and simple. The water in the tubing would reach the air temperature (or nearly so) with no flow. However, with flow, appreciably lower water temperature would be expected, due to temperature drop in the plastic, and poor contact with the metal pan. (In Table 4-4, the resistance R-2 could be excessively large.)

Loose plastic pipe is probably all right for a low water pressure system, but it is not recommended for pressures found in the house water lines. Copper would be needed for a domestic hot-water heater; the heat transfer question would remain, although it should be less of a problem than for plastic.

One way to increase the heat transfer is to force the pipe into contact with the pan, perhaps by wood separator strips, as shown in Fig. 6-5C. Under pressure and with the expected softening of the plastic, contact should be markedly better than for loose tubing. Finally, the tubing could be bonded to the metal pan by laying a seam of mastic, or similar material, along each side of the tubing, as shown in Fig. 6-5D. This should give quite good contact.

The final method, sketched in Fig. 6-5E, is to allow water to trickle into the upper end of the pan, and to flow in a thin film by gravity to a collector trough at the low end. This would eliminate any problem of poor heat transfer from the pan to the liquid, but would add two other problems. One would be corrosion, and the second would be the losses associated with condensation on the underside of the plastic film. The condensation would be unavoidable, but the loss should be relatively small. Corrosion can be avoided by using purified water with an anticorrosion additive.

Conversion of an existing patio roof, or installation of a new one, should be very simple. At the upper end, usually at the mobile home, a pipe would be installed, with holes drilled to give a small flow at two or three points on each pan. If not already equipped, the low end of the pan should be fitted with a gutter, easily installed

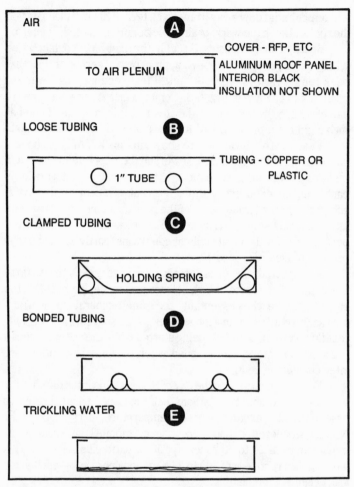

Fig. 6-5. Possible ways of using a roof panel for heating: A is the simplest, but the air passage routing is a problem. E should have the best performance, with D second.

with standard extrusion. Painting, insulating the bottom surface, and stretching plastic over the top would complete the absorber.

Incidentally, there is another "free" use available in all of these absorbers as a rain water catchment, for a cistern-based water supply. This thinking is contrary to the present practice of constantly expanding centralized water systems, but it may become desirable, even necessary. Aquifer depletion, salt-water intrusion, and chemically poisoned water sources are all too common. Hint—if you do decide on this, provide a valve system which will direct initial flow away from the cistern. This will clean dirt off the roof and keep the worst of airborne pollution out of the cistern.

Because heat transfer through the pan-pipe contact is so critical to several of the above approaches, a series of tests has been run on various types. A typical test section, less cover and insulation, is shown in Fig. 6-6. Common factors on all tests were use of 6 mil polyethylene for the cover plastic, and use of one-half inch rigid foam plastic board for the side and bottom insulation.

Results of a typical test are shown in Fig. 6-7. At A is shown a curve of water temperature rise versus the flow rate measured in minutes per gallon for a one-inch plastic pipe laid in a U formation in each pan, clamped every three feet but not cemented. Part B shows the water temperature in the pipe as a function of the time after flow was stopped. These results are sufficient to define the performance for the input sunlight conditions (partly hazy, about 50 percent of clear day input).

As expected, the water temperature is very sensitive to flow, partly the consequence of high contact resistance, but note that the stored water reaches essentially the same temperature in 15 minutes as it would reach in a longer time. This suggests an intermittent flow system, with flow being started when the water reaches a preset temperature, and stopped when the pipe is emptied (see later chapter on control).

For the conditions on the day of the test, this intermittent flow would produce about 70 gallons per hour, per panel, heated to essentially the maximum panel temperature, a rise of 26° F. Nothing wonderful, but note that a typical mobile home installation might run from 20 to 60 panels (patio or patio plus carport). This would give a recovery of 800 to 2400 gallons per hour—enough for appreciable home heating.

In clear air conditions the temperature rise would be greater, as shown by the data of Fig. 6-8. This was obtained for a fairly high flow followed by a lower one. The method of extrapolation to intermittent flow is shown by the dotted line. Note that it takes about twice as long for the temperature to reach essentially its final value, but that this temperature is nearly twice as high as before, a rise of 53°, water temperature of 115° to 120° F.

While these tests indicate that a workable system can be made with a simple design, the poor contact between pan and tubing definitely limit's performance. Further tests were made to see the result of improved contact. These are summarized in Table 6-1. Here, all results have been reduced to a common equivalent, watts

Fig. 6-6. A two-panel test section after a series of tests, and a season of uncovered exposure to temperatures between 25° F and 95° F. See text and later data for results.

heat into the water. For convenience, the ratio of this value to the solar input is also tabulated.

Bonding the plastic tubing to the pan definitely increases the heat input, but there are problems. Most bonds don't adhere well to

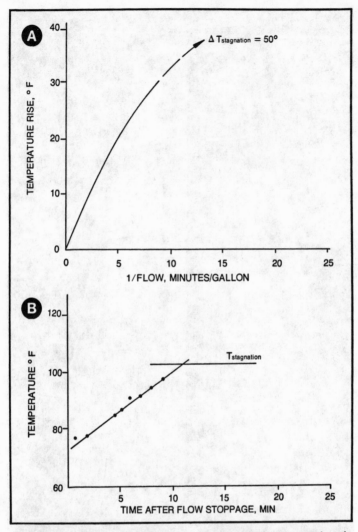

Fig. 6-7. Water flow test data and thermal and results for two panels as in Fig. 6-6, tubing clamped but not bonded. At *A*, water-temperature rise versus various flow rates; at *B*, temperature rise after flow is stopped. The data can be converted to the more usual rise versus output form. The flow performance is relatively low due to poor contact between tubing and metal.

polyethylene. Its expansion under high temperature makes bond failure likely. The result of this is shown in Fig. 6-9. Copper tubing would eliminate the problem and is required for water heating, but the expense is undesirable for heating system use.

174

Overall, at this time it appears that the best compromise is to use the design which holds the plastic tubing against the pan edges by mechanical means. A suitable design for this, and for the entire absorber, is shown in Fig. 6-10. An important factor in this design was ease of installation. The elements shown can be installed by one person, mostly working at the edge of the panels away from the roof, with no need to remove and replace panels. Long-handled brushes and rollers are used for cleaning and painting, and wooden pushers are used to position the tube clamps. Access to the roof is needed only for fastening the covering plastic.

The figure includes an area factor for size estimation. It is suggested that you run your own tests on a one- or two-panel

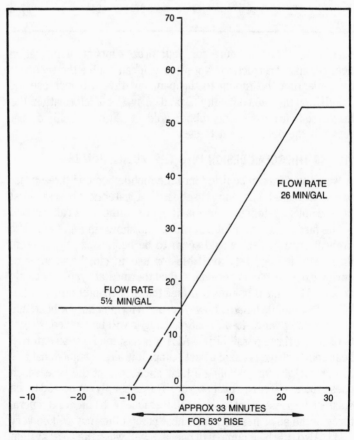

Fig. 6-8. Response to flow rate change. Temperature rise resulting from a change in flow rate, for the unbonded panel. See text for interpretation as an intermittent flow device.

Table 6-1. Effect of Thermal Contact, Insulation.

Summary of test results for a two-panel unit, all with one-inch foam plastic insulation at side and bottom, all made on clear days. Considering cost, the performance is favorable, nearly that of the lower performance commercial units for which data is available.

Incident solar energy on collector - 1780 watts ± 10%
Single-layer cover:

	Recovery	Ratio
Tubing clamped each 3'	100W	0.06
Tubing forced against sides	208W	0.12
Tubing cemented to panel	428W	0.25
Two-layer cover:		
Tubing cemented to panel	575W	0.33

Comparison: Commercial collectors (100 tested)

	Low	Average	High
Glazing			
FRP Cover	0.28	0.40	0.47
Glass Cover	0.29	0.47	0.54

section to obtain a figure for your area, amount of insulation needed, and construction. Note that you can double the recovery by cementing the tubing to the pan, but this will increase the installation time and difficulty. Based on available information, the black, self-curing silicone rubber sold for auto windshield leak repair is the best cement to use.

FITTING THE SOLAR DESIGN INTO THE MOBILE HOME

A water system can be fitted into the mobile home in three major ways. The rare home using baseboard hot water heat is easy—just tap the solar system into the existing one, either as an alternative to the furnace or as a preheater for it, as shown in Fig. 6-11. The preheat arrangement would seem to be best, since the present furnace is immediately available for use in cloudy weather or during extremely cold periods. A dual thermostat system is easily arranged to make this automatic (see the later chapter on controls).

Most mobile homes, however, use a form of hot-air heat, and some form of water-to-air heat exchanger will be needed. Figure 6-12 shows three possibilities. At A it is assumed that an external heat-cool package is used: a heat pump. It is also assumed that this has provisions for installing a heat exchanger of the type which uses ground water as a heat source. This is simply connected to the solar system instead of to the well. Because of the higher temperatures of the solar heater water, heat pump efficiency will be very good. Also, the heat pump will operate well when the solar system water temperature falls below the desired room temperature, something not possible with any other type.

Heat pump systems require expert knowledge, not only of the principles, but also of the specifics of a given design. Consult the local distributer-installer if you are considering such a system.

Many popular mobile-home furnace packages have a space at the bottom, intended for the evaporator of an air compressor. Others have a duct, to allow cold air to be fed to the distribution ducts. A water-to-air heat exchanger can be installed in the provided space, as pictured in Fig. 6-12B, or in a separate box. If separate, make provisions for returning air flow from the mobile home, rather than using cold outside air.

Heat exchangers follow the laws of heat transfer as outlined in Chapter 3. The most important factors are the surface area of the air-water interface, and the velocity of the air and water, which combine to determine the heat transfer rating and the water temperature drop and air transfer rise. The amount of friction, or head drop, is also important, since it determines the necessary pump and blower sizes. The relations are complex, and, again, expert help is recommended if you are planning such an installation.

These designs separate the hot-water storage and hot-water use. It is readily possible to combine the storage and use, as shown in Fig. 6-12C. This design uses common 55 gallon drums for storage and allows the heat leaking through the drum walls to be collected and fed into the regular mobile home ducting.

A feature in this particular design is an adjustable shutter in the hot-air line. This can be closed to shut off the heat source when not needed or it can be set partly open, to allow continuous heat

Fig. 6-9. Under the influence of thermal and pressure expansion, plastic tubing will break a bond to the aluminum in places, increasing the thermal resistance. Because of this bonding problem, and considering the cost of material and installation, it is best to accept the lower performance of an unbonded absorber, increasing absorber area accordingly. With most mobile home patio and carport areas, this is markedly lower in cost than bonded panels.

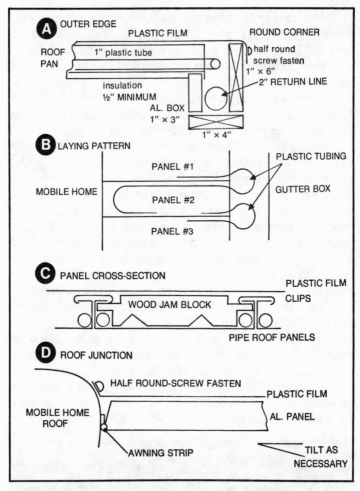

Fig. 6-10. Schematic diagrams of solar roof panel for mobile home. (A) View of outer edge of collector panel, showing component parts. (B) Top view of panel lay-out on roof of porch or carport. (C) Panel cross-section. (D) Side view of junction between panel and mobile home roof.

circulation due to temperature difference. It should be balanced and loaded to open completely when the furnace blower comes on.

Because of the weight of the water, these storage-interchange drums must be outside the mobile home. For most homes, the logical location is at the end away from the street. Most homes with hot air heat have a single duct under the floor for hot air, plus a return path along the floor to the furnace compartment door. It is relatively easy to connect to this from the end of the home. It might

178

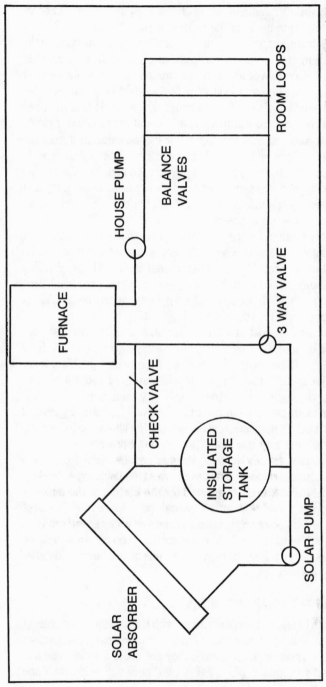

Fig. 6-11. Integration to an existing hot water system. Possible connections for adding a solar absorber-storage tank to an existing hot water system. Manual changeover to furnace-only operation is shown, but the furnace can also be used as an automatic back-up. There will be some heat loss in the furnace which can be avoided by added valving.

179

be worthwhile to add another duct, for cold air return. Alternatively, this could be from the furnace compartment only.

The drum compartment must be well insulated, as must be the ducting. It might be well to consider using the lost heat for another purpose: Rover would certainly appreciate a solar-heated doghouse, even better, the storage tanks might be installed under the plant benches of a small greenhouse. Even a little loss will keep the plant root system warm, a major element in greenhouse yield.

Heat loss and heat transfer to air can be calculated from the relations of Chapter 3. It probably will be necessary to provide some insulation for each drum, to prevent too high heat flow to the surrounding air when heat is not needed. If this is the case, try first placing the overall insulation directly on the top of the drums, so only their sides are exposed.

Water storage for the separate heat exchanger systems must also be outside the mobile home. This could still be a number of 55 gallon drums, probably the lowest cost approach. With filling stations being abandoned, it may be possible to secure used storage tanks, in sizes from 500 to 2500 gallons, at low cost. (This is the storage form for the home of Fig. 1-15.)

Another low-cost storage to investigate is the precast concrete tanks sold as septic tanks for sewage treatment. A 1000 gallon tank will be about 6 feet high by 5 feet wide by 10 feet long, and weigh about 4 tons empty. It will also hold about 4 tons of water, giving quite good storage capacity, sufficient for mobile homes in many parts of the country. Cost will typically be several times as much as for used steel drums, but life should be indefinite, whereas drums may rust out if not carefully protected.

Insulation for septic tank storage can be rigid foam, or a combination of rigid foam plus the cheapest available type, or even dry earth. Rigid foam is suggested for the bottom of the tank—it must support a load of about 250 pounds per square foot. Burial of the tank is satisfactory if rigid foam of the low water absorbent type is used, but wet insulation, like wet earth, is too good a conductor of heat. In heavy rainfall or high water table areas, surface installation may be necessary.

LOCATING THE SOLAR ABSORBERS

If you wish to equip an existing home with this type of solar heating system, it will be easiest to accept the existing patio and carport size and orientation, even though they are not at a good angle and are partially shaded. A photo every two hours will help determine

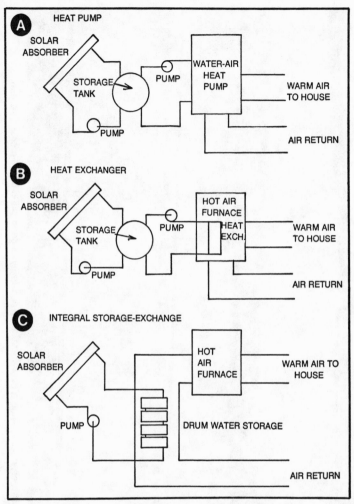

Fig. 6-12. Possible connections for integration of a solar system into three types of common hot air furnace systems. The system at *C* is probably lowest in cost.

shade factors. For example, Figs. 6-13 and 6-14 show two patio roofs, one at a poor angle since it slopes to the northeast, the second at a fair angle sloping to the south-southwest. The larger area of the first patio makes up for the poorer location, and the extra cost of increasing the absorber area is still less than the cost of making a change in the patio roof.

There is no reason why the combined use approach should not be used over the mobile home itself. This could also give you a new

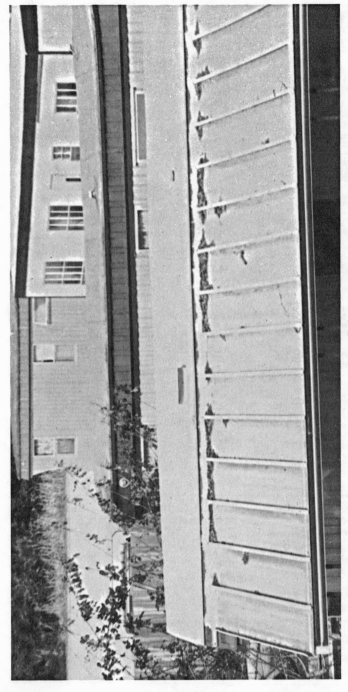

Fig. 6-13. Typical mobile home patio-carport roofs provide a good installation possibility: a good slope in the proper direction.

Fig. 6-14. A less desirable installation, partly shaded by trees and poorly sloped. Extra area, which is available, would be required for a solar installation here.

183

roof, eliminating any current leakage problems and increasing the roof insulation to performance as a solar absorber.

Ideas for these combined approaches are still being developed, and it is not yet clear what all of the problems and possibilities are, nor which is the best way to go. Because of this, you are very much on your own, doing quite a bit of pioneering.

NOTES ON WATER HEATING FOR DOMESTIC USE

Hot water for baths can be at 110° to 120° F if the supply is plentiful and should not be too hot because of danger of scalding. Temperatures of 150° to 160° F are good for laundry, with 200° F or so sometimes used. The lower desirable limit for laundry is about 120° F. In fossil fueled systems the compromise setting of 150° F is often used, with 130° F now being recommended for energy conservation.

During summer months, even 150° F temperature in a simple absorber is no problem. However, in winter the simplest designs won't even reach 120° F, since the rise needed would often be 100° F or so. Attaining this rise will require good insulation, at least. If the orientation is not near the optimum, around the latitude ± 10°, a double or triple layer cover section may be needed.

Because of these factors, it may be better to separate completely the absorbers for domestic hot water and for home heating. Alternately, it may be worthwhile to install a reflector, to increase the input to the absorber or to take advantage of an existing reflecting area (as an approximation, a white painted vertical surface the same size as a horizontal one will increase the solar input by one third).

If a section of an existing roof is to be used for domestic hot water, it should be the section with the least shading. The section will need to have extra insulation, as compared to the rest, perhaps two to three times as much. Copper tubing should be used for the water line. Tubing should be bonded to the roof metal. Silicone rubber would do, but it might be worthwhile to determine the relative cost of a high heat conductivity epoxy.

Consider also the relative costs of better cover material, glass or glass plus plastic film. The final choice of design can well be determined by the cost of available surplus material.

APPLICATION TO CONVENTIONAL HOUSES

While there is no rule saying that these low-cost ideas cannot be applied to conventional houses, it is expected that such applications will be in the nature of "special situations." Few houses use metal roofs, one of the factors in the low-cost approach; for those that do, the fact that the roof is usually corrugated is actually a benefit, giving better heat transfer to the pipe. Lay the tubing and paint the roof and tubing black or perhaps dark green, then fasten the frame carrying the cover in place, and the job is done.

For houses with wood or asphalt shingle, or built-up roof, it is possible to get acceptable results by increasing the amount of tubing to about 1 inch tubing spaced 4 inches on center. This would be covered with a frame carrying the cover. Compare the cost of this, plus storage, with the designs of the next chapter before undertaking a project.

For cold area homes with basements, the logical place to put a hot water storage tank is the basement. True, it does use some area, but it will make the rest of the area more livable, due to the leakage of heat from the tank. The heat is not wasted, since it reduces heat flow through the floor to the basement.

Making good use of this heat may require adding insulation to the basement walls. Make a check calculation for this and for the amount of insulation for the tank.

OPPORTUNITIES FOR MANUFACTURING

It would seem that there is a good field for both large- and small-scale manufacturing of these low-cost designs, both for new homes and for retrofit. Even relatively small shops make the mobile home roof panels from sheet stock in rolls and should find fabrication of special fasteners, clips, cover holders and such no great problem.

Prefabricated roof sections, perhaps 4 by 12 feet would be light enough to handle easily and should not be too expensive to produce. As patio roof panels, these would do better than the normal type, since the bottom insulation would keep the patio cooler.

With some ingenuity, curved panels to fit over the usual 12-wide or 14-wide roof could be worked out. Not only would these give ample absorber area, but they would markedly improve insulation and could also be designed to solve roof leak problems. Add water collection, and that would *really* be multiple use. There should be a large market for solar absorber roofs for conventional houses and buildings.

Following are some guidelines that should prove helpful in determining the type, size, and output of both air- and water-type solar collectors.

If flat-plate collectors are to be used for heating a house, they should be designed and installed for good performance and attention should be given to insulation. The following guidelines should help system sizing.

Water-Type Collectors

Tilt	Latitude + 10°
Orientation	South ± 15°
Number of glazings	1
Flow rate, per sq. ft. collector	10 lbs./hour
Insulation, per sq. ft. area	0.1 BTU/hr/°F
Pipe insulation, per sq. ft.	0.15 BTU/hr/°F
Storage, per sq. ft. collector	15 lbs. water

Air-Type Collectors

Flow rate per sq. ft. collector   2 c.ft./min.
Rock storage mass per sq. ft. collector   75 lbs.

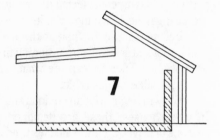

Don't Forget the Greenhouse

Let us now turn from active solar systems to look at low-cost passive designs. We will explore the hard part first—passive solar heat for existing conventional housing. In doing this we will want to see how much use we can make of what is already present. If this doesn't look attractive, we can see what can be added on, and preferably, what can be added and give a bonus in addition to solar heating.

With an existing house we have to accept its orientation with respect to the sun. To see again what this implies, look at Fig. 7-1. This estimates the relative size of solar absorbers for the four largest climate zones of the U.S.A., and for orientations from south to west. If the sky clearness factor is the same in the morning and afternoon, the curve also applies, changing the "wests" to "easts."

First, on a relative basis, note that the difference in the problems facing cool area versus hot area design isn't really enormous—a factor of two to one or so is needed for solar absorber area. Don't let the fact that you live in Maine or Montana steer you away from solar energy for heating.

Note also, as we have seen before, that there isn't much penalty for small departures from the best orientation of due south, but that the penalty increases rapidly as the departure becomes greater. Solar input never becomes zero, even for a north facing vertical window, but large misorientation definitely hurts. It can make the worst cool area problem nearly ten times as difficult as for a well-oriented southern home and over three times as difficult as a well-oriented home in the same location.

Because of orientation alone, it's not going to be possible to have a single prescription for the passive solar heating of existing homes. Instead, a family of ideas will be needed. The problem for the home owner will be to select the one which best fits his particular house, considering its orientation, its construction, and the changes he is willing or able to make.

Let us start by looking at the major elements of the home, walls, roof and so on and by assuming first that substantial changes are possible. Then we can see what can be done if major changes aren't possible or desirable.

We will begin with an obvious and fairly easy item, the walls. In older houses, these are designed to be opaque, usually for reasons of privacy. Newer houses tend to have more window area, but it is oriented for view, rather than for solar input.

An obvious step is to remove large sections of a southeast to southwest facing wall, and fill the space with glass. These can be single panes in the southern U.S.A. and double panes in the northern part. This is a simple operation, well known to contractors. It is not excessively expensive, and can be quite practical. Note that the glass needn't be perfectly transparent, but can be the type which distorts the image, as a way of retaining privacy.

This lets heat in, but, as shown in Fig. 7-2, something must be done to keep temperature excursions reasonable, which means some type of energy storage. Many newer houses built on a slab floor, provide this, but it must be added to older houses.

One method is to cover the existing floor with ceramic tile, or, if the weight and thickness can be tolerated, with brick. These surfaces are very practical and can be attractive.

At greater expense, the existing floor can be removed and replaced with precast concrete slabs. Again, these can be given a finish of tile, ceramic preferably, but even asphalt. This operation is also not uncommon and should certainly be considered if the existing floor is not in the best condition.

If the present floor is not too good an insulator, the heat storage can be installed below the flooring. An almost no cost trick here is to fasten one-gallon plastic milk bottles filled with water between the floor joists. Two hundred will give about a ton of heat capacity, but watch the extra weight. It may be necessary to add support posts, although most older houses are designed for rigidity and have ample strength.

If large windows seem impossible, consider the use of reflectors outside smaller windows, as pictured in Fig. 7-3. Up to three

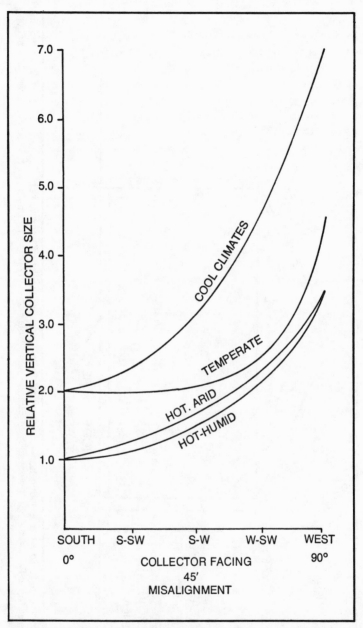

Fig. 7-1. The increase in size of a vertical collector as its azimuth is changed from the optimum south direction to the west. The curve for the east is identical if cloud cover is the same. For changes of 20° or less, the change can usually be neglected. However, the penalty for large misalignment is severe.

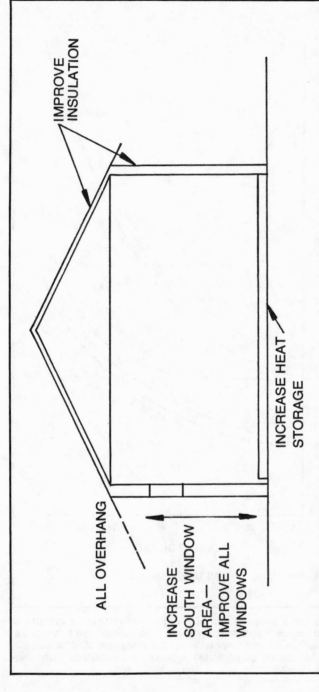

Fig. 7-2. Basic steps to adapt an existing home for direct gain solar heating. Insulation improvement should give R-19 insulation in southern areas, up to R-38 in the north. Heat storage addition is probably necessary with all frame houses. Watch the weight addition, however, adding floor support if needed.

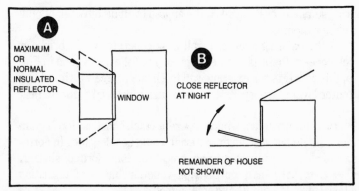

Fig. 7-3. In cold areas, it may be necessary (or easier) to keep window size down, adding solar input by a "drop" reflector panel, closed at night to reduce heat loss. While the daily changes are a nuisance, the method is effective.

times the heat input per unit of window area can be obtained with compound reflectors, or movable ones. Very simple ones may give a gain of 40 percent or so, as compared to the window alone.

Reflectors will usually change the location of heat storage to the room ceiling, or in the walls. The water jugs should work equally well, however,

Many substantial, older houses have porches of some form on the south, an important element of hot weather comfort control. Reflectors may be used with these, but it probably would be more practical to convert the porch roof to a grill, or to make a skylight, as shown in Fig. 7-4. Panels can be used to cover the opening

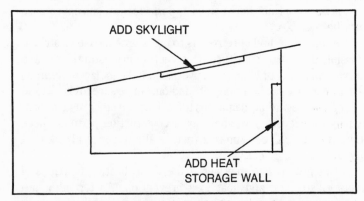

Fig. 7-4. Where rooms are large or blocked from southern exposure, a skylight can be added. It is usually indicated in passive systems for areas more than one and one-half times the height of the south wall. Wall-type heat storage is shown here, such as a mosaic panel.

during summer, or the grill can be angled to admit direct light only in winter months.

If the existing southern wall is of concrete block, brick, or brick veneer, there is another approach to follow. As seen in Fig. 7-5, this converts the existing wall to a heat storage wall by adding an outer layer of transparent or translucent material to form a heat trap.

In southern areas, where concrete block construction is common, a single layer of cover material would be adequate. In northern climates, two layers may be indicated. Some form of shutter, either external panels or perhaps venetian blinds of insulation material, would help in extreme climates.

This method works best with massive high heat capacity walls which are relatively poorly insulated. This is the situation for such items as row houses, factories, and public buildings in the older settled areas and for many newer buildings, such as schools. The approach offers an escape from high fuel costs for these as well as for homeowners.

It isn't necessary for the solar trap to completely cover the wall. Openings for windows would normally be left, although covering these gives an added control measure, in that they can be opened to let hot air circulate between the heat trap and the adjacent room. Alternatively, small vents can be provided.

The heat trap can be installed in panels, with variation in surface texture or color for appearance. If detail design, discussed later, shows that complete coverage is not needed, wall sections could be left in their original condition, or simply covered with insulation. A balance between cost, performance, and appearance may be possible.

Another method of retrofit is to use a greenhouse or atrium. Possibly this can be constructed by adapting an existing element, a porch, a balcony, or even a roof overhang. If the lot layout permits, the greenhouse can be a complete add-on, but be sure to check local zoning laws regarding clearances to lot lines and other restrictions. It may be necessary to apply for a construction permit. Check allowable uses, since a sun-room may be allowed by local codes but a greenhouse may not.

The greenhouse may serve the three heating functions of capture, storage, and heat loss prevention. As for other approaches, storage will require some mass; perhaps masonry or 55-gallon drums or 1-gallon jugs. This may be a problem for a wooden floor porch, but changing this to a well-supported concrete

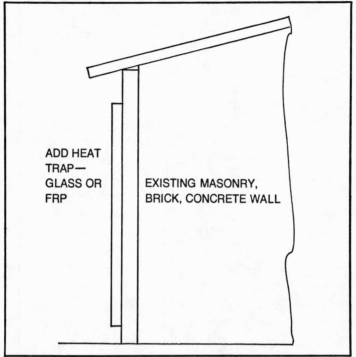

ADD HEAT
TRAP—
GLASS OR
FRP

EXISTING MASONRY,
BRICK, CONCRETE WALL

Fig. 7-5. Adding a heat trap facing to an existing masonry wall converts the area covered from a thermal loss point to a nearly neutral or even a thermal gain point, depending on construction. See Fig. 7-24.

floor should not be difficult. Double wall absorbers and some form of shutters may be indicated.

Unlike most of the other solar heat approaches, the greenhouse has the further advantage of being useful for another purpose; fresh vegetables in winter are always welcome, and the cost savings alone may pay for the entire add-on system.

Another add-on type is intended to give daytime heating only. From its appearance, as shown in Fig. 7-6, this can be called a *heating tongue*. It is simply an insulated box, divided horizontally into an upper and lower part, with the upper part being an air-heat solar absorber.

Installed at the bottom part of a window, the heat tongue draws cool air from the room through the bottom passage and returns warm air to the room through the upper part. Air temperature rise is determined by the absorber area, and by the size of the air passages. Good control of the amount by adjusting the window position, or closing it completely.

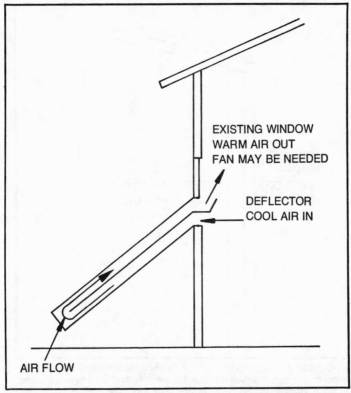

EXISTING WINDOW
WARM AIR OUT
FAN MAY BE NEEDED

DEFLECTOR
COOL AIR IN

AIR FLOW

Fig. 7-6. Principle of a heat tongue. A variation of the heat trap, designed to take cool air from a room, warm it, and feed the warmed air back. Shown as a window add-on, it can be cut into any wall. Unless storage is provided, this is a day-only heater, suitable for work shops, schools, and so on.

The heat tongue is simple, easy to fabricate, and requires no great installation effort. Schools, shops, and offices can use the system to advantage. Around the home, it can be used with various living zones to heat those which are used only in the day—play rooms, work shops, and so on.

Homes and other buildings which are on hillsides can use another form of air type solar heating that places the absorber on the hillside below the house (Fig. 7-7). This gives the necessary differential pressure required for circulation by the difference in density between hot and cold air.

In principle, heat storage can be integral with the collector, or it can be separate, say in the basement of the house. The integral collector, in the form of a massive floor to the absorber, is probably easiest. If a separate storage system is to be attempted, the air

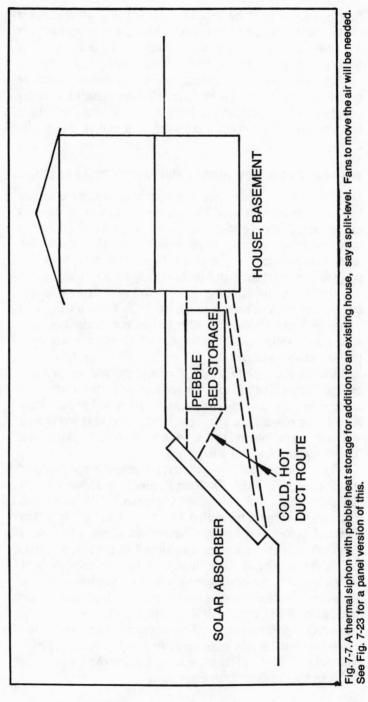

Fig. 7-7. A thermal siphon with pebble heat storage for addition to an existing house, say a split-level. Fans to move the air will be needed. See Fig. 7-23 for a panel version of this.

SOLAR ABSORBER

COLD, HOT
DUCT ROUTE

PEBBLE
BED STORAGE

HOUSE, BASEMENT

195

flow resistance must be kept low or there will be insufficient circulation. If the circulation is inadequate, it may be necessary to use powered fans. While both installation and operating cost of these is low, power failure may interrupt heating.

In the passive type system, air flow to the house can be controlled by manually operated shutters. Zoned heating is readily possible, with different temperatures during night and day. Where fans are used, thermostat control can give uniform heat, with zoning as desired.

THE PROBLEMS OF NEW HOUSES AND PASSIVE SOLAR DESIGNS

Let us now turn to passive systems for new houses. Here we face an easier situation since the house orientation, shape, and details can be varied over the wide limits necessary to reach acceptable solar operating conditions while retaining the other desired features. But remember—if you want to build a solar heated colonial, you will have to return to true colonial design concepts and not fall into the trap of thinking that a 1950 "colonial" represents the desired design. You must also accept the fact that a truly solar home may look different from other homes, but that isn't going to make it less livable. In fact, if it's a good solar home, it will be more livable and also less costly.

Design of complete homes is an art, and you will probably want professional help in this. It is recommended. It will save time and trouble if you do some preliminary homework. Not only will it be easier for your architect to see and understand what you want, it will make it possible to know if you are, or are not, getting your "dream house." And that's important.

Two volumes are especially recommended for background and idea material. One is *The First Passive Solar Homes Awards*, published by the Franklin Research Center for HUD, and available from the Government Printing Office. The second is *Village Homes: A Collection of Energy-Efficient Solar Housing Designs* by Judy Corbett, David Bambridge, and John Hofaire, available from Rodale Press. The HUD publication shows sketches, layouts, design, and performance data on 166 award-winning houses around the country; *Village Homes* shows sketches, plans, photos, and descriptions of 43 houses in Davis, California, which appears to be the site of the greatest single collection of new solar homes. *Village Homes* is unusual in that it discusses weaknesses of the design as well as good points. (There are other good books listed in the Bibliography—go over them if you can.)

Table 7-1. Solar System Use, 1978.

The type of solar system used in the 162 projects covered in the First Passive Solar Home Awards. A few homes used as many as four different systems. As seen, the simpler forms of passive systems are most popular. The average house used 1.87 means of solar heating. Only 27 percent used a single solar heating mode.

Solar System	Percent Usage*
Direct Gain	37%
Greenhouse/Solarium	26%
Storage Wall	24%
Skylight	10%
Thermosiphon	1.6%
Sun Catcher	1%

The data of the HUD volume can be used for some useful guidance, especially for the easiest and most popular designs. One way of looking at this is summarized by Table 7-1, which shows the usage of various types of collector-storage systems. An interesting and apparently important fact is that most houses used two or more different methods of solar heating. The average was 1.87 methods per house, and a few used three or four different techniques. Only 27 percent used a single method of heat collection.

The most popular method of solar heat absorption is the direct-gain system, with south facing windows, either at ground level, elevated (clerestory), or both. Heat-wall designs, either masonry or water, and the greenhouse or solarium were next. These three design types covered 87 percent of the solar absorber techniques. Of course, there were variations in details of design in all houses—after all, they were chosen for originality.

There seems to be three lessons in these degrees of popularity. One is that the simple approaches are good, perhaps even the best. Two the combinations of two modes of solar heat are possible, and probably desirable. However, the degree to which this is done appears to depend more on the concept of the house than on basic principles. (One important reason for this will be discussed shortly.) Three, special house features may indicate, or even dictate, use of one of the less popular solar heating approaches.

The HUD publication also gives the percentage of all heating derived by solar techniques. This varied from a low of 34 percent to several designs providing 100 percent. The distribution is tabulated in Fig. 7-8. The median and most probably values are fairly close, about 80 percent solar heating.

The current indication is that a higher percentage of solar heating is desirable. For the reasons discussed in the introduction, it seems best to strive for 100 percent solar capability, plus a 20 percent margin for above-average cold-month conditions. If this doesn't seem reasonable, zoning of the heated areas is suggested, with a sufficient area being completely solar heated to give adequate living space. Supplemental heating can then be concentrated in the cooler zoned areas, and used when fuel is available.

In studying these designs and others, pay attention to the measures which have been taken to secure comfort in summer. Shading of the absorber area and change of ventilation paths are the most common. Removable insulation, operable windows and vents, fans, and plantings are common.

PASSIVE HEATING GUIDELINES

Let us now look at guidelines for passive solar heating in some detail. As before, these are for use in the preliminary layouts of a design and also for determining that design approaches are reasonable. The final design should be prepared on the basis of detailed heat loss, heat gain, and heat storage calculations, but again, the guidelines are valuable checking tools.

By far the most articulate and extensive exponent of the guideline approach in passive systems has been Edward Mazria. Most of the following data is an adaptation of his published material, in different form but with attempt to preserve the values he gives.

The first guideline is of fundamental importance to all passive solar heat systems. It is simply that the maximum dependable penetration of heat from a passive system is in the range of 15 to 20 feet. This is related to the diffusion of illumination from windows, for which the usual recommendation is two to two and one-half times the window height, or 16 to 20 feet for the usual 8-foot high ceiling.

This guide tells quite a lot about the shape relations of the house. For example, if south windows are to be the main heating source, the primary zone of the house must be no more than 20 feet deep. There may be a secondary zone to the north of this, but it will not receive full heating. Such a house will need to be relatively long in the east-west direction and narrow in the north-south. It will require more insulation because of the shape factor.

If the house is to be nearly square for some reason, south windows alone will not provide good heating. Compensating changes will be needed, such as:

Clerestory windows, sky lights, or sun-catchers

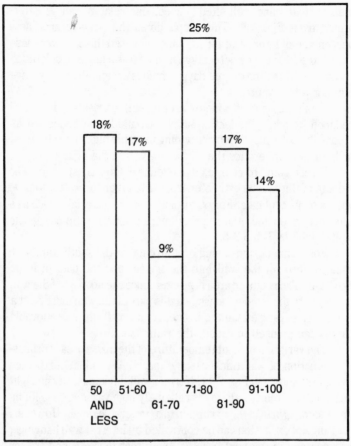

Fig. 7-8. The fraction of total home heating provided by solar energy for the 162 homes of Table 7-1. Many of the lower percentages were associated with retrofit of older homes, although one retrofit design attained 99% solar heating. The current recommendation is to design for a high solar fraction.

An elevated window wall to the south

Change to a different form, such as a roof pond

Use of a hybrid active-passive system

For the last, good practice would be to confine the active elements to the secondary zone, to the north of the 16 to 20 foot reach of the passive elements. In this way the effects of power or equipment failure will be a minimum.

Given this restriction on distance, the remaining guidelines can be based on the number of square feet of window needed per square foot of floor area of the house. For direct gain designs with well insulated and well sited houses, this relation can be determined from Fig. 7-9. This graph gives the window area as a percentage of floor area; for the range covered this is always less than 100 percent. The percentage is shown as a function of latitude and required heating degree days, which is essentially the average outdoor temperature.

If this amount of window area seems excessive, it can be reduced by adding reflecting surfaces outside the house, to increase the solar input, or by providing movable nighttime shutters, or both. Multipliers for the area are given in the figure.

Direct gain, of course, does require internal storage. The amount of this can be estimated from data given for water, for two values of absorptance. For other heat storage materials, such as a tile floor, determine the required mass from the ratio of specific heats given in Table 3-5.

For house designs using heat storage in the south wall, with transfer through the wall into the house, use the data of Figs. 7-10 A-B. The required area is greater since the hot part of the wall is closest to the outside, and since this part of the wall must be at a higher temperature than the inside. Again, reflectors or movable panels can be used to reduce the wall size.

The variation in input temperature of the house area is primarily a function of wall thickness and material. Guideline expected values are shown in Fig. 7-11. Normal wall thickness, say an eight inch concrete block wall, gives relatively high variation. Doubling the thickness brings the excursion to a preferable range. However, the range of excursion can be controlled by internal wall hangings, as discussed in the next chapter. Note that these values are for solid walls. If concrete block or tile is used, voids should be filled with grout, or packed sand. Cinder block is not good.

Time lag between maximum outside wall temperature and the inner surface temperature also varies with thickness and material. Guideline values are shown in Fig. 7-12. Remembering that a delay of eight hours or so will place maximum inner wall temperature in the late evening, wall thicknesses of eight to twelve inches or more are indicated. Extra thickness might be used for a bathroom wall, for morning comfort.

Greenhouses and atriums tend to have greater variation in form, since they extend from the house, or are separate. The importance of shape and construction can be seen from Fig. 7-13, which shows two greenhouses of conventional shape, one single-, the other double-insulated, together with a nearly optimum solar

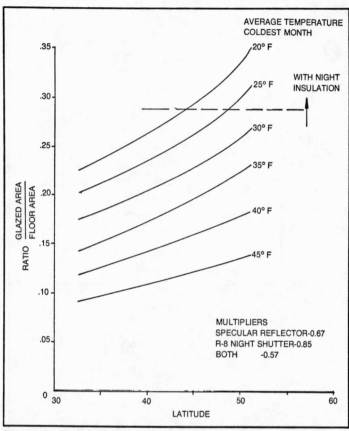

Fig. 7-9. Guidelines for direct gain systems I. Average glazed area of direct gain systems expressed in fraction of floor area, for different latitude and average exterior temperature. To use, move vertically from latitude to intersect the appropriate temperature curve, then horizontally to the fractional value. This and following curves are developed from data by Mazria.

shape. Heat gain and loss values are tabulated for each. Note that only the solar design captures excess heat, which can be used for house heating.

These data are for a detached greenhouse. Those attached to the house will have better characteristics, since heat will be fed to the house, rather than being lost to the outside. Figure 7-14A shows average temperatures expected for single and double glazed attached greenhouses of average design. For ambient temperatures below about 25° F, movable shutters can be used to increase the average indoor temperature. For the very cold climates, 10° or 15° F average, shutters are required.

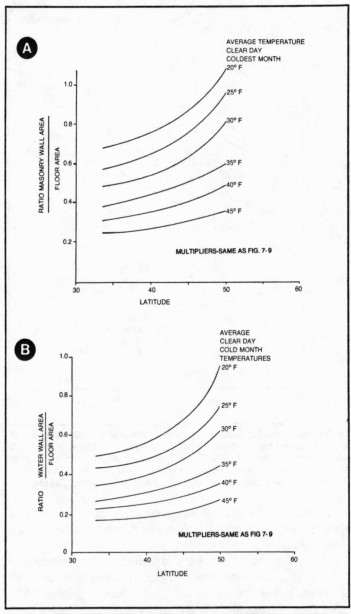

Fig. 7-10. Guidelines for direct gain systems II. (A) Masonry storage wall area in direct gain systems, expressed as fraction of floor area. The curves assume a masonry wall of eight inch thickness or more. This can be concrete block with spaces filled with sand, or solid. (B) Water storage wall area in direct gain systems, as before. If water containers essentially touch, use full area, otherwise projected area.

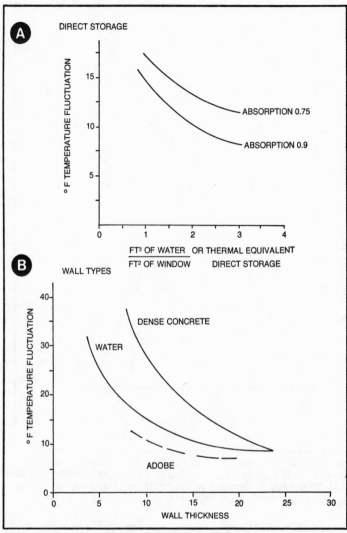

Fig. 7-11. The expected room temperature fluctuation in direct gain and wall systems. The variable for direct gain is the thermal equivalent of cubic feet of water per square feet of floor area.

The deviation from average temperature depends on the amount of storage. For water, the expected maximum departure from the average temperature is shown in Fig. 7-14B. The volumes can be converted to requirements for other material if needed.

Guideline values for greenhouse atrium design are summarized in Fig. 7-15, as the number of square feet of glass needed

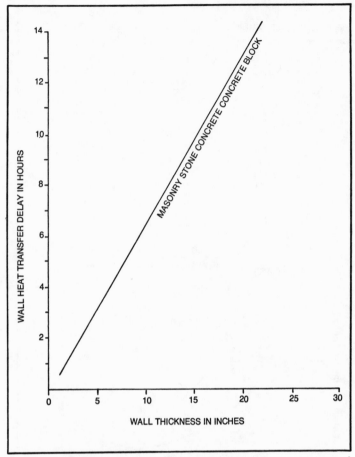

Fig. 7-12. Wall heat transfer delay. The time delay between the hour of maximum surface temperature on the sunlit surface and the hour of maximum surface temperature on the inside wall. Walls with long delay will also show smaller temperature excursions. See Fig. 7-11.

per square feet of floor area heated. This includes house and greenhouse areas. Because of the wide variation in construction, it would not be unusual for the requirement to vary by plus or minus one-third from the values shown. This is a warning—be careful with the detail analysis.

Roof ponds seem to be a neglected design—they are not even represented in the book of award-winning homes, yet the design is one of the best for climates where heating is needed for part of the year and cooling for another part. Also, the home interior can easily look like a conventional house. Perhaps it is the movable panels of the system which are considered too troublesome, but this is purely a mechanical problem. The performance record, heating and cooling, is impressive.

Guidelines for a roof pond system are given in Table 7-2. Normally, single glazing refers to the plastic bag which contains the water, with double glazing being secured by an additional sheet, or by an inflatable second skin. Double glazing is about twice as good for heating, but only one-half as good for cooling, as single glazing. Where both are needed, removable or deflatable second glazing is indicated.

The original roof pond design used a flat roof, as in Fig. 1-7. Some later designs have used reflectors to increase the capture in smaller ponds, as in Fig. 1-8. The reflector may be the underside of insulating panel flaps. Roof ponds on sloping roofs are not impossible. The heat gain is thereby increased, but the mechanical prob-

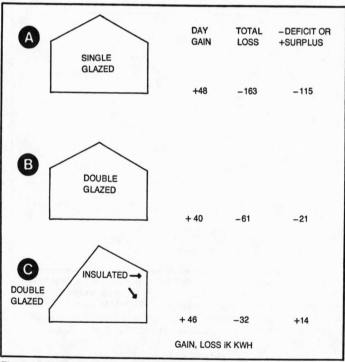

Fig. 7-13. Effect of shape on greenhouse performance. Relative gain and loss of single and double glazed conventional greenhouses, and of a double glazed solar design. The last produces a surplus of heat which can be used for house heating. If not so used, it must be vented. (Data for a winter day in Burlington, Vermont.)

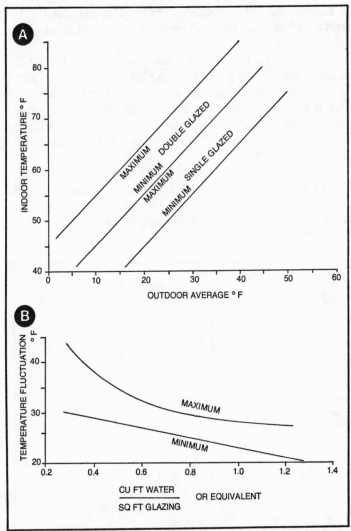

Fig. 7-14. Performance of greenhouse systems. At A, the expected indoor temperature as a function of outdoor temperature for single and double glazed greenhouse systems shown in Fig. 7-13C. At B, the expected thermal fluctuation as a function of the heat storage equivalent. Because of large areas, wind, and other loss factors cause appreciable variation in performance.

lem of containing the water must be solved. The forces are quite large. For a 10-foot slope, the pressure at the bottom amounts to about 700 pounds per square foot. This is not enormously high, but any small flaw is likely to produce a leak.

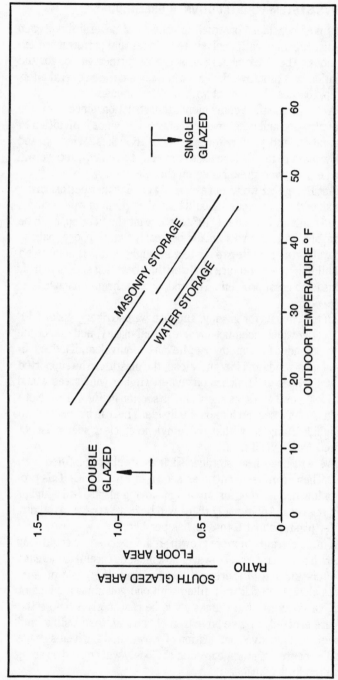

Fig. 7-15. Guidelines for attached greenhouses. The south exposed glazed area expressed as a fraction of floor area as a function of floor area, type of glazing and storage type. Expect the determined value to be within ± 30% of the value determined by detail calculations.

207

PASSIVE SYSTEM CONSTRUCTION: A GREENHOUSE

Let us now consider construction aspects of several direct gain systems, together with analysis techniques and performance expectations. These elements can serve as further guides for the evaluation of a tentative design, when considering several alternate approaches. Let's start with the greenhouse.

A 4' × 8' module is convenient in construction, since this is the size of plywood and other material sheets and since it divides into the standard stud/joist/rafter spacing of 16 inches. Windows and window glass to fit this size space are easy to come by, so we will base the prototype greenhouse on this element.

Assuming that we want reasonably good winter performance, one wall of the greenhouse should be at the optimum winter angle, or at an angle of Latitude + 10°. If we want the floor space to be reasonably large, the roof should be nearly flat. Suppose that the north wall is to be limited to ten feet in height. If this is not formed by a building, it will require splitting the sheathing sheets in half, but this is no great problem. The end view of the greenhouse is as in Fig. 7-16.

Of the choices for glazing, suppose we use fiberglass or RFP for a design which does not involve visual clarity, and one of the plastics intended for window use, Lexan or equivalent, if it does. In areas of light winds and low snow load, the plastic can be supported by 2 × 4's, spaced 24 inches on center. Higher wind areas would need 3 × 4's or 2 × 6's, as shown in the section in Fig. 7-16B. Note the addition of a second film on the inside. This can be identical to the outside film; very thin polyethylene if clear vision is not required, or vinyl, if it is.

We will need heat storage, such as steel drums filled with water. These can be arranged as shown in Fig. 7-16C. This provides a low bed in front for small light-loving plants, and a higher one in the rear. Additionally there will be heat storage in the dirt used for plants, about 6 to 8 inches per bed.

If more storage, or more growth area, is needed we could hang planters from the rafters. However, we must be careful to increase the rafter-stud size if there is a greater load. We could provide shelves along the back wall, filled with one-gallon plastic jugs of water. Or concrete water tanks could be cast in place before the walls are erected, to give an extremely strong, long lasting, and relatively inexpensive combination of growth bed and heat storage tank. The degree of storage needed obviously will depend on area, and on the heat demand.

Table 7-2. Guidelines for Roof Pond Systems.

Roof pond area per unit of floor area, for several methods of construction, and for heating and cooling. Several methods of detail performance calculation are given in the references.

Heating	Area Roof Pond* Area House		
Average Temperature	15°-25°	25°-35°	35°-45°
Construction			
Double-glazed, night insulated		.85-1.0	.60-.90
Single-glazed, night insulated reflector		.50-1.0	.25-.45
South sloping, night insulated	.60-1.0	.40-.60	.20-.45

Cooling	Area Roof Pond* Area House	
Climate	Hot-Humid	Hot-Dry
Single-glazed, day insulation	1.0	.75-1.0
Single-glazed, day insulation plus evaporative cooling	.75-1.0	.33-.50

*Pond should have unobstructed view of 75% of sky, or more.

209

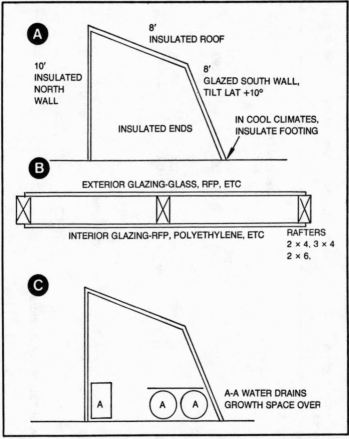

Fig. 7-16. Construction principles of a small greenhouse based on 4' × 8' panels. In A, the north wall can be an existing building. B shows two layer absorber construction, and C a possible location for water storage drums. As an alternate or adjunct, the north wall could be lined with one-gallon milk bottles painted and filled with water.

Performance calculations for such a greenhouse unit are summarized in Table 7-3. The agreement with the guideline values is reasonable. It is evident that the double glazing is a major item of performance in cold climates. Note that the approximately 40 square feet of greenhouse absorber can provide heat to about an equivalent house area, that is, to about a 10 foot deep room. Beyond this skylights would be needed.

We mustn't forget that we will need a way of transferring heat into the house and of controlling the flow. We must also have means of preventing excessive temperature rise within the greenhouse, especially in summer months. These control problems are covered in the next chapter.

EXAMPLES OF GREENHOUSE DESIGN

Greenhouses are becoming common and more can be expected as heating and food costs continue to rise, as they will. Figure 7-17 shows an unusual installation—an end greenhouse for a mobile home, the first such installation the writer had seen. Surprisingly, the second, shown in Fig. 7-18, was seen the same day. Both of these use translucent plastic glazing, since the wall they face is blank. The second is well integrated into the general layout of the home.

Integration of an add-on greenhouse to an existing home is not difficult, as shown by Fig. 7-19. This makes use of existing roof overhang. The solar captive area is accordingly smaller, in a relative sense, but the cost is also reduced.

If home design starts with the concept of a greenhouse, quite effective and spectacular results can be obtained, as shown in Fig. 7-20. This house uses a combination of greenhouse and direct gain

Table 7-3. Greenhouse Analysis.

Simplified performance analysis of a small greenhouse, primarily to check that the design is reasonable. This should be followed by a more complete analysis, with adjustments to the amount of insulation. The heat lost through the north wall, about 6 percent of the total, is available for house heating. For more severe climates or areas of lower solar input, night insulation is needed.

Assume floor = 12′ × 12′, Area = 144 sq. ft.
Area end = 8 × 8 + 2 × ½ × 4 + 8 = 64 + 32 = 96 sq. ft.
Area roof = 8 × 12 = 96 sq. ft.
Area north wall = 10 × 8 = 80 sq. ft.
Area glazing = 8 × 8 = 64 sq. ft.
Assume insulation = Rock wool batts   R = 12
Wall loss = (2 × 96 + 96 + 80) ÷ 12 = 24/deg/hr
Glazing insulation = 0.17 + 1.2 + 0.2 = 1.57
Glazing loss = 64 ÷ 1.57 = 40.76 BTU/deg/hr

At 30° average exterior, 70° average interior:
Loss = (40.76 + 24) × 40 × 24 = 62,170 BTU/day
With insulated perimeter, total loss ≈ 65,000 BTU/day

Energy captured, Bismarck, N.D. at 8 absorptance
1260 × 0.8 × 64 = 64,700 BTU/day

Fig. 7-17. Mobile home-greenhouse installation. An end mounted greenhouse on a mobile home in Arizona. Construction is obvious.

Fig. 7-18. A side mounted greenhouse on a mobile home-carport-storage wall assembly, also in Arizona. The greenhouse is primarily for winter garden, plus heat for the storage wall work area.

213

Fig. 7-19. A greenhouse added to a conventional house, taking advantage of roof overhang to reduce construction costs. Because of trees, this Arizona mountain home is not ideal for solar heating.

Fig. 7-20. A Davis, California, home with two greenhouse areas plus direct gain area. The photo is printed as a negative to emphasize the striking appearance.

heating, the direct gain windows being at the living room area. The greenhouses use widely advertised commercial components.

PASSIVE SYSTEM CONSTRUCTION: STORAGE WALLS

Now let us look at a storage wall system. Because of their basic similarity, we can use the same technique for a masonry wall, a water wall, or a retrofit formed by installing a heat trap over an existing brick or masonry wall. The construction is also similar to another retrofit device designed for air circulation, called a *TAP* for Thermo-syphon air panel.

Figure 7-21 shows a typical brick veneer house wall, with a solar heat trap added to it. This layout assumes that there is no window area involved in the space behind the trap. Most older houses with brick facing do have relatively small window areas, so it is usually easy to install heat panels which clear the window.

Because the panels are vertical and are add-ons, they do not need to carry major structural or wind loads, just their own weight and load. The load is very small when the wind is from the side and minor when the wind is head-on, since its force is holding the panel against the wall. Lag bolts and masonry fasteners are shown as holding devices in the drawing, but be certain that the box is well sealed to the wall, which prevents the fastenings from rusting out. Sealing is also needed to keep moisture from getting behind the trap.

Figure 7-21 shows two layers of plastic trap cover, the outer layer of fiberglass, the inner of a thin film. In warm areas, a single layer will probably suffice, and this may be sufficient for buildings which are occupied in the daytime only. On the other hand, in very cold climates additional thermal insulation may be needed. A simple one is a drop shutter, which can be reflective to increase the heat input. See the next chapter for some other heat loss control means.

A single trap, say 4 feet by 8 feet in size can make a measurable difference in heating costs. (The savings will be greater if the heat leakage from around the edges of the trap is prevented.) A layer of insulation some three times the thickness of the masonry is fairly effective, but the best, of course, is to cover the masonry completely. Provide insulation at windows and doors, or move already provided storm sash and doors flush with the outer face of the trap. Alternatively, for windows, install a second storm sash, and for doors, consider a new entry vestibule. These items reduce both heat conduction and air infiltration loss.

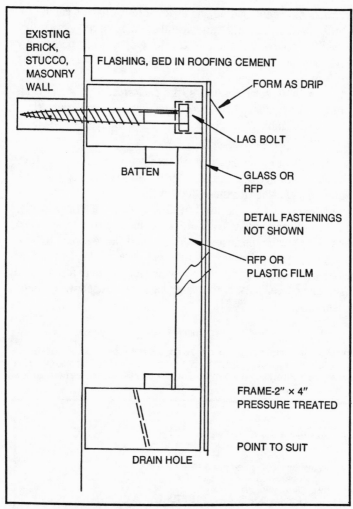

Fig. 7-21. Essential elements of a heat trap, an add-on solar absorber intended to increase input to an existing masonry wall, and to reduce heat loss. One 4' × 8' trap will save 30 to 60 gallons of fuel oil per season. Major construction problem is attaining a watertight seal.

If you build one of these, don't forget to include antirot treatment of the wood used. Pressure treated wood is best, but the paint-on liquids are adequate if the frame is kept well covered with paint.

These heat traps do change the appearance of the building. The effects can be minimized by using glass as the cover, but then there is a problem of glare, plus the problems of weight and cost.

Contrasts between covered and uncovered wall areas can be reduced by painting the wall before installation, say a very dark red or green. Alternatively, contrasts can be emphasized, perhaps by trim strips, but avoid light colors or reflective surfaces under the heat trap.

As with all solar absorbers, the performance is strongly affected by the number of layers of cover, leakage, and orientation, as shown in Table 7-4. The form in this table can be used for analysis of a particular design.

The effect on the heating will vary with the house construction, due to storage capacity and transfer time constants. Table 7-5 shows typical values for these, for typical wall construction. Some installation tricks can be used in this connection. For example, consider adding a second layer of brick to increase the capacity and delay. Or to make the absorber thicker, add shelves and fill these with plastic jugs of water. With some care, metal lath can be installed before the frame and covered with stucco to form a good absorber surface. This, or the water jugs, can be used with a frame house.

Table 7-4. Heat Trap Analysis.

Simplified analysis of a heat trap to show approximate solar input on an average day, and temperature at which the input reaches zero. Note that the trap is still showing net gain at this lower temperature, since it has reduced the net heat flow of its wall area to zero.

Area trap = 4′ × 8′ = 32 sq. ft.
Area frame = 2(4′ + 8′)× 4″/12″ = 8 sq. ft.

Insulation value, glazing = 0.17 + 1.2 + 0.2 = 1.57
    Loss = (32 ÷ 1.52) × 24 = 505 BTU/°F
Insulation value, frame = 2.0
    Loss = (8 ÷ 2) × 24 = 96 BTU/°F

At Grand Junction, CO, average January temperature = 27°F
Assume average wall surface equals 72°F.   ΔT= 45°
    Total loss = (505 + 96) × 45 = 27,000 BTU/day

At Grand Junction, vertical surface input is 1.3 × 848 = 1100 BTU/
    day/sq. ft. (Mazria)
    Total input = 1100 × 32 = 35,200 BTU/day

At assumed temperature, heat flow into house is
    35,200-27,000 = 8200 BTU/day

For zero flow, ΔT = 35,200 ÷ 601 = 58.6°, so exterior temperature
for lowered wall temperature is 72 − 58.6 = 13°F.

Table 7-5. Heat Penetration Delay.

Typical time delays for normal wood frame and brick veneer construction. If a heat trap is used with an uninsulated frame house, it would be advantageous to fill the voids with masonry to improve delay and heat storage capacity.

Type Construction	
Wood frame, inside plastered	
No insulation	0.8 hours
Insulated	3.0 hours
Brick veneer, wood frame, inside plastered	
No insulation	3.0 hours
Insulated	5.5 hours

It may be possible to work with storage constants and orientation, to give good timing control of heat. For example, low time constant on an eastern or southeastern wall will give quick morning heat. A long time constant on a west or south-west wall will give heat during evening and early night hours. The south wall could be short time constant, for day heating, or very long, for maintenance heat during the night.

The savings of these little add-ons can be appreciable. Over a heating season, from one to perhaps two gallons of fuel oil can be saved for each square foot of wall area covered. The cost-benefit ratio is good.

While the same idea can be used in new construction, it seems best to approach all new designs as a heat wall system, and to fully integrate heating into the house design. If the storage element is masonry, it can be load bearing, a form of double use. In principle, the tanks which form water walls can also be load bearing, although this seems to be rare.

With water walls, especially of culvert pipe, don't forget to provide strong anchors against overturning. This is an absolute must in earthquake areas. Put a layer of no-odor mineral oil on the top of the water, to prevent evaporation, and provide covers against insect entry. If there is the slightest possibility that small children can reach the tank top, fasten the covers securely.

Analysis of masonry or storage walls follows the techniques of Table 7-4 and 7-5. Again, there are real advantages in combining several types of heat storage; in particular, water walls with long time delays for sleeping areas and direct gain systems with short time constants for living areas are a good combination. Recommendation—try several preliminary designs before reaching construction decisions.

AIR-HEATING SYSTEM CONSTRUCTION

The final heating systems discussed in this chapter are for daytime heat only. Both work on the same principle, absorption, heat transfer to air, and air circulation by temperature differential. These differ most in orientation, and in construction details.

The term heat tongue is applied to an absorber which projects for a building, and which is normally oriented to the optimum angle for the heating season, that is, roughly due south and at a tilt of latitude minus 10°. Typical installation and construction is shown in Fig. 7-22. The tongue is divided into two nearly equal area passages, a hot air passage on top, and a cool air passage below. At the building, cool air is allowed to enter the bottom passage and warm air to escape from the top. The top may be installed at an existing window, or at a new opening. In any event, the openings must be closed when the sun is not shining.

The top of the tongue is the heat absorber. Double glazing is shown. To provide good heat transfer, the absorber needs vertical fins. A convenient and cheap source is aluminum drink cans with the top cut off, then cut in two vertically. These can be fastened to the bottom of the section with a single screw. Note the alignment sketched, intended to promote heat transfer. The cans and the inside of the top section are painted flat black to absorb heat.

The sides, ends, and bottom of the tongue are insulated, and, as usual, the performance is affected by the amount of insulation. But note also that there is a small amount of insulation between the top and bottom sections. If there is too much heat transfer between sections, the cool air will be warmed, reducing the temperature difference which causes the siphon effect, or draft.

There is a fairly complex relationship between the heat input, the amount of air moving, and the temperature rise. The dimensions shown were chosen to give good air flow. If the hot side air temperature rise seems too low, block off part of the outlet passage. If it seems to be too high, you can use a small fan to increase the flow. If quick heat-up is needed, the fan can be started as soon as the sun strikes the box.

Again, there is some freedom in orientation, to provide morning or afternoon heat. Also, it is not necessary to follow optimum orientation angles exactly. For example, a house or shop on a hillside might lay the tongue directly on the ground, increasing the area if orientation or slope are not the best.

The thermal-syphon can also be constructed in vertical form, the TAP already mentioned. While the heat input will be less for a

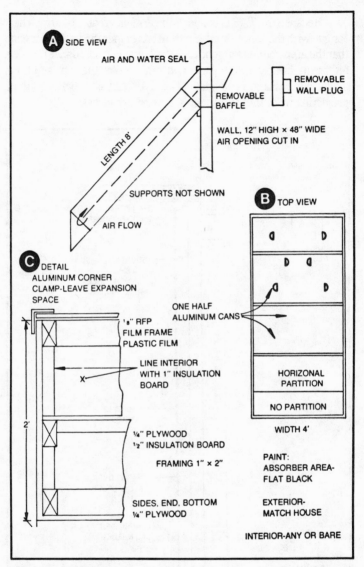

Fig. 7-22. Essential elements of a day-only variation of the heat trap, (heat tongue) using a box extended from a window or new opening. Air circulation due to difference in temperature gives room heating.

given area of glazing, the construction cost can be less, by using the outside wall of a building to form one side of the siphon. Heat loss through this goes into the building, partially making up for the lower input.

Because the TAP is vertical, the draft is greater than for a heat tongue with the same air inlet and outlet temperatures. This means that the area needed for good air circulation is less. Also, air can be fed at the bottom of the panel and removed at the top, so only a single air passage is needed. The TAP can be relatively thin, projecting from the wall by only four to six inches.

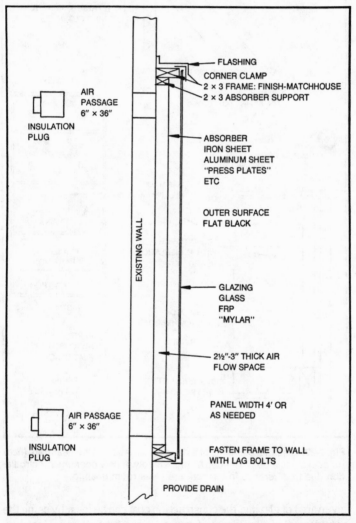

Fig. 7-23. A variation of the thermal syphon, using a vertical panel attached to a new or existing dwelling. Heat waste is less than for the heat tongue, and cost is probably lower. Night insulation is by insertion of insulation plugs.

Fig. 7-24. "Subdued" solar heating in a new Arizona mountain house, using a skylight and internal phase change heat storage. The design looks like a conventional house from most directions.

223

Fig. 7-25. "Exalted" solar heating in a nearly new Arizona mountain house using the entire roof for solar heating, a variation of roof pond and direct gain ideas. Site was chosen to emphasize the solar aspect as seen from the approach roadway.

The TAP design of Fig. 7-23 is based on one which appeared in *Organic Gardening* magazine. The original design was a high-performance unit, using double plate glass for the absorber cover and aluminum for the absorber plate. The modification replaces the inner glass with plastic film, for lower cost and weight. It also allows iron or aluminum for the absorber plate. In fact, an old piece of rusty galvanized roofing is perfectly good—it doesn't even need paint on the back.

Note that the spacing between the absorber plate and the plastic is small. This is to prevent the excessive vertical circulation on this side of the panel which would increase heat loss. Note also that this design heats the air by transfer from the back of the absorber panel, whereas the tongue heats in from the front.

The savings from a tongue or TAP should be essentially the same as for the thermal wall, about one and one-half gallons of fuel oil per square foot of panel per year. However, the tongue and TAP are daytime only heating devices, whereas the thermal wall is for day and night or evening heating, as optimized.

There is another form of air heater, sometimes called a solar furnace. It is essentially a greenhouse filled with heat storage material, with the material arranged to give good air passage. The material is heated by direct sunlight, with the heat distributed by conduction and circulation. It can be used with a hot air furnace whose blower provides the necessary air flow. Some designs also provide a small separate fan to keep air circulating in the absorber area.

Let us close this discussion of passive and hybrid solar heating systems by noting that the effect on the appearance of the house is quite controllable. By design choice, the house can be made to fit into a group of conventional houses. Alternatively, the house may be designed to emphasize some aspect of solar heating.

This architectural freedom is well illustrated by Figs. 7-24 and 7-25. Both use a form of skylight, but in one it is subdued and in the other, emphasized. Both are equally attractive in their mountain setting.

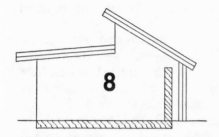

Controls for Solar Systems

In the past chapters, several references have been made to the matter of solar system control. Let us review the need for it and the options available for installing control functions.

Figure 8-1 is a schematic of the heat gain/heat loss paths of a typical solar house, showing the inputs to the house and the losses from it. Here, to emphasize the variable elements which exist, many of the resistors which represent heat loss have been shown as variable, and variable attenuators have been added to the heat inputs which vary. A symbol has been added to show that the ambient temperature varies with respect to the fundamental reference, zero degrees absolute.

Also, three new symbols have been introduced, and are placed alongside each variable item. One consists of two cycles of a sine wave, representing the fact that the item shows a daily cycle of variation. The second, a single cycle of a sine wave, representing items which vary with a yearly cycle. The final one, a line with two peaks of different size, represents the irregular variations of "weather."

In the house, the problem is to keep the temperature at "H," within the human comfort zone, as defined in Chapter 2. This is a relatively narrow range, say 65 to 75° optimum, as compared to the ambient range of 30 to 85° in the south and 0 to 80° in the north, or more.

In the conventional house, this narrow comfort range is attained by a simple step, a furnace, represented by the input line

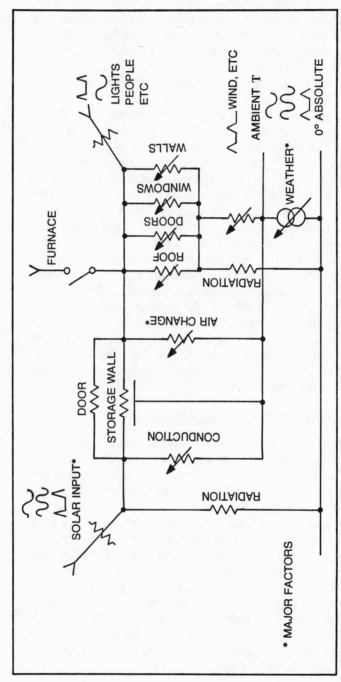

Fig. 8-1. Schematic of a storage wall solar system, showing major variable quantities. Dominant ones are the weather and the solar input. Most losses are affected by wind, and also by details such as the number of people, window, and door openings, and so on.

227

with a switch. Under control of a thermostat, the furnace feeds heat to the house interior for variable periods, the temperature going slightly above the desired value at the end of an operating period, and being somewhat below it just before the furnace starts. In the conventional house, the comfort zone is maintained quite well, as long as fuel is supplied to the furnace and there is power to run the motors and controls, barring equipment failure.

In "olden" days, the heating system operation was somewhat different. The furnace, stove, or fireplace operated continuously, or nearly so, feeding heat all of the time. The amount of heat was manually controlled, primarily by changing the amount of air fed to the furnace, but also by changing the amount of fuel fed. As long as there was fuel, and someone to feed and control the furnace, comfort was reasonably well maintained, again barring equipment failure. (Records and recollection seem to indicate there were fewer failures in the older systems, but that the consequences were apt to be more severe, even including burning of the house.)

In our solar house we also need to maintain the comfort zone temperatures. And we would like to do this without dependence on the furnace, which is primarily for extreme weather backup. It would be nice not to have to use the fireplace, if provided, but we might want to use it without upsetting the comfort zone conditions. And it would be nice to do this without dependence on outside power, but it would also be nice if air manual elements were simple and not demanding of attention.

FUNDAMENTAL CONTROL CONSIDERATIONS

The approach to meeting these needs and desires depends on a fundamental factor of control, the fact that any variable element which can be controlled in some way is a possible element of a control system. Thus, in Fig. 8-1, any element which can be changed is a possibility.

Of course, while there is a possible control use, not all of these are really practical. For example, varying the size of a massive storage wall is completely impractical. Even the usual annual control variation in window heat loss leakage, by putting up and taking down storm sash, is a chore that most of us put off.

But there are a number of relatively simple control steps which can be used. The major ones are indicated in Fig. 8-2, which is the schematic of Fig. 8-1, with the elements which are usually varied for control indicated by enclosing them in a circle. For our purposes, these can be regarded as:

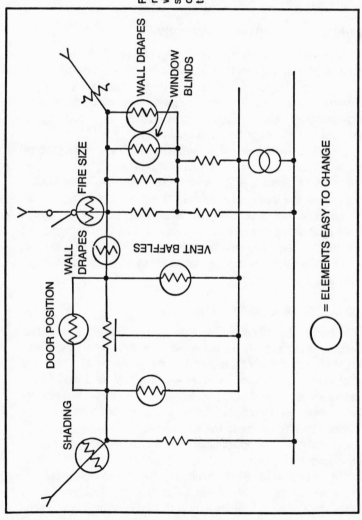

Fig. 8-2. The schematic of Fig. 8-1 modified to indicate elements which are easily varied, and can serve as control elements. These can be varied manually or by automatic devices.

229

Input control items, which regulate the amount of solar heat absorbed

Transfer control items, which regulate the amount of heat transferred from storage

Loss control items, which regulate the amount of heat loss
Usually, the input control items are made effective with respect to the long term variations, and the transfer control items with respect to short term and unpredictable ones. Loss control items are usually made effective with respect to long term variations but are a useful way to supplement other controls for unpredictable variations, especially the extreme occurrences.

MANUAL VERSUS AUTOMATIC CONTROL

We have said that it would be nice to avoid dependence on outside power systems. This is often taken to mean that manual operation is a necessity, but this is not necessarily so. There are a family of self-power control devices available, most working on differences in temperature. They can be used to avoid the trouble, tedium, and forgetfulness associated with manual control.

However, we should also bear in mind a fundamental precept of the field called *reliability,* the art of making things work. Stated simply, this precept is—"If it's not there, it can't fail." Practically, this implies the more common rule, "Keep it simple." Automatic devices tend to violate this rule. So a good, *reliable* solar house probably should use manual control extensively. Certainly, manual operation, or backup of any automatic element should be possible.

With these items in mind, let's turn to practical control concepts and design.

CONTROL OF SOLAR INPUT

The basic method of controlling solar input is shading, placing the absorber in shadow when input is not wanted. In passive systems this shading is usually inherently automatic, (self-auto), obtained by choice of geometry. As described in Chapters 1 and 4, the control is usually seasonal, giving solar heat in winter and removing it in summer. Occasionally, hour of the day self-auto control is provided by orientation to the east or west.

A secondary method of input control is by positioning a reflector. Again, this may be seasonal, self-auto, as in the sun-catcher design of Fig. 1-10. More commonly the reflector is manually positioned, as in the bread-box water heaters of Chapter 5. In these, the reflector doubles as a heat loss control when closed.

Some roof pond systems have these dual use elements, others only shading panels.

In active solar systems, heat input control is rarely found. The absorber, whether using air or water, sits exposed to sunlight at all times. True, a modest degree of self-automatic control results from the fact that the absorber is usually oriented for best winter season input, but this is in the direction of equalizing the input over the annual cycle. Because of this lack of control, there are special requirements for materials, as discussed in Chapter 5.

If you consider some form of heat input systems necessary or find after a summer season that you have an excessive heat problem, a number of approaches to shading are available. Probably the easiest is deciduous planting, growth which gives leafy shade in summer and no shade or minimum shade in winter. These can be trees, but they tend to grow too large, so pick the species carefully. Vines on a trellis are good—they can be heavily pruned types, such as a grape trellis, or an annual such as morning glory. If winter heating is critical, make the trellis removable. Don't forget that a trellis can also serve as a privacy screen if vertical, or allow clear vision if horizontal.

Several other heat input control elements are sketched in Fig. 8-3. One family is based on a roll-up reflector, the second on rigid slats. Combinations are possible, as in the venetian blind. Each family is shown in three positions: behind the absorber face, in front of it, and horizontal.

Of these two families, the roll type seems superior. It is easier to fabricate and gives no shading when rolled up. The slat type would reduce the winter input appreciably if left in place. However, an outside slat type, removable, with the slats nearly horizontal, is a good way of obtaining summer vision, shading, and a degree of privacy.

These reflector and shading systems could be made automatic in operation, using some of the sensor and control mechanisms described later. It seems best to leave these systems manual. The trouble and work of rolling a shade once a season, or perhaps adjusting its position to compensate for an unusually warm or cold week, is just not that great.

We should note that shading may be a refinement in some systems, but is often a necessity with the greenhouse or atrium during summer months. Deciduous planting, including vines, seem to be the preferred techniques. Often the shading will be provided only for the horizontal, or near horizontal, parts of the greenhouse.

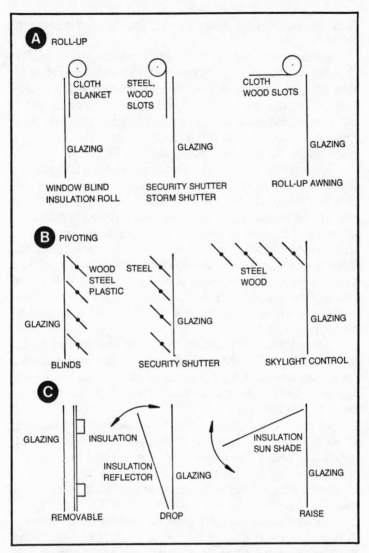

Fig. 8-3. Sketch of three families of heat control possibilities, as they are usually found. If the heat input is direct solar radiation, the type ahead of the glazing with a reflective surface would be preferred.

CONTROL OF HEAT TRANSFER

The largest percentage of passive systems and all active systems use a working fluid to transfer heat, and control of this flow is common. Let's look first at passive systems using simple control elements.

Figure 8-4 shows techniques for air type heat trap collectors, including a greenhouse or atrium, or a storage wall, as pictured. At the top and bottom are air vents, as shown at A. Removable plugs block these vents when air circulation is not desired. Typically, the plugs could be removed during the early morning hours, to give increased heat flow into the house area. As it warms up, the plugs are inserted, letting the trap-wall function for storage and delay.

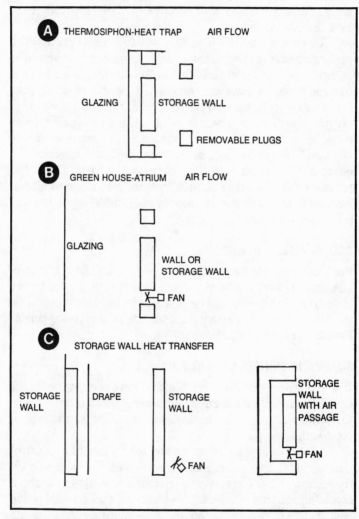

Fig. 8-4. Schematic of several methods of varying heat transfer. The wall plug and drape designs are best for manual control, the types with a fan, for automatic control.

The plugs would be left in place at night and during long cloudy periods.

The early day heat flow can be increased by installing a fan in one passage. This can be controlled manually or automatically by means discussed later.

Another method of controlling heat flow is shown at C, in the form of a barrier on the inside of a storage wall. This can be an insulating material, but any material which will reduce air flow across the wall surface is also effective—the goal is to reduce the heat circulation.

This use of a barrier is an easy way to bring a system which performs better than expected into the design range ("I should be so lucky!"). If the system is intentionally oversized, it can be used to compensate for extra cold weather, or periods of cloudiness.

Storage wall heat flow can also be increased. One way is to provide one or more passages in the wall, blowing air through these as in Fig. 8-4C. (Some increase in heat transfer can be obtained by simply turning a fan blast on the wall, which reduces the effect of the still air wall film, increasing the heat flow.) The passages could be some unfilled core areas in concrete blocks. Remember that both storage capacity and time delay will be different if the cores are filled or unfilled.

GREENHOUSES AND ATRIUMS

For greenhouses and similar structures, the simplest heat control element is a door. If it is open, there is heat flow, if closed, very little. The effectiveness can be increased by making the door floor to ceiling, or providing a transom panel extending to ceiling height. Fans can also be used, of course.

AUTOMATIC CONTROL OF HEAT FLOW

It would appear that a market could be developed for automatic devices to control the amount of heat transfer and, therefore, house temperature. Pending this, home mechanics might want to experiment with some possibilities.

An obvious approach is to use small electric motors to control the position of drapes over a heat storage wall, or vent position in the air flow path to a greenhouse or atrium. It would appear that a control which, in effect, includes a triple integration would be the best, as it could hold the house temperature constant despite outside variations. A double integration system allows the house temperature to fall as the outside temperature falls.

It would also seem possible to develop a set of control elements which are temperature operated, requiring no outside power. Bimetal strips, discussed later, can provide appreciable force, as can the expansion of a number of solids and liquids. A well balanced air vent on good bearings requires very little force to adjust its position. For small vents, it might be possible to use a mechanical type of automobile radiator thermostat as the working part.

For some discussion of other automatic control possibilities, see a later section.

THERMAL SENSORS AND OTHER CONTROL ELEMENTS

Before starting on control of active systems, let us look at the devices which are needed for control, the thermal sensors and other elements. Following current practice, these will be largely electrical in nature, but realize that other sources of power for control use are perfectly feasible. Water pressure and air pressure could serve equally well. Their use might be indicated in special situations, for example, a home built to do without electric power.

The basic control element of the conventional heating system is the thermostat. This is a temperature sensitive control device which opens an electrical circuit if the temperature is at or above a preset point, and closes the circuit if it is below this point.

The usual operating principle is shown in Fig. 8-5A. A thin strip of metal is shaped into a spiral, with an extended arm at one end which bears a contact. The center of the spiral is attached to a post, and to a wire lead. The strip of metal is formed by welding two different metals together, one having high expansion when the temperature changes, the other low expansion. As a result, when the strip warms up, it bends, as shown in the right part of the figure. Those two-metal elements are called *bimetals*. Iron and copper are a typical pair.

Because of the bending, the contact arm moves with temperature, to the left when hot, to the right when cold. The center post is made movable, and a setting arm is provided for it. This allows the temperature at which the contacts close to be set to the desired value. Sometimes a scale is provided to indicate the setting temperature.

If the device is used in this form, a problem arises. At exactly the set temperature, the contacts may make and break very often, due to air currents, or to vibration, say footsteps. Also, as the temperature rises, the contacts separate slowly, which makes a lasting arc which burns and pits or destroys the contacts.

To prevent this, a small magnet is placed near the arm section. Now, as the contacts approach each other the attraction of the magnet increases as the arm comes closer to it. At some point the arm will suddenly jump to the closed position, and is firmly held there by the magnet. When the air and the bimetal warm up, the arm is restrained from moving by the magnetic force. This holds the arm until the expansion force exceeds it, when the arm suddenly jumps to the open position. This distance is chosen to quench any electrical arc which develops. There may be another contact in the open position, and another magnet, but these are not usually found in home thermostats.

As a result of the magnet, the temperature at which the contact opens is not the same as the closing temperature. This effect is called *hysteresis*. This is the reason for the action of the furnace described by Fig. 3-12. Too much hysteresis would mean that the house is alternately too hot or too cold, but a little is not noticeable and greatly reduces wear on the contacts and on the motors which are controlled by the thermostat.

There is another form of bimetal commonly used in furnace systems. Here, as in Fig. 8-5B, the bimetal is formed into a slightly cup-shaped disk. As the upper surface tends to expand, the shape is first maintained, then suddenly changed to a cup of opposite curvature. On cooling, the second disk is maintained until a lower temperature than that of the first change (built-in hysteresis). These elements are sometimes used as an advertising stunt, a "flying saucer," at room temperature, and another shape when warmed by the hands.

In the furnace system, these disks are held at the edge. A small insulated plunger transfers the center motion to contact movement, open or closed.

While the thermostat is by far the most common control element, two other forms are found. One uses the change in resistance with temperature, as sketched in Fig. 8-6A. The resistance is compared to that of a reference whose value does not change with temperature. If the difference in resistance exceeds a preset amount, this is detected, the excess amplified and used to provide a control signal. The amplifier may be completely electronic, using transistors, or it may be electromechanical, a sensitive relay.

A new special form of thermometer uses the temperature change of a semiconductor function, one of the family which includes the transistor. The change is small, but it is very linear with

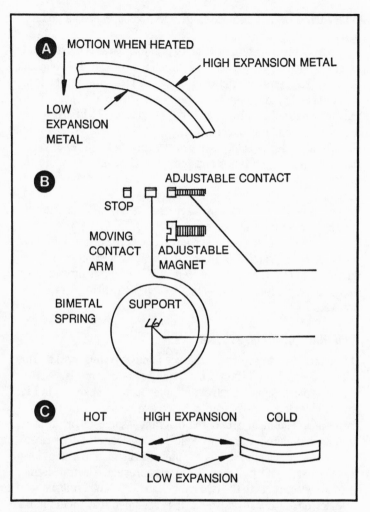

Fig. 8-5. Elements of thermostats. *A* shows the construction of a bimetal thermostat, two metals of different thermal expansion bonded together. *B* is a schematic of a typical thermostat. *C* shows the working element of many control and safety devices, a bimetal disk which inverts at specific temperatures.

temperature. The units are not at all expensive. The connections, Fig. 8-6B, are the same as for a resistance thermometer, but the voltages are different. Expect to see more of this type in the future.

The other major control system element is the electric motor. It may be used to turn a fan or a pump. It is sometimes found in an actuator, geared down and fitted with stop contacts to give linear or rotary force over a distance (a garage door opener is a common actuator).

Any control system relating to possible hazards must include safety devices. A common one is a form of the disk bimetal, designed to open an electrical circuit if the temperature rise is too great. Usually, the disk must be reset to the ON position by pushing a button, generally red in color and labeled RESET. These are often found on electric motors.

Another set of safety devices are the pressure relief valves found on hot water tanks and furnaces. These open when the pressure becomes too high, and are important for explosion prevention if the tank or furnace runs out of water. Sometimes there is a high temperature relief also, often operated by the expansion of a wax as temperature increases.

Fuses in the electrical system are also important safety devices. A good practice is to put the heating system on its own circuit, fused for the load expected. If it is on a circuit with other items, good practice requires that it have its own fuses or circuit breakers.

A FURNACE CONTROL SYSTEM

It is instructive to see how a furnace control system works. This will be useful later, when considering back-up controls.

A typical, simple control for an air furnace is shown in Fig. 8-7. All elements are labeled, and the symbols used are the standard ones. The main part of the diagram assumes a gas furnace, with an add-on indicating the typical change for an oil furnace.

When the main switch is on, power is applied to a step-down transformer, a safety element not always present. The transformer secondary connects to the two limit switches, the thermostat, and an electromechanical gas valve. It is assumed that this is in the operating position, feeding gas to the pilot, which is lit, and ready to feed gas to the main burner. In these valves, the main flow is blocked if the pilot is out by an expanding liquid heated by the pilot flame.

When the thermostat closes, gas is fed to the burner and ignites. The furnace starts to heat up. At a preset temperature, commonly around 135° F, the fan thermal switch closes and heat delivery to the house starts.

If the furnace air temperature becomes too high, the low-limit thermal switch opens, shutting off the fuel supply until the temperature drops. This can happen, for example, from a blocked hot air

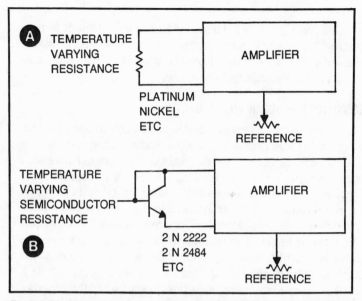

Fig. 8-6. Thermostat elements used for precision and proportional control, that is, a system in which the response varies as the input varies. A shows a "resistance thermometer," and B a newer type, using the resistance variation of a semiconductor.

duct. This switch is "backed up" by a second or auxiliary limit thermal switch, set to a slightly higher temperature. This one may require manual reset.

When the house heat has risen sufficiently, the thermostat opens and the gas is shut off. The fan continues to run, however, until the fan thermal switch reaches its lower limit. This cools down the furnace, and prevents the fan from starting and stopping several times.

An oil furnace replaces the gas valve with a relay, which applies power to the combined pump and blower, which feeds air and oil to the combustion chamber, and to the igniter, which produces a steady stream of sparks to ignite the oil. The igniter is shut off by a thermal detector after flame starts.

In hot water systems, the fan is replaced by the circulator pump. There may be low water pressure shut-offs in addition to overtemperature protection.

There are many variations in these designs with the details of component connections varying. Some omit the transformer, using the thermostat for switch control. Mechanical design of the various elements is also a major variable.

Incidentally, it should be noted that these automatic furnace controls aren't just a convenience. They are also energy-saving elements. The savings over manual control is estimated to be as much as 15 percent in fuel consumed.

CONTROLS FOR SOLAR WATER HEATING

Let us review the factors involved in solar water heating, first for domestic hot water, then for an active home heating system. The first factor is the effect of the day-night cycle. Obviously, we don't want the water circulating when the sun is not shining, or more precisely, when the water in the solar absorber is lower in temperature than the water in the tank. This will require a pump which does not allow reverse flow, or a reverse flow "check valve." The valve is required in thermosyphon systems which need no pump, but circulate water by virtue of the decrease in density as it heats up. (This reverses flow when the tank water is the hottest.)

For pump systems we want flow to start when the absorber water is hotter than the tank water. One way to do this is to put a resistance thermometer in the absorber and another in the tank, and use the difference between these as the control signal. This is called a *differential thermostat*, and exists in several forms. One is shown in Fig. 8-8. The thermal elements are resistance change material, called *thermistors*, encased in a metal pressure shell. The two signals are compared by a special amplifier, called an *operational amplifier*, because it is designed to perform operations that add or compare signals. The output drives a sensitive relay. Whenever the absorber temperature exceeds the tank temperature by an amount ΔT, the relay operates, starting the circulation pump. The size of ΔT is set by the characteristics of the relay, and the gain of the amplifier, which is controlled by the ratio of resistors R1 and R3. The diode at the output prevents operation when the tank temperature is the highest.

Current practice is to replace the relay with solid state devices. If you encounter one of these designs, be careful. The amplifier circuits may be at or near the potential of the ac line.

Recently a simpler approach has been introduced that eliminates the thermometers and the differential action. Instead, an absorber thermostat is used, starting the pump whenever water temperature at the outlet exceeds a prechosen value. Pumping continues until all absorber water has been replaced, at which point the outlet temperature drops and the pump shuts off.

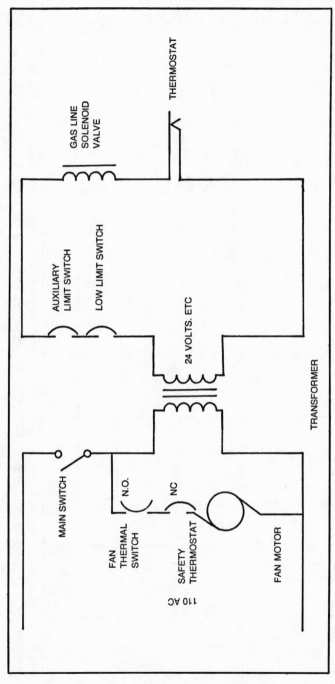

Fig. 8-7. Schematic of the controls for home gas furnace which includes both operating and safety controls. The limit, thermal, and safety elements are of the bimetal disk type in most designs.

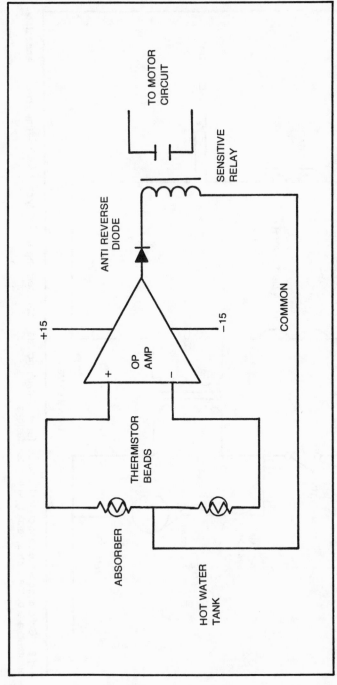

Fig. 8-8. Schematic of one form of temperature comparison or differential thermostat, using electronic amplification. When the absorber becomes warmer than the hot water tank, the motor starts, pumping water around the heat loop.

242

This system has both advantages and disadvantages. It is simpler, and less expensive to install. It gives the largest supply of hot water, and it may actually capture more energy. However, under marginal conditions, there is not even warm water. Also, the pump must be larger than for the differential system, and must be designed for start-stop operation. It is likely to require repair more often.

Based on experience so far, the simple or "bang-bang" thermostat system is suggested for the home owner.

An item to consider in this intermittently pumped system is the desirability of providing a two-temperature control, one effective on cloudy days, the second when there is good sunlight. The decision should be based on the amount and cost of auxiliary heat, the amount of storage provided, and the expected occurrence of low heating hours.

A simple way of setting up the controls for a two-temperature absorber is shown in Fig. 8-9. This is based on the use of a blackened bimetal temperature switch, which could be adapted from the type found in temperature controlled electric heater fans. The magnet position should be adjusted until the bimetal is always in contact with one or the other of the stationary contacts.

We have considered briefly the matter of absorber freezing in cold weather. Manual draining is the simplest, but requires careful pipe layout to avoid trapping water at some point in the exposed line. It is a nuisance, as is the other manual approach, a shutter or blanket over the absorber.

With some care in layout, we can use water from the tank to prevent freezing without losing any of the hot water. The approach is shown in Fig. 8-10, (which also shows the other elements of the

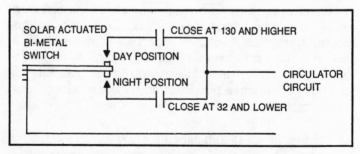

Fig. 8-9. Schematic of a form of two-temperature thermostat, using a solar heated bimetal to start the pump at the hot water temperature in daytime. At night, pump starts if the absorber reaches freezing temperature. Electronic versions of the circuit are possible.

bang-bang circulator). Water is taken from the middle point of the tank when needed to raise the absorber temperature above freezing, and the colder water is returned to the bottom of the tank. Since the flow rate is low, the water in the upper half of the tank is undisturbed.

Of course, this doesn't come for free. Calculate the expected absorber loss and allow for it by increasing the size of the tank, and the size of the absorber. Good absorber insulation, plus double or triple glazing will keep the size increases to the acceptable range.

You might also think about a back-up system, say a water heating coil at the back of a fireplace. This would give a back-up hot-water source, and the fireplace would probably be used anyhow on those very cold winter nights when the absorber needs extra protection.

In thinking about these hot-water control systems, don't forget the benefit of placing the water tank at or above the absorber, say on the roof. Thermal-syphon action moves the water to the tank, eliminating the need for valves, thermostats, and pump. The system works if the tank is at least 1 foot above the collector. Don't forget to provide good insulation for connecting lines as well as for the tank.

CONTROLS FOR HOT-WATER HOUSE HEATING

For house heating, the problems are the same as for water heating for that half of the system from absorber to tank. While the absorber, tank, and pump will be larger, controls can be just the same.

The control of the process of moving heat from the storage tank to the house isn't much different from the conventional house system where heat is moved from the furnace to the house. A pump moves the heat, with floor pipes, radiators, or baseboard strips handling distribution. A water-air system will need, in addition, a fan to move heat from the water- air interchanger to the house. Existing hot water systems will have valves for flow control at each radiator, or baseboard section. Don't forget these in a new system, to allow balancing of heating, and shut-off if needed.

INTEGRATION OF SOLAR AND BACK-UP SYSTEMS

Since the action of heat transfer from storage to house is so similar to conventional furnace operation, the storage tank seems to be the best place to integrate the solar back-up control (in one sense the

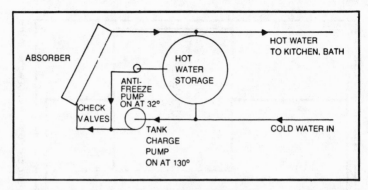

Fig. 8-10. Schematic of piping to use stored hot water to prevent absorber freezing in cold weather. The control of Fig. 8-9 can be used, modified to start the small pump when needed. Note that this uses water from the cooler part of the storage tank.

problem is identical since the conventional system is also using heat from stored fuel).

Probably the easiest way to make the control integration is to use a water thermostat at the top of the solar water storage tank, as shown in Fig. 8-11. This assumes that independent circulators are used for the solar tank and the conventional furnace. If a single circulator were used, electrically operated flow valves (solenoid valves) would be in the position of the two circulators shown, and the circulator would be in the common line to the furnace.

Another way to handle the control problem is to use a two thermostat system, the main thermostat controlling the solar elements, and a secondary thermostat controlling the furnace. Such a system is pictured in Fig. 8-12, for a hot water-hot air solar system interchange design. The second thermostat is installed adjacent to the regular one, and is set for a lower temperature. As long as the solar system provides ample heat, the furnace remains in standby. If the house temperature drops because the solar heating is insufficient, the furnace comes on.

In this simple system the blower will remain in operation until solar input is again sufficient for heating. This extracts maximum heat from the stored water. If it is considered undesirable, a special thermostat can be fabricated in which the furnace or low-temperature circuit remains in the on position until the main thermostat goes to off. This action can be secured by a small actuating arm attached to the moving element of the main thermostat, and pulling the other thermostat arm away from its holding magnet. An electromagnet can do the same job.

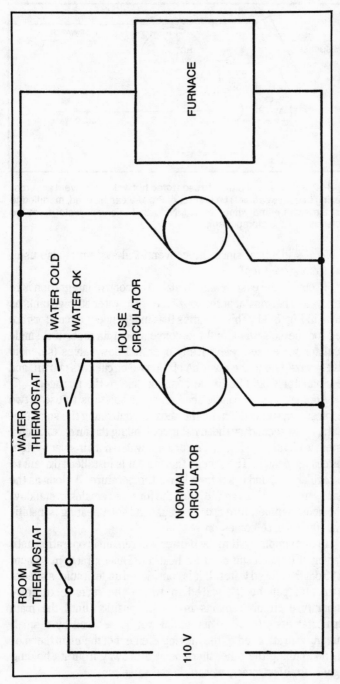

Fig. 8-11. Back-up furnace control I. Schematic of control which starts the furnace if there is a heat demand but no stored hot water. In this form, the residual hot water is not used.

246

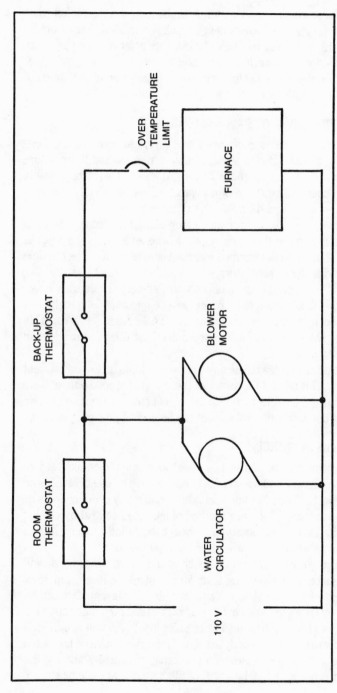

Fig. 8-12. Back-up furnace control II. Schematic of another control, starting the furnace if there is insufficient hot water (in a water-air system). This design continues to draw on the storage tank, to provide furnace preheat.

These combination systems can become very complex when the full spectrum of solar energy capability is used. For example, Fig. 8-13 shows a school installation, with solar or back-up energy available for domestic hot water, building heat, and swimming-pool heat. See the quoted references for a description of the states of operation possible.

CONTROLS FOR ACTIVE AIR SYSTEMS

Air control systems don't need to be very different from these water systems. Of course, fans replace pumps, and temperature sensors are air only, rather than air and water. There are probably fewer "check valves" and flow control valves, which take the form of flappers, balanced to give the desired action.

In the solar-absorber/air-heater element, common practice seems to turn on the circulation fan whenever the solar input is above some limit determined by a light sensor. It would be possible to provide some heat storage in the absorber and use the "hot enough" bang-bang control of the water system. To be truly effective, this would need to be based on a compound which melts at a selected temperature, with a large exposed surface area. This would give a period of full temperature heat flow, followed by an idle period.

It is a good idea to use air vents with a built-in flow adjustment feature. This permits a balance of the system for good temperature distribution, and allows the closing off of house sections when they are not used, or when solar input has been cut by a cloudy period.

HEAT LOSS CONTROL

In the conventional house, basic heat loss tends to be fixed at two values, summer and winter, the conditions set by use of screens or storm sash. There is some secondary control, by opening doors or a few windows. The older method of heat loss control by closing shutters isn't even possible, although so-called modern homes with large glass areas will often have pull drapes.

The solar home, being closer to the natural variations, will need more provisions for heat loss control. It is an important element of system sizing. Very considerable investment can be saved by sizing the system for near normal solar input and compensating by reducing heat loss when solar input is low. It is perfectly possible to do this on a daily basis, but the extent must be tempered by the cost and complexity of automatic controls, and by the nuisance of the manual control of more than a few elements.

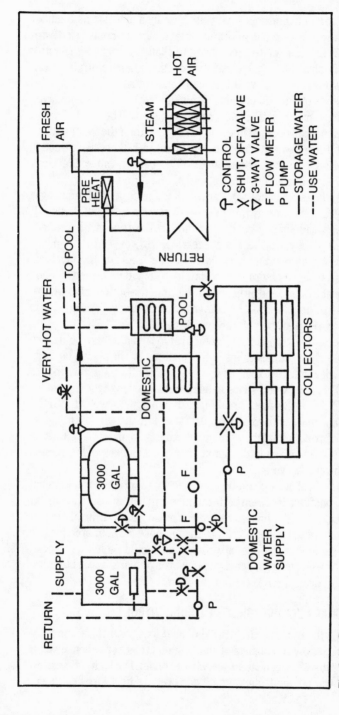

Fig. 8-13. Schematic of a school solar system, using stored solar energy for domestic hot water, special hot water lines, pool heating and building air conditioning. Automatic control and manual back-up are provided. Controls for the back-up systems are not shown. See the Flat-Plate Conference reference for more data.

249

When deciding this, use your heat loss analysis as a guide, especially the percent allocation mentioned in connection with Table 3-8. Don't waste time trying to change a heat loss quantity which is already low. For most houses, the air infiltration, the window loss, and the wall loss will be dominant.

Be very cautious in reducing air infiltration loss if it involves reducing ventilation. Probably auxiliary heat will be needed in bad periods, perhaps open flames. Death can result if the ventilation is bad, and health problems can be expected if there isn't enough ventilation to remove carbon dioxide, carbon monoxide (less likely), fumes from cooking, plastics, and so on.

On the other hand, window loss itself is large, and reducing it at night is very worthwhile. The easiest way is to pull drapes. If these are made of several plies of cloth and batting, with a reflective liner, they can be very effective. However, the standard design isn't as good as it could be, since it allows too much air circulation between drape and window. Provide a closed top box valance at the top, and either another box at the bottom or allow the drapes to touch the floor. Or use a roller type drapery rod moving in a side track. See the references for details.

Better than drapes to prevent heat loss, but more trouble, are movable rigid panels of insulating material. These can be very light. A design with excellent insulating properties is shown in Fig. 8-14. This uses wood strips to support the edges of the plastic, to prevent the edges from breaking. Small magnets are set into the wood, and mate with small iron plates set into the window frame to keep the panels in place at night. Figure 8-15 shows an alternate clip. You can certainly design your own—even use old fashioned turn buttons of wood.

Wall heat loss could be controlled with drapes or additional panels, but it would seem better to invest in better insulation in the first place. In older houses this might mean installing insulation on the inside of the current wall, at the expense of room-area loss. It would seem that the use of wall drapes should be left for special situations—covering a set of game boards or blackboards built into the wall, or as a large decorative map.

TEMPORARY ZONING FOR HEAT LOSS CONTROL

Possibly the most useful method of heat loss control is temporary zoning. Simply, it consists of shutting off areas of the house when there is insufficient heat for the whole house. The shut off areas do cool down, but shutting them off does reduce heat loss because of

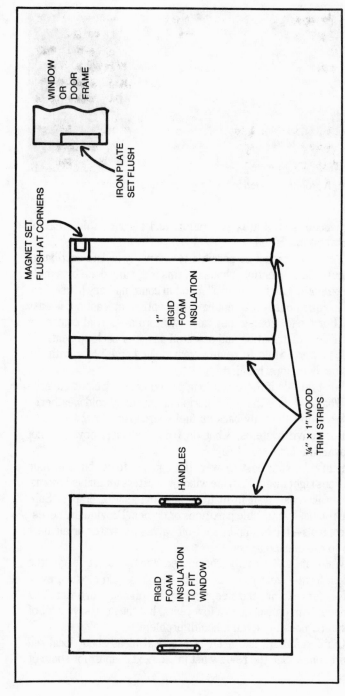

Fig. 8-14. Elements of a rugged lightweight night shutter, using wood edging to give strength. The shutter is held in place by small magnets.

251

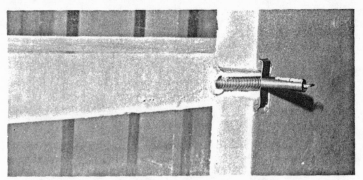
Fig. 8-15. A proprietary latch to hold night shutters in place.

the reduced heated area perimeter, and because this area has better total insulation.

To work, it must be possible to thermally isolate sections of the house. In conventional housing, this is usually done by simply closing doors. The "open plan" found in contemporary houses and often in solar houses may not have this option, at least not in easy form. For these, zoning may take two forms—partial control of regular heat distribution and selected usage of back-up heat.

It is worthwhile to review your solar home plans with the following questions in mind:

What do I do if there is a long period of heavy cloud cover?

What do I do if there is a period of unusually cold weather?

What do I do if my back up fuel source runs low?

For active systems, what do I do if electric power is not available for several days?

Zoning may be your best answer. If it appears to be, build in your provisions right away. Provide window shutters for unused rooms. Possibly increase wall insulation, or provide wall drapes. Subdivide rooms, by movable partitions or drapes. Provide the necessary controls—for example, shut-off valves for water or air heat ducts to the unused areas.

While it isn't usually considered zoning, don't forget the simplest form—wear more clothing. Sweaters, ski clothes, even snuggies for reading, and sleeping bags for night are in order. You may need them only once in a few years, but they can save a lot of discomfort, possibly even a health problem.

Our forefathers had a lot of practical ideas about localized comfort zones. See the review list in the next chapter for some of these.

EXTERIOR HEAT LOSS CONTROL

One of the important ways of heat loss control is exterior planting to reduce the effect of winter wind. The normal way of handling this is a line of trees between the prevailing wind and the house. Fencing can also be used, if high enough. Figure 8-16 shows the reduction in air flow velocity which results from an obstruction. The effect is given at obstruction height—it is less above the height, somewhat greater below it. For a swimming pool, a 6-foot board fence would help, but for a house, a bank of 30-foot trees might be indicated.

WARM WEATHER HEAT LOSS CONTROL

In addition to providing heat loss reduction for cold weather, heat loss increase for warm weather is needed. Again, the solar house

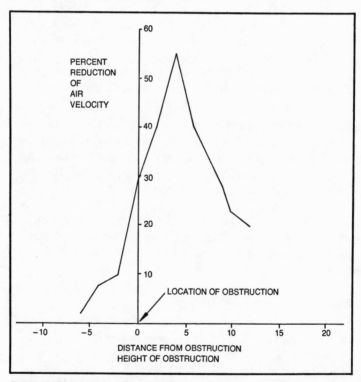

Fig. 8-16. Effect of an obstruction on air velocity. Velocity reduction by an obstruction, showing the best location for a wind-break line of trees, a swimming pool fence, or for evaluating an exposed location. The effect on heat loss can be evaluated by relations given in basic air conditioning and heating handbook.

needs excellent capability. It may need this on a daily basis, but more likely, from season to season.

In all houses which do not depend on air conditioning, the fundamental way of handling heat increase is by increased ventilation, with increased window heat loss the secondary factor. The solar house is no different. Provide windows or air vents which can be opened, and make sure that there is good air flow even when your requirements for privacy are met. Don't forget the old fundamental—cross ventilation.

The solar house may well require more ventilation capability than conventional houses. Often this is provided by skylights, which are also air vents, and/or by opening clerestory windows. Good design is needed to meet the requirements of water and air tightness when closed and good circulation when open. A hint from the marine field may help here. Expect the window (or skylight) to leak—then catch the water, and gently lead it away to a safe place. Practically, this means an indoor gutter, and a drain to the roof. Take precautions against repeatedly wetting wood, or you will have a dry-rot problem.

AUTOMATIC CONTROL OF HEAT LOSS/HEAT GAIN

In conventional houses, automatic operation of heat loss or heat-gain control methods isn't seen. It is sometimes found in solar houses. For example, Fig. 8-17 shows the essential element of a Steve Bayer concept for a self-opening flap for nighttime insulation of a solar absorber. This is actuated by sunlight. Figure 8-18 shows a variation of the idea, a thermally operated skylight vent.

These automatic elements do have their place. They are convenient and may be necessary if an area must operate "on its own," as for greenhouses. But don't forget the fundamental principles of reliability. At least, be certain that manual operation is possible.

Computer Controlled Solar Systems

Many business and industries are computer controlling their heating, air conditioning, and lighting to save money by reducing fuel and electric bills. It works, and works just as well for solar systems as for conventional ones.

However, it seems at present that it is best to avoid this for the home. For one thing, the system is a slave to a power source. Also, even though the basic central processor chip costs only ten dollars or so, the entire system will run to at least ten times, and

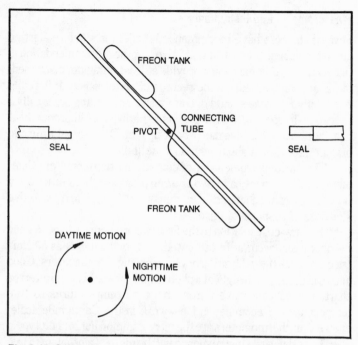

Fig. 8-17. Schematics of device to automate air vent control. Two tanks contain freon; when sunlight falls on the upper one, the freon becomes gas, forcing liquid into the lower tank, thus shifting weight and causing the balanced damper to open.

probably 100 times as much. At this time it seems best to put the money into simplified manual controls, better insulation, and the solar absorber itself.

It's an interesting field, however, and you might want to look into it as a hobby, or as a possible base for a future business activity. The references include some entries for the field. An example is a computer control for a wood stove, a field which has had no changes for scores of years. In this application, if you are using wood for back-up heat, watch the temperature in the flue. If this is below about 220° F, creosote will condense out of the stack gas. It produces a strong odor, will stain if it drips on anything, and is a fire hazard if it accumulates. If the temperature is above 380° F, heat is being lost above the chimney, soot and creosote may catch fire, and there is danger of ignition of surrounding objects if they have a low temperature fire point. The optimum temperature is between 220° and 380° F. Special thermometers to monitor stove pipe temperature are available.

Measurements and Instruments

Several chapters have recommended model tests before starting complete design or construction. Also, another recommendation is that every solar home owner provide at least minimum instrumentation and keep at least some records of performance. It is really helpful if your home should become a show place. It's practically a necessity if you run into a problem, perhaps of improper heat distribution or excessive use of back-up fuel. Don't forget its use in bragging to friends about your low fuel bills.

The basic instrument is, of course, the thermometer. Commonly available ones have two or three problems. Lack of accuracy is one, lack of adequate scale markings is a second, and excessive slowness of response a third.

The low-cost solution to the first two problems is to get a good thermometer, accurately calibrated, and to use it *only* as a reference, to check the calibration of your working thermometers. Good ones can usually be bought at a photo supply shop. Make up an error chart, so you can convert from indicated temperatures to true temperatures. Recommendation—work in the Centigrade scale, even if your thermometers are the more common Fahrenheit type.

Time delay or slow response will be more of a problem in test than in performance monitoring. Check the time it takes your thermometer to change reading, say when changing from a bowl of hot water to a cold one, or from oven to room temperature. Then set up experiment conditions so the temperature change is less than one-tenth as fast as the thermometer response. If this is too long, get another thermometer, smaller and less insulated from the working fluid.

Probably the second most important item to have is a good timepiece. A stopwatch is necessary. One of the digital wristwatches with a chronograph is excellent. The alarm feature can be helpful, as when you are checking temperature rise every ten minutes.

Solar energy meters are available, but expensive. For the homeowner, a useful substitute is a photographic exposure meter. Some read directly in light units. Others read in one of the exposure scales, but the reading can be converted to light intensity. A useful meter can be made from a piece of photovoltaic cell and a milliammeter, both available at radio equipment stores. While the reading is actually nonlinear, useful results can be obtained by adjusting the amount of cell exposed to give full scale meter

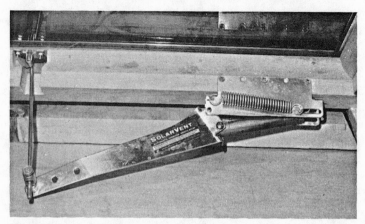

Fig. 8-18. Photo of an automatic control device, designed to open a sky vent when air temperature becomes too high. The unit operates on expansion of a semiliquid, and can produce appreciable force.

reading on a clear day and recording the light as percentage of clear day value.

In experiments, flow meters will be needed. Several types are available for air, usually sold as wind speed gauges. The type with the moving plastic ball is surprisingly accurate.

Water flow is more difficult, since commercial flow meters are expensive. One trick is to measure the time for a given flow, say one or five gallons. For small flows, use one of the tapered plastic rain gauges. The accuracy remains good even for a very small quantity of water.

Record keeping is a vital part of a measuring program. Make up a form, and keep your data together. When you run an experiment, make a sketch of the layout and record conditions. Make entries neatly, and keep the results in a notebook. It's likely you will have many occasions to refer to it.

For performance monitoring, indoor and outdoor temperatures, estimated cloudiness, and amount of back-up fuel used are the fundamentals. Occasional measurements of temperature several places in the home, wind speed, actual light level readings, and so on are helpful, but it is suggested that you do not try to keep such extensive data regularly. Unless you are very dedicated, you are likely to get fed up and stop completely.

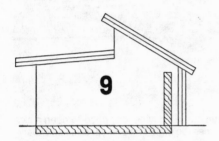

Other Low-Cost Ideas

As we have said before, solar heating is both very new and very old. One result of his phenomenon is that old ideas and concepts have had to be developed again, often after they had been brought to a high state of perfection then allowed to fall into disuse and forgotten. Then too many ideas never got into practical use, for a variety of reasons. Perhaps what seemed to be a better idea showed up, or perhaps the idea depended on materials or technology not available.

It is at least interesting, and it may be worthwhile to leaf through old magazines and books, to see if something useful shows up. Or simply to keep a sketch pad available, to record ideas as they appear. Or consciously review old methods, to see if they will trigger a new approach.

The remainder of this chapter is devoted to additional solar ideas. A few have been tested, and, where possible, actual embodiment is shown. Others are presented in concept form only. Where known, the source or originator of the idea is given.

STANDARD INVENTIONS FROM THE ENERGY VIEW

We take for granted many fairly sophisticated energy-oriented devices. The device came into being to fill a specific need, or to solve a specific problem relating to energy.

An example of this is the ordinary wing-backed chair. This high-backed, upholstered chair with extensions or wings projecting from the back at an angle of 45 to 60°, is an excellent energy invention. It generates a microclimate of comfort when used in its natural location in front of a fireplace. The wings serve the dual function of deflecting drafts and reflecting the radiant energy from the fire and the fireplace, especially to the face. Upholstery makes for comfortable sitting, but also for good insulation and good heat capacity. In a wing chair, you can be comfortably warm long after the fire has died to coals.

There are many others. Table 9-1 gives a table of those which immediately come to mind. These are not grouped in any order and no attempt has been made to organize them into families, or to trace their time sequence. You might want to try such an approach; and by all means, extend the list, and place your own inventions on it. Think about using the concept in your home.

TEMPERATURE RANGE OF SOLAR APPLICATIONS

Different uses of solar energy have a different range of values of temperature which give best results. This is an important element in design, since, as we have seen, it is much easier to get a

Table 9-1. Energy-oriented Inventions for the Home.

An incomplete listing of energy related inventions for personal comfort, health and well being. Clothing and fire are basics from which other inventions stem.

Four-poster bed	Patio
Alcove bed	Overhang roof
Stove	Fur lining
Brazier	Wall hangings
Fireplace	Paneling
Furnace	Rugs
Radiator	Straw
Firepit	Rushes
Lamp	Screens
House over stable	Entryway
High ceiling	Self-closing doors
Sod roof	Wing chair
Berm house	Hypocaust
Small window	Bed warmer
High window	Raised bed
Thick wall	Electric blanket
Selective paint	Blankets
Window glazing	Clothing
Glass	Mackinaw
Isinglass	Mukluks
Sheep gut	Heat wall
Fish bladder	Water wall
Parchment	Curtains
Shutters	Drapes

relatively small temperature rise than a high one. In fact, it's so easy that we often have to work to avoid a temperature rise, as during those hot, sunny summer days.

Figure 9-1 shows a number of possible uses of solar heating techniques, organized with respect to the approximate optimum temperature for the application. Note that the list also implies a low-temperature range made possible by the last entry at the high-temperature end, that is, ammonia absorption refrigeration, for food preservation, or for air conditioning. (See later notes regarding this.) Note also that applications exist for temperatures beyond those listed, and that solar energy can provide these high temperatures by concentrators, or by solar radiation to electric conversion.

For the home owner, many of the items on the list aren't of interest. But home heating, hot water, swimming pool heating, gardening, and air conditioning certainly are. And perhaps you have a farm or a shop or factory problem which would be a worthwhile solar application.

LOW-COST SOLAR ABSORBER/STORAGE SYSTEM

You will recall that a way of maintaining low cost is to make each element do double duty. One way of doing this is to combine the solar absorption and the storage tank. To be worthwhile, the tank must not be too large, or the area as an absorber will be too low. On the other hand, small tanks have a large exposed area for heat loss. The latter can be reduced by surrounding the tanks by an insulating box. For a given amount of insulation, there is an optimum tank size. (You might want to work this out as an exercise, although the optimum is fairly broad, and can be ignored completely if you get a low cost design which gives the desired performance.)

Figure 9-2 shows the essential elements of such a combined absorber-storage system. This is based on a design commercially available in Japan, where it is sold especially for the famous hot-tub bath. Since this is an end-of-the-day event, storage is only for the heating period.

Figure 9-3 gives typical performance data for such a heater, showing the average and hot point water temperature by month. These data are for latitudes around 35° N. Since hot tub temperatures of around 40° C or 103° F are often used, the heat will be a little low during the winter months.

The bread-box heater of Chapter 5 is, of course, a member of this family. As for these, there is no reason why metal tanks cannot

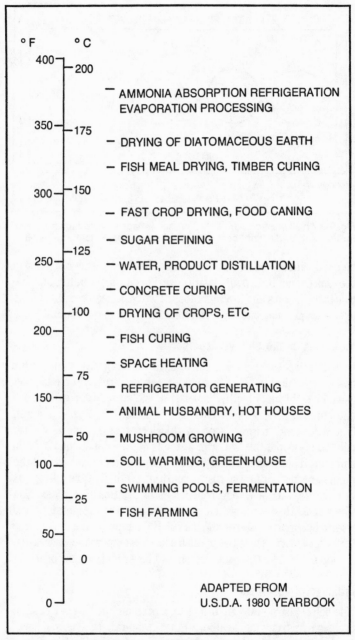

°F   °C

400 — 200

— AMMONIA ABSORPTION REFRIGERATION
  EVAPORATION PROCESSING

350 — 175

— DRYING OF DIATOMACEOUS EARTH

— FISH MEAL DRYING, TIMBER CURING

300 — 150

— FAST CROP DRYING, FOOD CANING

— SUGAR REFINING

250 — 125

— WATER, PRODUCT DISTILLATION

— CONCRETE CURING

— 100 — DRYING OF CROPS, ETC

200 —

— FISH CURING

— SPACE HEATING

— 75

— REFRIGERATOR GENERATING

150 —

— ANIMAL HUSBANDRY, HOT HOUSES

— 50 — MUSHROOM GROWING

100 —

— SOIL WARMING, GREENHOUSE

— SWIMMING POOLS, FERMENTATION

— 25

— FISH FARMING

50 —

— 0

ADAPTED FROM
U.S.D.A. 1980 YEARBOOK

0 —

Fig. 9-1. Thermal range of solar energy application. A list, arranged in order of temperature, of possible and/or proven solar energy applications on farms and in homes. Salt making is another extensive solar application.

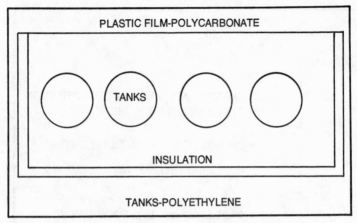

PLASTIC FILM-POLYCARBONATE

TANKS

INSULATION

TANKS-POLYETHYLENE

Fig. 9-2. An all plastic solar absorber, used in Japan to produce hot water for the "end-of-day" hot-bath ritual. Tanks are approximately 12" × 48".

be used with the basic configuration. Also, there is no reason why the tank cannot be provided with covering doors, for better absorption by reflectors and low night loss. Two tank-heater units may be used, for preheat one day, and final heat and use the next.

Variations on the Storage Absorber

It is not necessary to use tanks as the storage element. If the absorber tubing is large enough, it serves nicely. For example, 2-inch I.D. black polyethylene plastic pipe stores 0.16 gallons per one-hundred feet of pipe. One design places the pipe in a spiral, held with wood strips. Placed on a black roof, or on a piece of black painted plywood, this will give a supply of water at about 120° F in summer. The temperature will be higher if a "fence" surrounds the pipe, to reduce air flow across it, and higher still if the resulting box is covered with a transparent sheet of plastic, as discussed in Chapter 5. However, watch the combination of temperature and internal pressure. Above about 160° F the pipe cannot carry rated "cold" pressure. Drop the pressure as the temperature increases. At about 200° F, the pressure should be essentially zero.

Drainage of Absorbers

The spiral just mentioned brings up a problem in absorber design, drainage in freezing weather. For the spiral, this is a manual operation, involving turning the spiral as sketched in Fig. 9-4.

The figure also shows other common patterns. The one at B will not drain. The orientation should be changed to that at C. Even this will not drain unless the pipe has a definite downward slope at all points. The arrangements of *D, E,* and *F* are self-draining if the simple requirement of downward slope is met.

SWIMMING-POOL HEATERS REVISITED

Solar heating for swimming pools is a simple, low-cost undertaking. Temperatures needed are low, and a circulation pump is already available in any pool in operation. Major requirements are that a sufficient area of collector and sufficient pipe size be provided to keep the hydraulic load on the pump low.

Tests at the Florida Solar Energy Center suggest the following guidelines, based on areas with 5 kWh/m^2/day solar irradiation. See Fig. 4-3, and increase the area if the irradiation is less than this. For a collector of bare plastic pipe, in contact with the adjacent pieces and tilted at Latitude $-10°$, expect:

Absorber Area	Pool-Temperature Increase
½ Pool Area	6° to 8°
Pool Area	10° to 12°
2 × Pool Area	20° to 25°

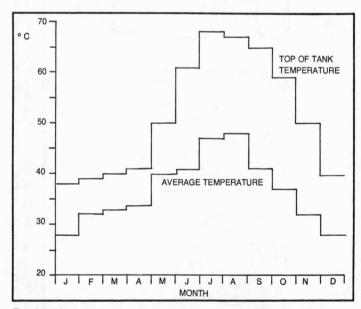

Fig. 9-3. Measured temperatures produced in the absorber of Fig. 9-2 in the vicinity of Tokyo, for one year. System is designed to produce at least some hot (38° to 40° C) water in even the coldest months.

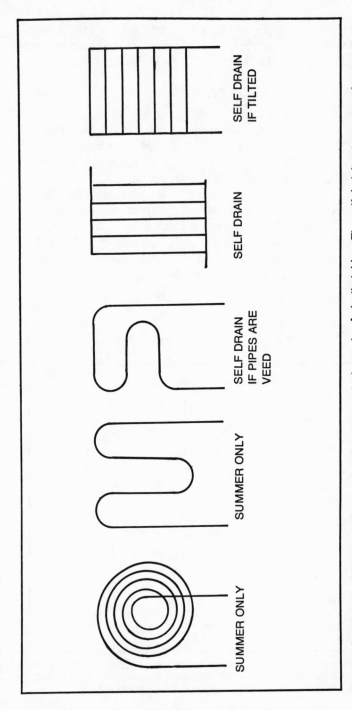

SUMMER ONLY

SUMMER ONLY

SELF DRAIN
IF PIPES ARE
VEED

SELF DRAIN

SELF DRAIN
IF TILTED

Fig. 9-4. Possible layouts of absorber or absorber-storage tanks made of plastic tubing. The self-draining types are, of course, more convenient at the end of a summer swimming season, or when used for hot water heating in cold weather with nighttime freezing.

Which are plotted in Table 9-2. This figure also gives a correction factor to be used if the pipe is spaced, rather than touching. The area needed can be reduced if the pipe is cemented to a metal plate, or if a metal plate collector is used.

Figure 9-5 is a photo of such a swimming pool collector on test. This is a commercial unit, using a special plastic compound to reduce deterioration due to ultraviolet.

The performance of these collectors can be increased a small amount by stretching a clear plastic sheet across the assembly. Its primary function is to reduce heat loss due to moving air and also to reduce heat loss during cloudy periods. (However, greater gain can be secured by covering the pool at night with a plastic or cloth sheet.)

These swimming pool heaters are an excellent project for the home craftsman. They are very undemanding and really pay off.

DESIGNS FOR A CORRUGATED IRON ROOF

There are an enormous number of corrugated iron roofs in the world—barns, sheds, even houses. Since one of the major costs of a solar absorber is the absorber sheet, these roofs represent a good start for low cost design.

One idea is to overlay the existing corrugated iron with a second layer, of translucent plastic (fiberglass) formed to the same corrugation size and having small studs cemented in the grooves to

Table 9-2. Guidelines for Swimming Pool Heating.

Absorber areas required to increase average swimming pool temperature by stated amounts. The correction factors shown apply to all exposed tube absorbers. Note that a swimming pool cover can also increase average temperatures. For children, pool temperatures above 80°F are now considered good.

SWIMMING POOL SOLAR HEATERS BARE BLACK PLASTIC TUBE TYPE	
Desired Pool Temperature Increase	Absorber Area for Tubing in Contact
6° - 8°F	One-half pool surface
10° - 12°F	Equal to pool surface
20° - 23°F	Twice pool surface
Corrections Tube spacing	Absorber Area Multiplier
One diameter	1.3
Two diameters	2.1
Three diameters	2.9

Fig. 9-5. A pipe-type swimming pool heater on test at the Florida Solar Energy Center. The pipe and fittings used are specially compounded for long life under direct solar exposure.

form a set of spacers, as sketched in Fig. 9-6. The working fluid could be air, blown between the sheets, or it could be water, allowed to trickle into each corrugation at the top and collected in a trough at the bottom. A second trough, or gutter, could collect rainwater.

The major problem would seem to be sealing at the edges. The figure also shows a possible solution to this problem, based on the use of preformed strips now used where the corrugated sheets abut a vertical surface. Better designs should be possible.

If you have an existing roof of ample area and need relatively low performance, a very low-cost absorber can be made by simply stretching plastic film across the roof. (Be certain that all loose and protruding nails have been taken care of first, or you will soon have holes.) Allow water to trickle down the corrugations.

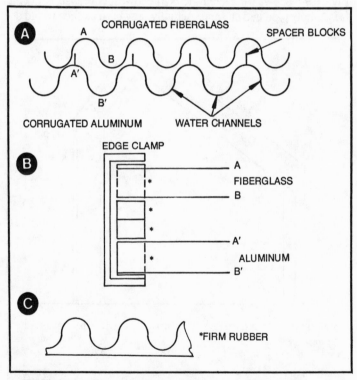

Fig. 9-6. A solar water heating drip-collector designed for a small flow of water in confined channels. Possible basis for a roofing panel series, incorporating solar water heating, skylights, and opaque roofing in a low pressure design. Enclosed tubes could be used for the high pressure domestic water supply.

A friend is working out a design for a house based on the fact that he likes the sound of rain on a sheet iron roof, a la the old Beachcomber in Hollywood. Key elements of his concept are shown in Fig. 9-7. This is to be an active system with a fan to move hot air from the under-the-roof heat trap to the masonry storage wall during the day, and from the wall to the rooms during the night. Since this is to be a Florida home, the heat trap is vented in summer, and the wall is used as a daytime heat sink, being cooled at night.

The possibility of a business based on a good design of a combined solar absorber-roof panel has been mentioned. It's an open field.

A SUPER LOW-COST ABSORBER

Figure 9-8 shows what seems to be the lowest cost absorber of all. It is simply pipe laid on sand. Actually, any bare surface would do.

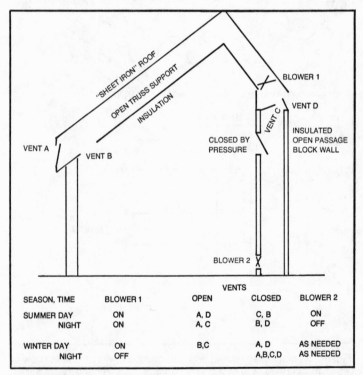

SEASON, TIME	BLOWER 1	VENTS OPEN	VENTS CLOSED	BLOWER 2
SUMMER DAY	ON	A, D	C, B	ON
NIGHT	ON	A, C	B, D	OFF
WINTER DAY	ON	B,C	A, D	AS NEEDED
NIGHT	OFF		A,B,C,D	AS NEEDED

Fig. 9-7. An air heated storage wall concept, intended to give the sound of rain on a metal roof, winter heating plus summer air circulation and thermal averaging. A fireplace is planned for back-up heating.

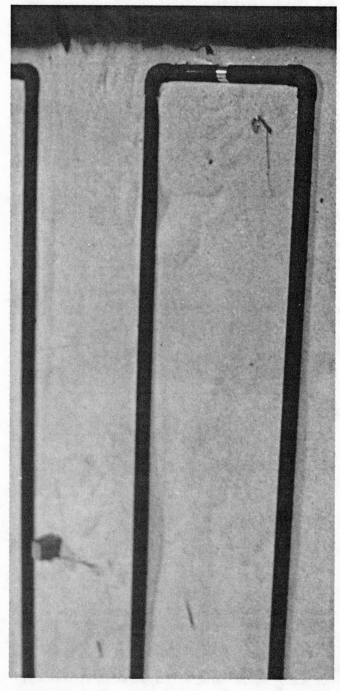

Fig. 9-8. A minimum cost hot water absorber, formed by laying copper tubing on dry sand—a reasonable insulator. A possibility for flat roofs.

Sand, dirt, even stone, is a reasonably good insulator, and quickly comes to temperature equilibrium. Even pipe laid on grass will do. Temperatures around 120° are to be expected on any sunny, summer day.

SOLAR COOKING

Figure 9-9 shows the essential elements of a solar cooking device which won a prize for two local Sierra Club members. This uses the relatively rare heat-concentrator technique, the concentrator being two sheets of plywood bent into a parabola, and covered with aluminum foil, glued on.

Heat is captured at the focus, in a black-painted oil tank about six inches in diameter and four feet long. The top of the tank is well insulated, and the bottom part provided with a window made of three glass panes. If a piece of glass of circular shape can be found, it would be ideal. Oil is lifted from a cooking pan into the tank by a small pump.

In use, the collector is first tilted and oriented to aim at the sun, and is rotated from time to time, to keep the concentrated sunlight focused on the tank. With good design, baking temperatures are possible.

Figure 9-10 shows a solar oven design, based on one-half of an empty steel drum, insulated on the back by dry sand, and provided

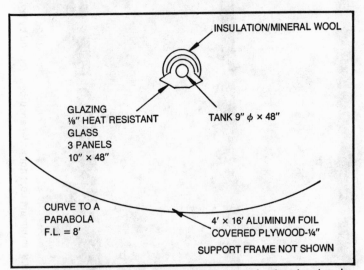

Fig. 9-9. A high temperature concentrating type of solar absorber, intended to heat a quantity of oil to cooking temperature. Concentrating collectors must be aimed at the sun, which is done manually in this design.

270

Fig. 9-10. A concentrating solar oven collector based on one-half of an oil drum, with a pyramidical concentrator to increase absorber area. Designed for near tropical regions, aimed upward for baking shortly after solar noon.

with four wings of aluminum foil covered wood, which essentially double the solar input (a two-sun collector). Depending on the amount of insulation and the number of glass covers used, interior temperatures can range from the low-heat cooking of the "Crock Pot," to fast baking temperatures.

The unit is small enough to allow rotation about an inclined north-south axis, to give useful cooking temperatures from about 9 AM to 3 PM, or it can be fixed, giving maximum temperatures between about 11 AM and 1 PM, all sun time. If the unit is to be used year around, and fixed, optimum tilt angle is about latitude $-10°$. For summer only use, the unit can be horizontal.

SELECTIVE PAINTS

In these high temperature designs, appreciable performance improvement can be secured with selective paint covering the absorber. These are available commercially, but difficult to obtain in small quantities. This is another area where you might want to do some experimentation and where there appears to be a business opportunity.

If you want a starting point for experiment, a relatively simple preparation is given in U. S. Patent 4,011,190. It is issued to M. Telkes, one of the pioneers of "modern" solar heating. The preparation process is: Dissolve 20 gms. $CuSO_4 \cdot 5 H_2O$ in 100 gms. of boiling distilled water, then add 0.05 normal NaOH to give 2 gm. of solid NaOH. A precipitate forms, then dissolves. Add this solution to a suspension of 5 micron powdered metallic zinc in hot distilled water and stir. A selective black coating is formed. Decant after settling, wash the solid several times with distilled water, and dry in air. Use the powder as a pigment in a clear silicon resin—xylene solvent varnish.

In test, this gave an open air stagnation temperature of 199° F. As a comparison, the flat black recommended earlier gives a stagnation of 186° F when mounted in an insulating box with a single Plexiglas cover.

If you do experiment with paints, a test box is worthwhile. It can be of one inch insulation board, lined with aluminum foil, and with a one-eighth inch low-iron cover glass. The test panel should be mounted 1 inch above the foil, with 1 inch of space around it and 1 inch clearance to the glass. A 1-foot square panel is good. Use an accurate thermometer inside the box, and record ambient temperature and light intensity.

ULTRAMODERN SOLAR APPLICATION: EPROM ERASURE

In the computer field, there is a series of data memory storage devices called *Programmable Read-Only Memories*, or PROMs for short. These accept data written in electricly once, then read it out by other signals as many times as desired. If a mistake is made, the simple ones must be scrapped. But there is a second family— *Erasable PROMs*, or EPROMS, in which the storage elements can be reset by exposure to ultraviolet light.

The normal source of the ultraviolet is short-wave radiation from a mercury arc lamp in a quartz tube, but these are expensive. Ultraviolet from the sun will do the job, with an investment of a few cents plus a little time. True, the erasure is slower, about five to seven days, as compared to fifteen to thirty minutes, but it could be shortened if necessary. Anyhow, "the price is right."

Figure 9-11 shows the construction of a solar-activated EPROM eraser, made from a piece of aluminum plus a few screws or rivets. The piece forms a truncated pyramid, plus the flat top of the pyramid. The top is drilled with holes on an 0.1 inch spacing, as shown, to provide clearance. The inside of the pyramid should be polished, the outside painted any color.

To use, one or two EPROMs to be erased are coated on the bottom side with heat transfer silicon grease and then inserted into the holes, from the inside. The pyramid is then placed where it will catch full sun at noon, and for as much of the day as possible. In a week it will be ready for a new set of input data.

The time can be reduced by moving the eraser, say each two hours. Very highly polished aluminum is also helpful. More concentration is possible, but it may be necessary to use radiator fins or even water cooling if the high temperature of the high concentration ratio is attempted, as would be needed for, say, eight-hour erasure. However, note that some manufacturers recommend a high temperature "annealing" process if erasure of any type is to be attempted often. See device application notes for details.

PHASE-CHANGE HEAT STORAGE

If it will be some time before you build a solar home, plan on reviewing the state of *phase-change heat storage,* those compounds which give off a lot of heat when going from the liquid to the solid state. Use of these makes it possible to hold the house temperature closer to the design comfort temperature than is possible with masonry or water type passive storage.

Unfortunately, there have been problems with passive storage systems, not universal, but common enough to require a recommendation of care. Container leakage is not unknown. Usually phase change materials change volume when they change phase. Water is an example, increasing in volume by over eight percent when it freezes. Enormous forces are developed in closed containers—for water, in excess of 30,000 pounds per square foot of area. The container must either be extremely strong, or it must be expandable. And the expansion introduces another problem—fatigue failure due to repeated expansion and contraction.

Some of the materials used are corrosive, usually mildly so, but enough to restrict choice of container material. Additionally, a combination of stress and a corrosion tendency accelerates failures in many materials.

There is also an anomaly in the thermal performance, due to the phenomena of supercooling. Many substances, including water, will remain in their liquid state when cooled slowly, to well below the normal freezing temperature. Then, suddenly, they solidify, at the same time releasing the energy of transition. As they cool down, they release energy only at the liquid rate. It isn't until the sudden change point that the desired heat is released. The result is that the home cools to below its desired temperature, then suddenly partly recovers to the design value.

Materials which are a combination of a solid plus water, such as Glaubers Salts, display another problem. The "water of hydration" tends to separate out, giving a mixture of three substances, two having poor thermal properties.

Still another problem is the natural one of the freezing starting at the lowest temperature point, which is the outside wall in convection and conduction cooling. The layer of solid material which results may have poor heat conductivity, slowing down further release of energy.

Much work is being done on these problems, partly by seeking new materials, and partly by improving the packaging of existing ones. A few installations are being made. If you are interested in the approach, a visit to an actual installation, and/or careful study of the test data would be worthwhile. This would seem to be an interesting and worthwhile field for your own experimental work.

A few specific results are reported in the references.

AN EXERCISE IN SELF-HEATING CAPABILITY
The fact that a human releases heat at the rate of 150 watts or so has been mentioned. As we know from experience, we can keep com-

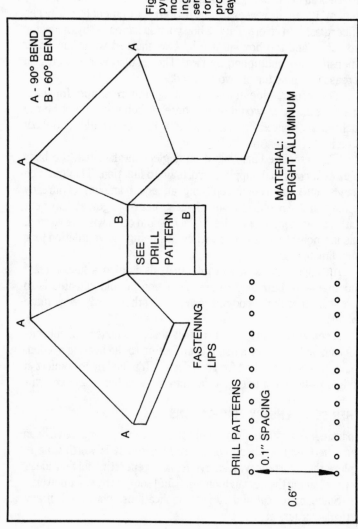

Fig. 9-11. EPROM eraser using a pyramidal concentrator for a modern application; concentrating solar ultraviolet on a semiconductor memory to reset it for reprogramming. While de-programming requires two to five days, cost is negligible.

A - 90° BEND
B - 60° BEND

MATERIAL:
BRIGHT ALUMINUM

SEE DRILL PATTERN

FASTENING LIPS

DRILL PATTERNS

0.1" SPACING

0.6"

275

fortable at almost any temperature if we wear sufficiently warm clothing, that is, if we have sufficient personal insulation. A question arises—how much insulation would be needed if this body heat were used to keep a room at comfort temperature?

A little work with a slide rule or calculator gives the answer. For an ultra minimum room, a closet 1 foot by 2 feet by 6 feet, just over 1 inch of fiberglass insulation will give a comfortable inside temperature when the outside is 50°F lower. (We don't need 1 inch of clothing, since the body surface area is much less than the surface area of the box.) Doubling the size of the closet to 2 feet by 4 feet by 12 feet increases the insulation requirement to 4.2 inches of fiberglass batt. Note that the box volume increases by the factor two cubed and the box surface by two squared when the linear dimensions are multiplied by two. The insulation required also increases by a factor of two squared.

The closet doesn't have an optimum shape for heat conservation—that would be a sphere. A cube would not be too much worse. For example, a 12′ × 12′ × 12′ room would need about 23 inches of insulation.

This simplified analysis does neglect the fact that the body requires a continual supply of fresh air to function. This must be brought into the room, replacing an equal amount of already warmed air. An efficient air/air-heat interchanger at the vent would recover some of the heat which would otherwise be wasted. This is a point to bear in mind when designing the ventilation for a cold climate house.

An important lesson in this analysis is also a fundamental guideline—the best way to use insulation in cold climates is to place it as close to the body as possible. In other words, wear more clothes.

A second lesson is that in a well-designed house, the inhabitants can, and do, make a major contribution to the heating needed. In fact, this is a good test for good design. It's the key to comfort in the igloo—the most energy-efficient cold-weather house known.

OTHER SOLAR ENERGY APPLICATIONS

In passing, several nonhome applications of solar energy have been mentioned, or have been considered briefly. It is worthwhile to explore them further with an eye toward generating further ideas about replacing the demands on fossil fuel sources by solar power.

Some historical and current applications, not listed in any particular order, are:

276

Making salt from sea water
Making fresh water from sea or mineralized water
Drying grain, fruit, and so on
Air heating
Water heating
Bio-mass growth activation
Catalyst replacement, usually by ultraviolet
Solar-thermal saline ponds power generation
Algae growth pond
Greenhouse heating
Swimming pool heating
Car washer heating
Farm livestock food heating
Animal shelter heating
Solar air conditioning
EPROM erasure
Disinfection
Sewage treatment
Photovoltaic power generation

Some of these areas have an extensive literature, and more is being issued on many other topics.

SOLAR HEATING AND PUBLIC BUILDINGS

The factors of low-cost fuel and desire for comfort have led public building programs down the same "energy dog" path as have home building programs. Schools, courthouses, and law centers, in particular, and even maintenance buildings have "turned their backs on nature," requiring power 24 hours a day for operation. At the extreme, one system requires that both the heating and air-conditioning systems be in operation continuously, mixing warmed and cooled air to meet the comfort zone requirements with respect to both temperature and humidity. It is elegant, yes, and it is comfortable, but it is also extremely expensive.

As you work with solar heating, you will certainly have an increasing concern about this waste of energy, and its current and future impact on your taxes. It will affect you more than the average person, because your energy efficient home will be more valuable than conventionally heated ones, which will be reflected in higher taxes for you—a penalty for foresight, if you will.

It would seem wise to start working with your local governments on this general problem. Push for "energy audits" of all public buildings in existence, showing how much energy is used, and for what purposes. Experience shows that from 10 to 50 percent savings in energy costs are no great problem; 10 percent savings seems simple, and 20 percent readily attainable. Larger savings usually require some capital investment, which may be worthwhile.

Pay particular attention to new construction programs. Increasingly, designs are reflecting an awareness of energy conservation, too often, designs attempt to attain this ideal by small improvements in conventional high energy use techniques. Habits developed over the past 50 years prevent designers from looking at the naturally comfortable period, first extending it, then using simple low energy approaches for the rest of the time. The problem is compounded by the low regard contractors have for the life of a tree.

You'll probably want to look at other energy waste also.

NATURAL COOLING

Let's close this volume with a review of a factor not really touched on so far, the matter of reducing temperatures during the summer months, when temperature and humidity are too high for comfort in much of the U.S.A.

Actually, if you are following the common solar approach, you will have made some progress towards summer comfort as well as winter since insulation is just as effective at keeping heat out of a box as in keeping it in. But this doesn't help the problem of air temperature. Recall that moving air is much more effective in cooling than stationary air, so part of the time moving air will handle the cooling problem. This requires a good area of windows (or walls) that open. This type of cooling fails when the temperature of the air approaches body temperature and the humidity is high. That 150 watts the body produces can't escape, and we are uncomfortable, perhaps dangerously so.

The passive storage line of solar heating offers some additional benefit. The temperature of the heat storage mass will tend towards the average air temperature. In areas where the day-night variation is large, at high elevations in particular, the average temperature is well below the maximum temperatures, and storage wall or storage floor designs are also comfortable in summer.

For other areas it is necessary to make use of different principles if passive cooling is desired. A well-insulated horizontal surface facing a clear sky receives almost no incoming radiation, but radiates to "cold, outer space." As a result, its temperature goes below the ambient air temperature. This is the reason the roof pond design cools in summer, this being accomplished by closing the insulating panels during the day and opening them at night. (Note that this technique doesn't work if the sky is heavily clouded at night.)

One of the original Harold Hay designs of a roof pond house is located in Atascadero, California. The appearance of the house is not the same as a solar house. This is emphasized in Fig. 9-12.

This house has an excellent performance record, holding temperatures five feet from the floor to within ±2° F of 70° F during winter, and keeping the indoor temperature between 66° F and 74° F all year.

On a recent visit, it was found that the house had recently been sold, and that the new owner was making some changes to make the design less different in appearance from conventional homes. It was notable that the changes were entirely cosmetic—the basic roof-pond/roof-panel system was left intact.

There have been some problems with the roof pond system due to water leakage. The metal support panels should form a watertight layer. Originally, there were problems with the movable insulation and with the seal between panels when these were in the closed position, but these were eliminated long ago.

It would appear that a masonry roof would work just as well as a water roof, just as masonry storage walls can be used instead of water walls. Figure 9-13 shows a possible design that has not yet been analyzed for performance.

Other forms of solar heating do not work for cooling. The usual reason for this is the presence of the heat trap, the transparent or translucent covering. Associated with this is the matter of orientation. To truly cool, the radiator must be shielded from surrounding objects. It must see only the sky, or nearly so. Vertical or inclined solar absorbers just are not properly oriented.

It would be possible to provide an alternate element in active liquid solar heating systems to accomplish the cooling function. This would resemble a simple absorber—that is, would have a set of liquid lines fastened to a metal sheet. The sheet would serve as a radiator. Now, however, we want low absorption and high radiation properties, so white paint, or even bare metal would be used.

The cost of this radiator would not be excessive, and it would seem worthwhile to study the design further. Sky cooling definitely depends on a clear sky. You can check this for your area by measuring the night temperatures of a 1-foot square metal plate

Fig. 9-12. The Hay Roof Pond solar-heated and radiation-cooled house in the hills of Central California. Printed as a negative to emphasize the difference in lines as compared to conventional houses. Currently refinished, colorful and attractive.

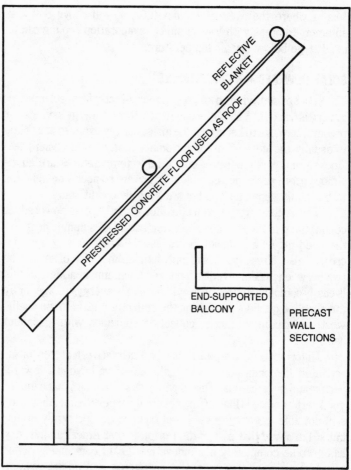

Fig. 9-13. A variation on roof storage, using precast concrete panels as storage elements. Shown with a sloping roof and roll-up insulation, it could be used with a flat roof and panel insulation.

placed in an open box with side and bottom insulation. Unless this goes well below the temperature of the air, don't try to use radiational cooling.

However, even if radiational cooling doesn't work, you can get some cooling gain by introducing an active cooling element. In simplest form this can be a fan blowing outside air over a heat storage surface whenever the air is cooler than the storage. With a well-designed system, capable of cooling down the storage rapidly, the storage temperature can be brought to nearly the minimum air temperature of the day—typically close to 75° to 80° F even in

Miami where the average temperature is well above 80° F in summer. In areas with low humidity, evaporation cooling can be used to go below dry air temperature.

SOLAR POWERED AIR CONDITIONING

The concept of driving an air conditioner directly from solar power is very attractive. First, there is the matter of energy savings. At present, in warm to hot areas, the major energy expense of a family is usually the cost of air conditioning. Many home owners feel "locked in," partly because comfortable temperatures are an insidious habit, partly because their homes are so poorly designed as to be totally dependent on hot weather air conditioning.

The second attractive feature for directly solar-powered air conditioning is the self-compensating nature of summer heat. As the need for heat removal increases, the solar energy level increases also. True, there is usually a time difference of an hour or two between maximum solar input and maximum heating, but this is easily compensated for by providing a little energy storage, or by the simple expedient of aligning the collector a little to the southwest, so maximum energy collection coincides with maximum heat.

Unfortunately, despite these two attractive features, solar activated air conditioning is virtually unknown beyond a few experimental installations. This is partly due to the fact that a unit of good performance is likely to be relatively expensive and therefore still not able to compete on a cost basis with electrically driven units. I'm afraid that part of the reason is that American industry has become completely non-innovative. Giant companies, dominated by their financial or legal departments, just do not go after "strange" lines of business. They prefer to let someone else do the pioneering, then to buy them up, a process encouraged by current tax laws. There are two lessons here if you are thinking of solar powered air conditioning as a possible new business venture.

Because of this situation, there isn't any solar air conditioning "now." There isn't even any "soon," at least as far as the author has been able to determine. But the concept is so attractive that it seems there is a real pent-up demand, which seems likely to be satisfied sometime. As a result, it seems worthwhile to spend a little time on the basics, as currently understood, to help evaluate designs when they do appear.

There are two major lines of approach to solar air conditioning, with each line having two members. Crudely, these may be

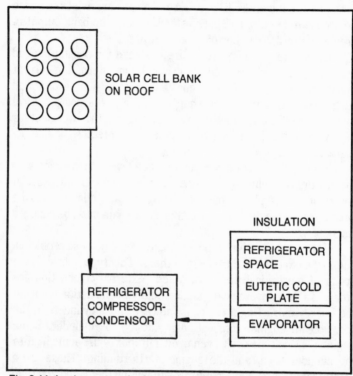

Fig. 9-14. A solar powered refrigerator design using a dc motor to operate the refrigerator compressor, and a "cold plate" to give refrigeration overnight. Batteries could be used as an alternate, allowing a conventional refrigerator to be operated from a dc-ac inverter. Not cost attractive for extensive use at this time.

called the active approach, involving moving machinery, and the passive approach, having no moving mechanical parts.

One straightforward approach is to substitute a solar electric generator for the power line of a conventional air conditioner (or refrigerator), as shown in Fig. 9-14. The solar cells shown here are available, and the remainder of the design is reasonably conventional, so it appears that the success of the approach hinges on the cost of solar cells. Their price is coming down, and this decrease is projected to continue—after all, a solar cell is made from silica—or common sand. The reason the cost is high is the extreme purity required, plus the fact that the yield of current processes is low. The cost seems certain to decrease as our technology increases so it seems certain that the technique will become attractive.

There are a few points to watch for. Conventional solar cells are arranged in banks, and shading just one cell of the bank reduces

283

the output of the entire bank to zero. Designs are available which do not have this problem but, instead, reduce the bank output in proportion to the number of cells shadowed.

Conventional compressors are designed for constant speed operation, or nearly so, and are driven by an alternating current induction motor, fed from a constant voltage line. Motor and compression rotation stops when the voltage reaches a critical lower limit. The drive motor may be damaged if the voltage stays below this limit for a long time, unless a protective device actuates.

Solar cells put out direct current, at a level which varies with the amount of sunlight present. A dc to ac converter with special control features plus some oversizing of the collector will be necessary, or the drive motor-compressor chain must be changed frequently.

The second "active" type eliminates some of these problems, but at the expense of introducing others. This type is based on a group of mechanical elements called "external combustion engines." In the conventional gasoline engine, combustion is inside the energy extracting area, or is internal to the cylinder. In the "old" steam engine, combustion is outside the cylinder. Some engines of this type don't even need a firebox—just apply heat to the cylinder head, and the engine starts running. These are a natural for solar power—just focus sunlight on them, and you're in business.

One type of solar, external combustion engine was in operation in 1878, and a larger one of another type in 1906. The last one was claimed to have essentially zero operating cost, and require only twice the investment of a conventional steam engine. The work seems to have died as a result of cheap fuel and low cost convenient electrical power. It is known that work is going on in a few laboratories, but it's very quiet. Progress is unknown.

A "passive" version of an external combustion cycle was used in a commercial refrigerator unit in the 1930s. This was the Crosley "Icy Ball," which, while passive, did require some manual work. The design, as shown in Fig. 9-15, is very simple: two sealed tanks contain a low boiling point liquid, a Freon, and an expansion valve. In use, at the start, one tank contains liquid under pressure. This expands through the valve, boils, and produces a cooled vapor which is trapped in the second tank. The process stops when the pressure in the two tanks becomes equal. The system must then be recharged, by heating the second tank while cooling the first, as also shown.

284

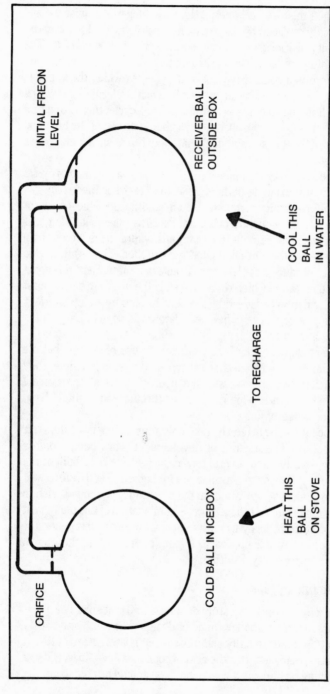

INITIAL FREON LEVEL

RECEIVER BALL OUTSIDE BOX

COOL THIS BALL IN WATER

TO RECHARGE

HEAT THIS BALL ON STOVE

COLD BALL IN ICEBOX

ORIFICE

Fig. 9-15. Ultra-simple refrigerator. Basis of a refrigerator using two tanks plus a connecting line containing an orifice, a needle value. The cycle is made continuous in the conventional refrigerator, and in the heat pump. The cycle can be reversed to secure mechanical power, giving a solar heat to refrigerator/air conditioner family.

While this device is perfectly workable, it is a nuisance and was rapidly replaced by the mechanical refrigerator. Recently the University of Florida has made some working models of it. The device awaits redesign with solar heat in mind, and size expansion.

There is a related type of flow cycle, in which the vapor is trapped, for example, by absorption by a material. Silica gel works well with sulphur dioxide as the fluid. After a cycle, there must be a regeneration cycle, the absorbed gas being driven off by heat and condensed in the storage tank. At one time, such units were commercially available.

The second type of passive unit works on a continuous cycle. A well known example of this type is the Servel or Electrolux gas refrigerator—similar units are often sold as portable or motor home units. They operate on a complex cycle, the major elements being shown in Fig. 9-16. Ammonia vapor is driven off an ammonia—water solution, cooled and liquefied. This is allowed to expand to produce a cooled vapor in an evaporator. Here it is again absorbed in water, which returns to start the cycle. In small units, water circulation is caused by the head formed by an intermittent heat pump, a geyser or coffee percolator type device. Large units may use a mechanical pump.

These units are not highly efficient in use of energy, but are cost competitive with mechanical types. While, in principle, they can run forever, they must have hydrogen gas at the correct pressure to operate. This gas escapes through the slightest flaw, the major cause of failure.

Since it can be driven by heat only, this device is a natural for solar cooling. The amount of development work being done is unknown—units up to several tons capacity have been built at the University of Florida, but availability for home use will have to wait on some business innovation. In the meantime, you might wish to experiment on an old refrigerator. A combination of this plus a heat pipe to transfer energy from the solar absorber to the generator would seem a simple approach. Again, it appears that there is an excellent opportunity awaiting.

CONCLUDING REMARKS

It would seem to be adequately demonstrated that solar heating is here now, with a sufficient range of design possibilities to satisfy any heating need partially and most home heating needs fully. It would also seem clear that the cost is not out of line—in fact, if you are planning on building a new home, you should be able to get the

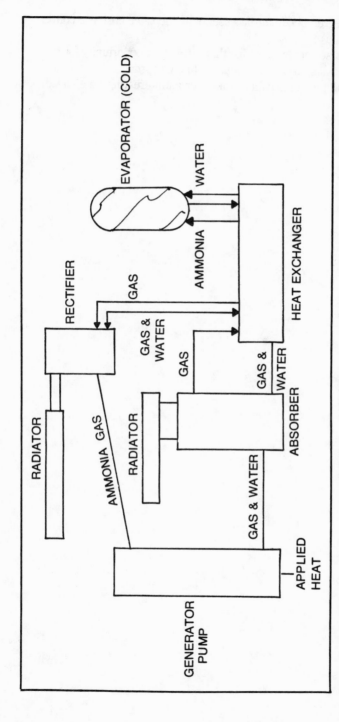

Fig. 9-16. Essential elements of a heat operated absorption refrigerator, based on selective absorption/de-absorption of ammonia gas by water at different temperatures and pressures. Usually operated by a gas flame or electric heat, the unit could be designed for solar heat, applied directly or by a working fluid. Possible basis for a family of solar air conditioners.

287

same degree of comfort at essentially the same cost as a conventional house.

It also seems clear that there is a great opportunity for creative thinking, creative design, and new approaches.

And the combination makes for an interesting time ahead.

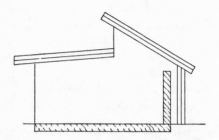

Bibliography

RECOMMENDED FOR HISTORICAL CONCEPTS

Butti, Ken and Perlin, John. *A Golden Thread, 2,000 Years of Solar Architecture and Technology.* New York: Van Nostrand Reinhold, 1980.

Rudofsky, Bernard. *Architecture without Architects.* Garden City, NY: Doubleday, 1964.

RECOMMENDED FOR DESIGN DATA

ASHRAE. *ASHRAE Handbook of Fundamentals.* New York: ASHRAE Printing, current ed.

Dubin, F.S., et al. *How to Save Energy and Cut Costs in Existing Industrial and Commercial Buildings.* Park Ridge, NJ: Noyes Data, 1976.

Governor's Energy Office. *Residential Energy Work Book; South, Central and North Florida Editions.* Tallahassee, FL.

Los Alamos Scientific Laboratory Report. *Passive Solar Heating and Cooling, Report LA-6637-C.* Los Alamos, NM, 1976.

Mazria, Edward. *The Passive Solar Energy Book.* Emmaus, PA: Rodale Press, 1979.

Popular Science. *Solar Energy Handbook, 1979.* New York, 1979.

Portola Institute. *Energy Primer.* Menlo Park, CA: Portola Institute Printing, 1974.

Riffner, James A. and Blair, Frank E., ed. *The Weather Almanac.* New York: Avon, 1977.

Sandia Corporation. *Passive Solar Buildings, Report 79-0824.* Albuquerque, NM, 1979.

U.S. Department of Housing and Urban Development. *Intermediate Minimum Property Standards Supplement, v. 5, Solar Heating and Domestic Hot Water Systems.* Washington, D.C.: Govt. Printing Office, 1977.

U.S. Department of Housing and Urban Development. *Regional Guidelines for Building Passive Energy Conserving Homes, Report HUD-PDR-355(2).* Washington, D.C.: Govt. Printing Office, 1980.

Ward, Delbert B., ed. *Proceedings, 1977 Flat Plate Conference.* Cape Canaveral, FL: Florida Solar Energy Center, 1977.

RECOMMENDED FOR ARCHITECTURAL CONCEPTS

Corbett, Judy et al. *Village Homes: A Collection of Energy-Efficient Housing Designs.* Emmaus, PA: Rodale Press, 1979.

Beck, C.A. *Designing with the Environment.* Cape Canaveral, FL: Florida Solar Energy Center, 1980.

Goddard, Murray C. *How To Be Your Own Architect.* Blue Ridge Summit, PA: TAB Books, 1977.

Lane Publishing. *Sunset Homeowners Guide to Solar Heating.* Menlo Park, CA: Lane Publishing, 1978.

Mazria, Edward. *The Passive Solar Energy Book.* Emmaus, PA: Rodale Press, 1979.

Scott, Ray G. *How to Build Your Own Underground House.* Blue Ridge Summit, PA: TAB Books, 1980.

Shurcliff, William A. *Solar Heated Building of North America.* Harrisville, NH: Brick House Publishing, 1978.

U.S. Department of Housing and Urban Development. *The First Passive Solar Home Awards, Report HUD-PDR-376.* Washington, D.C.: Govt. Printing Office, 1979.

U.S. Department of Housing and Urban Development. *A Survey of Passive Solar Buildings, Report HUD-PDR-287(2).* Washington, D.C.: Govt. Printing Office, 1979.

Watson, Donald. *Designing and Building a Solar House.* Charlotte, VT: Garden Way Publishing, 1977.

ADDITIONAL REFERENCES

Eccli, Eugene. *Low-Cost Energy Efficient Shelter for the Owner and Builder.* Emmaus, PA: Rodale Press, 1976.

McCullagh, James C., ed. *The Solar Greenhouse Book.* Emmaus, PA: Rodale Press, 1978.

U.S. Department of Commerce. *Solar Heating and Cooling of Residental Buildings: Design of Systems; Sizing, Installation and Operation of Systems.* Washington, D.C: Govt. Printing Office, 1980.

U.S. Department of Housing and Urban Development. *Solar Dwelling Design Concepts, Report HUD-PDR-156 (2),* Washington, D.C., Govt. Printing Office, 1980.

USEFUL ARTICLES AND SHORT REPORTS

Andes, F. Stephen III and Sher, Brian. *An Insulation Optimization.* Interface Age, July, 1980.

Bainbridge, David and Long, Denny. *Easy to Build Heat Trapping Shutters.* Organic Gardening, January, 1980.

Carstens, Dean. *Control the Sun with Your Micro.* Interface Age, July, 1980.

Carter, Joe. *Build a Solar Water Heater.* Organic Gardening, July, 1979.

Chandler, Subrato and Root, Douglass E. *Calculation of Heating and Cooling Loads for Florida Residences.* Cape Canaveral, FL: Florida Solar Energy Center, 1979.

Ciarcia, Steve. *A Computer Controlled Wood Stove.* Byte, January, 1980.

Cogswell, Jerald M. *Build a Solar Controller.* Popular Electronics, July, 1980.

Electronics Experimenters Handbook. *Differential-Temperature Basement Ventilators.* Winter, 1975.

Federal Energy Administration. *Home Energy Savers Workbook, Report FEA/D-77/177.* Washington, D.C.: Govt. Printing Office, 1977.

Florida Solar Energy Center. *Design Notes.*

Florida Solar Energy Center. *Summary Information Sheet.*

Florida Solar Energy Center. *Technical Notes.*

Hall, Tom. *A Heating and Cooling Management System.* Byte, February, 1981.

Hetherington, Richard. *Energy-Saving Cost/Benefit Analysis.* Byte, February, 1981.

Klapper, Sheldon. *A Solar Panel for Hot Air Heating.* Organic Gardening, January, 1981.

Krenter, Rodney A. *Solar Controller.* Radio Electronics, December, 1980.

May, Elaine. *Solar Goes Underground.* Popular Science, May, 1980.

National Bureau of Standards. *Retrofitting an Existing Wood-Frame Residence for Energy Conservation, An Experimental Study, Report 105.* Washington D.C.: Govt. Printing Office, 1978.

National Bureau of Standards. *The Thermal Performance of a Two Bedroom Mobile Home, Building Science Series Report 102.* Washington, D.C.: Govt. Printing Office, 1978.

National Solar Heating and Cooling Information Center. *Solar Hot Water and Your Home.* Rockville, MD.

Packard, Hewlett H. *Solar Engineering Users Library Solutions, HP41C; Energy Conservation Users Library Solution, HP67/97.* Corvallis, OR.

Solar Energy Research Institute. *Analysis Methods for Solar Heating and Cooling Applications, Third Ed.* Rockville, MD.

Spitz, William J. *Heat Loss Audit.* Interface Age, November, 1980.

Tolwar, Rajesh. *A Guide to Solar Pool Heating in Florida.* Cape Canaveral, FL: Florida Solar Energy Center, 1978.

U.S. Department of Housing and Urban Development. *Solar Fact Sheet.* Washington, D.C.: Govt. Printing Office.

Wierenga, Theron. *A Furnace Watchdog.* Byte, January, 1980.

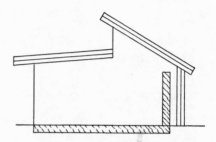

Sources of Information

Solar Energy Hotline
(800) 462-4983
   Recent government sponsored research, reports and publications, lists of architects and engineers, aid on specific questions

Florida Solar Energy Center
(305) 783-0300
   Information on sponsored programs, reports and publications, in-house programs, seminars and classes, design aid (generally Florida residents)

Solar Heating and Cooling Information Center
(800) 532-2929
   Reports and publications, scheduled conferences and seminars, location of specialists

Energy Hotline
(800) 424-9246
   At time of writing, hydrocarbon fuel availability only

Sandia Corporation
(505) 844-5678
Los Alamos Scientific Laboratory
(505) 667-5061

Information on recent in-house and sponsored programs, (re-search and design), reports and publications, location of specialists

Village Homes
(916) 758-4534
Information on developments in Davis, CA area, on own home design and performance, architectural service

Index

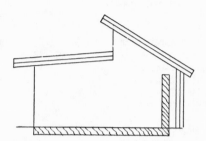

Index

DATE DUE

FEB 28 '84			